Old Holland Maggi Sharp's Palette

Cad yellow light.

Cad red l[illegible]

Alizar[illegible]

French ultramarine blue

Cerulean blue Hue

Raw umber

Medium

1 part dama Varnish

2 parts stand oil.

3 parts turpentine

few drops of Venice Turpentine

(or 1: 2: 2) for large paintings session.

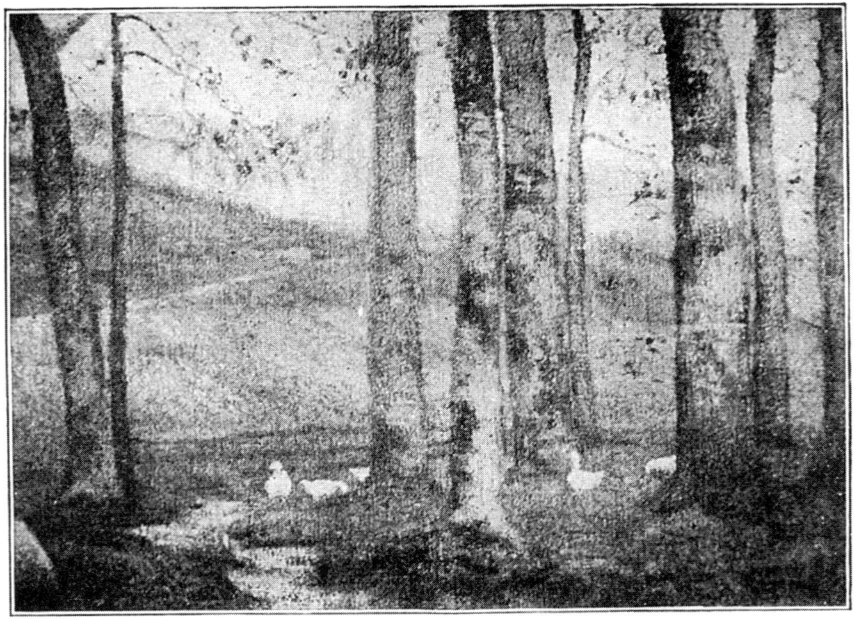

November Beechwood. *D. Burleigh Parkhurst.*

The Painter in Oil

Daniel Burleigh Parkhurst

Dover Publications, Inc.
Mineola, New York

Bibliographical Note

This Dover edition, first published in 2006, is an unabridged republication of the edition published as *The Painter in Oil: A Complete Treatise on the Principles and Technique Necessary to the Painting of Pictures in Oil Colors* by Lothrop, Lee & Shepard, Boston, 1930 (revised editon). Some of the original full-page illustrations have been replaced by versions of better quality. The color plates showing Speciman Tints of Artists' Oil Colors, from the original 1898 edition, are reproduced on the inside front and back covers of the Dover edition.

International Standard Book Number: 0-486-44847-9

Manufactured in the United States of America
Dover Publications, Inc., 31 East 2nd Street, Mineola, N.Y. 11501

PREFACE TO THE SECOND EDITION

AFTER thirty years it has been interesting to re-read a book and see how much or how little you would like to change it. In bringing out a new edition I have done this, and made those changes which the different point of view, either of the time or in my own mind, has suggested.

The time has seen many fads, and some discoveries: but nothing that should alter the character of this book, or that calls for especial elucidation beyond what has already been written. I find that I have laid a ground work of principle and technique which can serve as well the fads and fancies of our time as the things of the older tradition. Here and there I have added or subtracted something which seemed to make for improvement; but I have been surprised to find how little I cared to alter — how well it still represents what I think ought to be said to the student. And I can only hope that the book will continue in the future to be as helpful as the fact that it is still alive would seem to indicate that it has been in the past.

D. B. P.

OGUNQUIT, MAINE
November 25, 1929.

PREFACE

Books of instruction in the practice of painting have rarely been successful. Chiefly because they have been too narrow in their point of view, and have dealt more with recipes than with principles. It is not possible to give any one manner of painting that shall be right for all men and all subjects. To say "do thus and so" will not teach any one to paint. But there are certain principles which underlie all painting, and all schools of painting; and to state clearly the most important of these will surely be helpful, and may accomplish something.

It is the purpose of this book to deal practically with the problems which are the study of the painter, and to make clear, as far as may be, the principles which are involved in them. I believe that this is the only way in which written instruction on painting can be of any use.

It is impossible to understand principles without some statement of theory; and a book in order to be practical must therefore be to some extent theoretical. I have been as concise and brief in the theoretical parts as clearness would permit of, and I trust they are not out of proportion to the practical parts. Either to paint well, or to judge well of a painting, requires an understanding of the same things: namely, the theoretical standpoint of the painter; the technical problems of color, composition, etc.; and the practical means, processes, and materials through which and with which these are worked out.

It is obvious that one cannot become a good painter without the ability to know what is good painting, and to prefer it to bad painting. Therefore, I have taken space to cover, in some sort, the whole ground, as the best way to help the student towards becoming a good painter. If, also, the student of pictures should find in this book what will help him to appreciate more truly and more critically, I shall be gratified.

D. B. P.

December 4, 1897

CONTENTS

PART I.—MATERIALS

PART II.—GENERAL PRINCIPLES

PART III.—TECHNICAL PRINCIPLES

LIST OF ILLUSTRATIONS

The Painter in Oil

PART I

MATERIALS

THE PAINTER IN OIL

CHAPTER I

GENERAL OBSERVATIONS

THERE is a false implication in the saying that "a poor workman blames his tools." It is not true that a good workman can do good work with bad tools. On the contrary, the good workman sees to it that he has good tools, and makes it a part of his good workmanship that they are in good condition.

In painting there is nothing that will cause you more trouble than bad materials. You can get along with few materials, but you cannot get along with bad ones. That is not the place to economize. To do good work is difficult at best. Economize where it will not be a hindrance to you. Your tools can make your work harder or easier according to your selection of them. The relative cost of good and bad materials is of slight importance compared with the relative effect on your work.

The way to economize is not to get anything which you do not need. Save on the non-essentials, and get as good a quality as you can of the essentials.

Save on the number of things you get, not on the quantity you use. You must feel free in your use of material. There is nothing which hampers you more than parsimony in the use of things needful to your painting. If it is worth your while to paint at all, it is worth your while to be generous enough with yourself to insure ordinary freedom of use of material.

The essentials of painting are few, but these cannot be dispensed with. Put it out of your mind that any one of these five things can be got along without : —

You must have something to paint *on*, canvas or panel. Have plenty of these.

You must have something to set this canvas on — something to hold it up and in position. Your knees won't do, and you can't hold it in one hand. The lack of a practical easel will cost you far more in trouble and discouragement than the saving will make up for.

You must have something to paint with. The brushes are most important ; in kind, variety, and number. You cannot economize safely here.

You must have paints. And you must have good ones. The best are none too good. Get the best. Pay a good price for them, use them freely, but don't waste them.

And you must have something to hold them, and to mix them on; but here the quality and kind has less effect on your work than any other of your tools. But as the cost of the best of palettes is slight, you may as well get a good one.

Now, if you will be economical, the way to do it is to take proper care of your tools *after you have got them.* Form the habit of using good tools as they should be used, and that will save you a great deal of money.

CHAPTER II

CANVASES AND PANELS

You should have plenty of canvas on hand, and it would be well if you had it all stretched ready for use. Many a good day's work is lost because of the time wasted in getting a canvas ready. It is not necessary to have many kinds or sizes. It is better in fact to settle on one kind of surface which suits you, and to have a few practical sizes of stretchers which will pack together well, and work always on these. You will find that by getting accustomed to these sizes you work more freely on them. You can pack them better, and you can frame them more conveniently, because one frame will always do for many pictures. Perhaps there is no one piece of advice which I can give you which will be of more practical use outside of the principles of painting, than this of keeping to a few well-chosen sizes of canvas, and the keeping of a number of each always on hand.

It is all well enough to talk about not showing one's work too soon. But we all do, and always will like to see our work under as favorable conditions as possible. And a good frame is one of the favorable conditions. But good frames are expensive, and it is a great advantage to be able to have a frame always at hand which you can see your work in from time to time; and if you only work on four sizes of canvas, say, then four frames, one for each size, will suit all your pictures and sketches. Use the same sizes for all kinds of work too, and the freedom will come, as I say, in the working on those sizes.

Don't have odd sizes about. You can just as well as not use the regular sizes and proportions which colormen keep in stock, and there is an advantage in being able to get a canvas at short notice, and it will be one of your own sizes, and will fit your frame. All artists have gone through the experience of eliminating odd sizes from their stock, and it is one of the practical things that we all have to come down to sooner or later, and the sooner the better, — to have the sizes which we find we like best, not too many, and stick to them. I would have you take advantage of this, and decide early in your work, and so get rid of one source of bother.

Rough and Smooth. — The best canvas is of linen. Cotton is used for sketching canvas. But you would do well always to use good grounds to work on. You can never tell beforehand how your work will turn out; and if you should want to keep your work, or find it worth while to go on with it, you would be glad that you had begun it on a good linen canvas. The linen is stronger and firmer, and when it has a "grain," the grain is better.

Grain.—The question of grain is not easy to speak about without the canvas, yet it is often a matter of importance. There are many kinds of surface, from the most smooth to the most rugged. Some grain it is well the canvas should have; too great smoothness will tend to make the painting "slick," which is not a pleasant quality. A grain gives the canvas a "tooth," and takes the paint better. Just what grain is best depends on the work. If you are going to have very fine detail in the picture use a smoothish canvas; but whenever you are going to paint heavily, roughly, or loosely, the rough canvas takes the paint better. The grain of the canvas takes up the paint, helps to hold it, and to disguise, in a way, the body of it. For large pictures, too, the canvas must necessarily be strong, and the mere weight of the fabric will give it a rough surface.

Knots.—For ordinary work do not be afraid of a canvas which has some irregularities and knots on it. If they are not too marked they will not be unpleasantly noticeable in the picture, and may even give a relief to too great evenness.

Twilled Canvas.—The diagonal twill which some canvases have has always been a favorite surface with painters, particularly the portrait painters.

This grain is a sympathetic one to work on, takes paint well, and is not in any way objectionable in the finished picture.

The best. — The best way is to try several kinds, and when you find one which has a sympathetic working quality, and which has a good effect in the finished picture, note the quality and use it. You will find such a canvas among both the rough and smooth kinds, and so you can use either, as the character of your work suggests. It is well to have both rough and smooth ready at hand.

Absorbent. — Some canvases are primed so as to absorb the oil during the process of painting. They are very useful for some kinds of work, and many painters choose them; but unless you have some experience with the working of them, they are apt to add another source of perplexity to the difficulties of painting, so you had better not experiment with them, but use the regular non-absorbent kinds.

Old and New. — The canvas you work on should not be too freshly primed. The painting is likely to crack if the priming is not well dried. You cannot always be sure that the canvas you get at stores is old, so you have an additional reason for getting a good stock and keeping it on hand. Then, if you have had it in your own possession a long while, you know it is not fresh. Canvas is all the better if it is a year old.

Grounds. — The color of the grounds should be

of interest to you. Canvases are prepared for the market usually in three colors, — a sort of cool gray, a warm light ochrish yellow, and a cool pinkish gray. Which is best is a matter of personal liking. It would be well to consider what the effect of the ground will be on the future condition of the picture when the colors begin to effect each other, as they inevitably will sooner or later.

Vibert in his "*La Science de la Peinture*" advocates a white ground. He says that as the color will be sure to darken somewhat with time, it is well that the ground should have as little to do with it as possible. If the ground is white there is so much the less dark pigment to influence your painting. He is right in this; but white is a most unsympathetic color to work over, and if you do not want to lay in your work with *frottées*, a tint is pleasanter. For most work the light ochrish ground will be found best; but you may be helped in deciding by the general tone of your picture. If the picture is to be bright and lively, use a light canvas, and if it is to be sombre, use a dark one. Remember, too, that the color of your ground will influence the appearance of every touch of paint you put on it by contrast, until the priming is covered and out of sight.

Stretchers. — The keyed stretcher, with wedges to force the corners open and so tighten the canvas when necessary, is the only proper one to use.

For convenience of use many kinds have been invented, but you will find the one here illustrated the best for general purposes. The sides may be used for ends, and *vice versa.* If you arrange your sizes well, you will have the sides of one size the right length for the ends of another. Then you need fewer sizes, and they are surer to pack evenly.

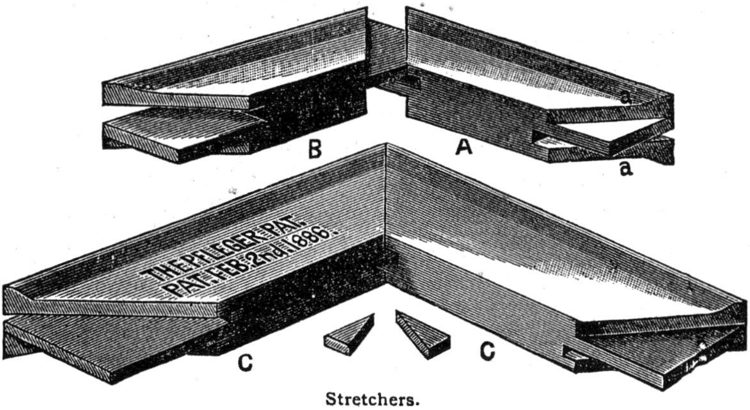

Stretchers.

Stretching. — You will often have to stretch your own canvases, so you should know how to do it There is only one way to make the canvas lay smoothly without wrinkles: Cut the canvas about two inches longer and wider than the stretcher, so that it will easily turn down over the edges. Begin by putting in *one tack* to hold the *middle* of one end. Then turn the whole thing round, and stretch tightly lengthwise, and put a tack to hold it into the *middle* of the other end. Do the same way with the two sides. Only four tacks so far, which have stretched the canvas in the middle two ways. As you do this, you must see that the canvas is on square. Don't drive the tacks all the way in at first till you know that this is so. Then give each another blow, so that the head binds the canvas more than the body of the tack does; for the pull of the canvas against the side of the tack will tear, while the head will hold more strands. This first two ways stretching must be as tight as any after stretching will be or you will have wrinkles in the middle, while the purpose is to pull out the wrinkles towards the corners. Now go back to the ends: stretch, and place one tack each side of the first one. In a large canvas you may put two each side, but not more, and you must be sure that the strain is even on both sides. Don't pull too much; for next you must do the same with the other end which should bear *half* of the whole stretch. Do just the same now with the two sides. Now continue stretching and tacking, — each side of the middle tacks on each end, then on each side, then to the ends again, and so gradually working towards the corners, when as you put in the last tacks the wrinkles will disappear, if you have done your work well. Don't hurry and try to drive too many tacks into a side at a time, for to have to do it all over again would take more time than to have worked slowly and done it properly. You may of course stretch a small canvas with your hands, but it will make your fingers sore, and you cannot get large can-

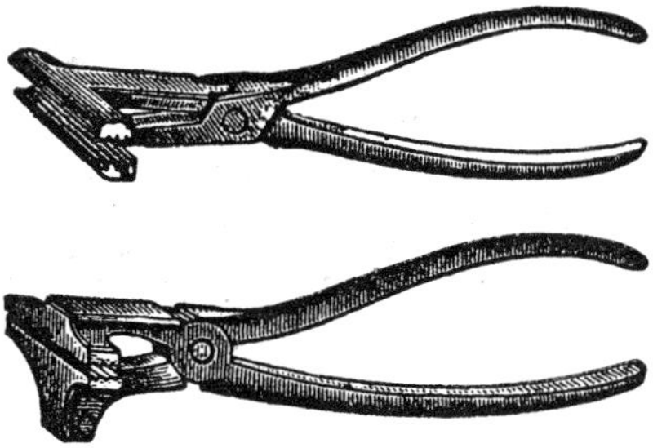

Canvas Pliers.

vases tight without help. You will do well to have a pair of "canvas pliers" which are specially shaped to pull the canvas and hold it strongly without tearing it, as other pliers are sure to do.

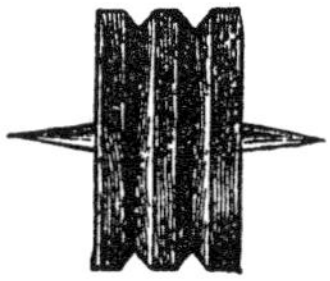

Double-pointed Tack.

When you take canvases outdoors to work, you will find it useful to strap two together, face inwards, with a double-pointed tack like this in each corner to keep them apart. You will not have any trouble with the fresh paint, as each canvas will then protect the other. You can pack freshly painted canvases for shipping in the same way.

Panels. — For small pictures panels are very useful, and when great detail is desirable, and fine, smooth work would make an accidental tear impossible to mend well, they are most valuable. They are made of mahogany and oak generally.

Panels are useful, too, for sketching, as you can easily pack them. They are light, and the sun does not shine through the backs. You can get them for about the same cost as canvas for small sizes, which are what you would be likely to use, and they are often more convenient, particularly for use in the sketch-box.

CHAPTER III

EASELS

THE important thing in an easel is that it should be steady and firm; that it should hold the canvas without trembling, and so that it will not fall as you paint out towards the edges. You often paint with a heavy hand, and you must not have to hold on to your picture with one hand and paint with the other. Nothing is more annoying than a poor easel, and nothing will give you more solid satisfaction, than the result of a little generosity in paying for a good one. The ideal thing for the studio is, of course, the great "screw easel," which is heavy, safe, convenient, and expensive. We would like to have one, but we can't afford it, so we won't speak of it. The next best thing is an ordinary easel which doesn't cost a great deal, but which is firm and solid and practical. Don't get one of the various three-legged folding easels which cost about seventy-five cents or a dollar. They tumble down too often and too easily. The wear and tear on the temper they cause is more than they are worth. It is true that they fold up out of the way. But they fold up when you don't expect them to; and you ought to be able to afford room enough for an easel anyway, if you paint at all.

The illustration shows one of the firmest of the inexpensive easels, and one which will fold up into as small a compass as any practical easel will. It will hold perfectly well a good-sized canvas, even with its frame, and will not tumble over on slight provocation.

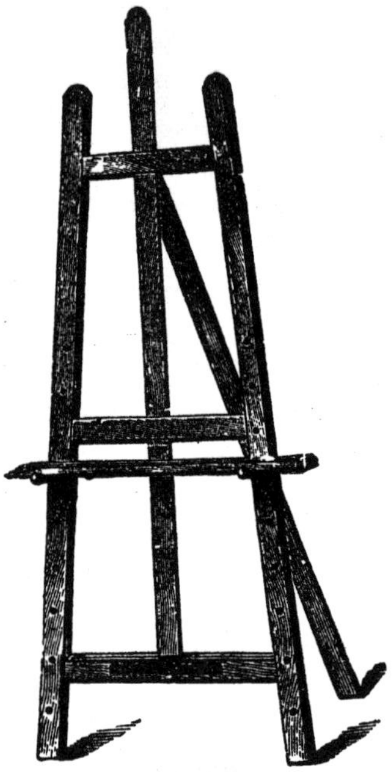

Another good easel is shown on p. 17. It is more lightly made, not so well braced, but is more convenient for raising and lowering the picture, as the catch allows the whole thing to be raised and lowered at once.

If you are to save money on your easel, don't save on the construction and strength of it, but on the finish. Let the polish and varnish go, but get a well-made easel with solid wood. The heavier it is, the less easily it packs away, to be sure, but the more steadily it will hold your picture.

Sketching Easels.—The same things are of importance in an easel for out-of-door work that are needed in a studio easel, except that it must also be portable. So if you must have a folding easel, get a *good* sketching easel; or if you can't have one for in-doors and one for out-doors, then pay a good price for a sketching easel, and use it in doors and out also. There are two things which are absolutely essential in a sketching easel. It *must* have legs which may be made longer and shorter, and it *must hold* the canvas firmly. It is not enough to lean the canvas on it. The wind blows it over just when you are putting on an interesting touch, or the touch itself upsets it, either of which is most aggravat-

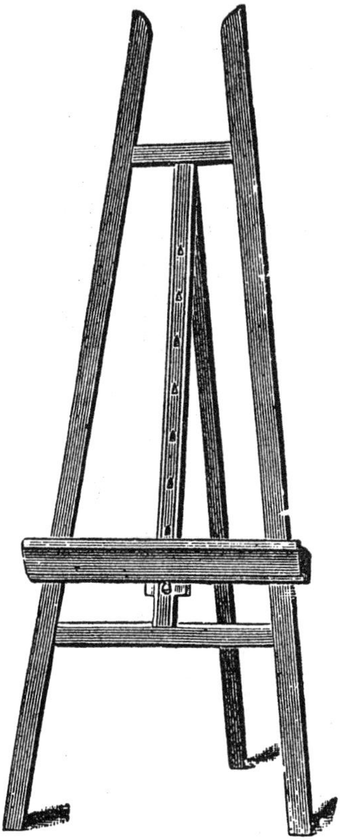

ing, and does not tend to satisfactory work. You must not be obliged to sit down to work just where you don't want to, a little this side or a little that side of the chosen spot, because the ground isn't even there and the easel will not stand straight. You must be able to make a leg longer or shorter as the unevenness of the ground necessitates. It is impossible to work among rocks or on hillsides if you cannot make your easel stand as you want it. These things are not to be got round. You might as well not work as to sketch with a poor sketching easel. And you must pay a good price for it. The sketching easel that is good for anything has never been made to sell for a dollar and a half. Pay three or four dollars for it, at any rate, and use it the rest of your life. I use an easel every day that I have worked on every summer for twelve years. Most artists are doing much the same. The easel is not expensive *per year* at that rate! It is such

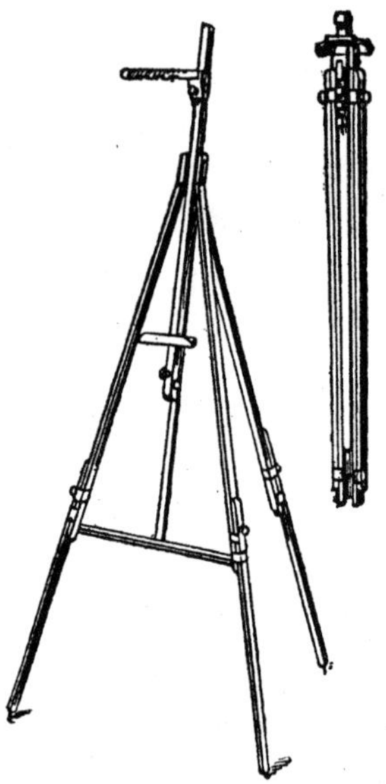

an easel as that shown on the opposite page, and is satisfactory for all sorts of work.

If you are working in a strong wind, or if you have a large canvas, such an easel as this illustration shows is the best and safest yet invented, and it is as good for other work, and particularly when you want to stand up. And either of these easels will be perfectly satisfactory to use in the house.

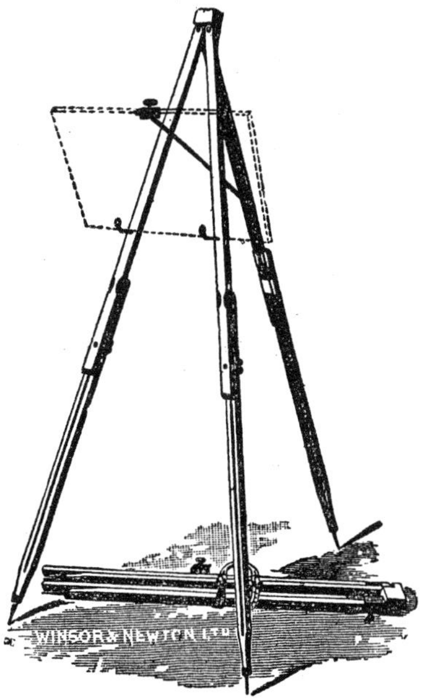

CHAPTER IV

BRUSHES

An old brush that has been properly cared for is generally better than a new one. It seems to have accommodated itself to your way of painting, and falls in with your peculiarities. It is astonishing how attached you get to your favorite brushes, and how loath you are to finally give them up. What if you have no others to take their places?

Don't look upon your brushes as something to get as few of as possible, and which you would not get at all if you could help it. There is nothing which comes nearer to yourself than the brush which carries out your idea in paint. You should be always on the lookout for a good brush; and whenever you run across one, buy it, no matter how many you have already. Don't look twice at a bad brush, and don't begrudge an extra ten cents in the buying of a good one. If you are sorry to have to pay so much for your brushes, then take the more care of them. Use them well and they will last a long while; then don't always use the same handful. Break in new ones now and again. Keep a dozen or two in use, and lay some aside before they are worn out, and use newer ones. So when at last you cannot use one any more, you have others of the same kind which will fill its place.

Have all kinds and sizes of brushes. Have a couple of dozen in use, and a couple of dozen which you are not using, and a couple of dozen more that have never been used.

What! six dozen?

Well, why not? Every time you paint you look over your brushes and pick out those which look friendly to what you are going to do. You want all sorts of brushes. You can't paint all sorts of pictures with the same kind of brush. Your brush represents your hand. You must give every kind of touch with it. You want to change sometimes, and you want a clean brush from time to time. You don't want to feel that you are limited; that whether you want to or not these four brushes you must use because they are all you have! You can't paint that way. That six dozen you will not buy all at once. When you get your first outfit, get at least a dozen brushes. As you look over the stock and pick out two or three of this kind, and two or three of that, you will be astonished to see how many you have—yet you don't know which to discard. Don't discard any. Buy them all. Then, if you don't paint, it will not be the fault of your brushes. And from time to time get a half a dozen which have just struck you as especially good ones, and quite unconsciously you acquire your six dozen—and even more, I hope!

Bristle and Sable.— The brushes suitable for oil painting are of two kinds,—bristle and sable hair. Of the latter, *red* sable are the only ones you should get. They are expensive, but they have a spring and firmness that the black sable does not have. Camel's hair is out of the question. Don't get any, if you can only have camel's hair. It is soft and flabby when used in oil and you can't work well with such brushes. The same is true of the black sable. But though the

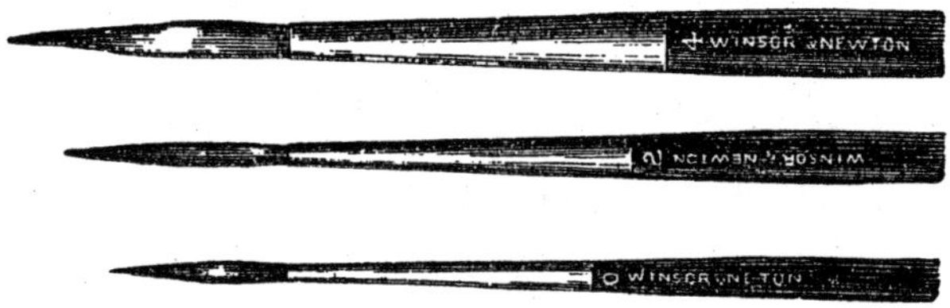

red sables are expensive, you do not need many of them, nor large ones, so the cost of those you will need is slight.

The only sables which are in any degree indispensable to you are the smaller sizes of *riggers*. These are thin, long brushes which are useful for outlining, and all sorts of fine, sharp touches.

You use them to go over a drawing with paint in laying in a picture, and for branches, twigs, etc. As their name implies, you must have them for the rigging of vessels in marine painting also. The three sizes shown in the cut on the opposite page are those you should have, and if you get two of each, you will find them useful in all sorts of places. When you buy them, see that they are elastic and firm, that they come naturally and easily to a good point, without any scraggy hairs. Test them by moistening them, and then pressing the point on the thumb-nail. They should bend evenly through the whole length of the hair. Reject any which seem "weak in the back." If it lays flat toward the point and bends all in one place near the ferrule, it is a poor brush.

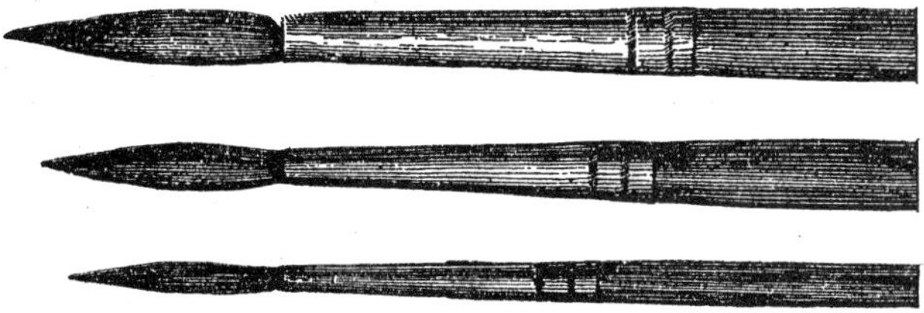

These three larger and thicker sizes come in very useful often and it would be well if you were to have these too. Sometimes a thick, long sable brush will serve better than another for heavy lines, etc.

All these brushes are round. One largish flat sable like this it would be well to have; but these are all the sables necessary.

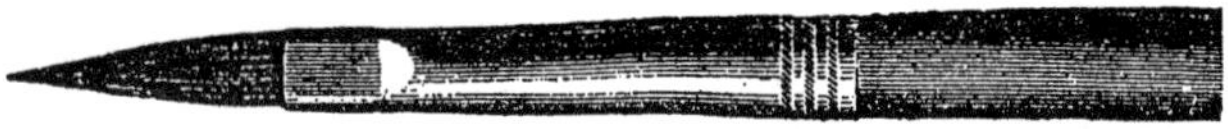

Bristle Brushes.—The sable brush or pencil is often necessary; but oil painting is practically always done with the bristle, or "hog hair," brush. These are the ones which will make up the variety of kinds in your six dozen. A good bristle brush is not to be bought merely by taking the first which comes to hand. Good brushes have very definite qualities, and you should have no trouble in picking them out. Nevertheless, you will take the trouble to select them, if you care to have any satisfaction in using them.

The Bristle. — You want your brush to be made of the hair just as it grew on the hog. All hair, in its natural state, has what is called the "flag." That is the fine, smooth taper towards the natural end of it, and generally the division into two parts. This gives the bristle, no matter how thick it may be, a silky fineness towards the end; and when this part only of the bristle is used in the brush, you will have all the firmness and elasticity of the bristle, and also a delicacy and smoothness and softness quite equal to a sable. But this, in the short hair of an artist's brush, wastes all the rest of the length of the hair; for it is only by cutting off the "flag," and using that, which is only an inch or so long, that you can make the brush. Yet the bristle may be several inches long, and all this is sacrificed for that little inch of "flag." Naturally the "flag" is expensive, and naturally also the manufacturer uses the rest of the hair for inferior brushes. These latter you should avoid. These inferior brushes are made from the part of the bristle remaining, by sandpapering, or otherwise making the ends fine again after they are cut off. But it is impossible to make a brush which has the right quality in this way.

Selection. — Never buy a brush without testing its evenness, as has been advised in the care of sables. Feel carefully the end of the bristles also, and see that the "flag" is there. All brushes are kept together for packing by paste in the bristles. See that this is soaked off before you test your brush.

Round or Flat. — It will make little difference whether you use round or flat brushes. The flat brush is most commonly preferred now, and most brushes are made that way. So you had better get that kind, unless you have some special reason for preferring the round ones.

Handles. — Whether the handles are nicely polished, also, is of no importance. What you are to look to is the quality of the bristles and of the making; the best brushes are likely to be nicely finished all over. But if you do find a really good brush which is cheaper because of the plain handle, and you wish to save money, do it by buying the plain-handled one.

Sizes and Shapes. — You will need some quite large brushes and some smaller ones, some square ones and some pointed.

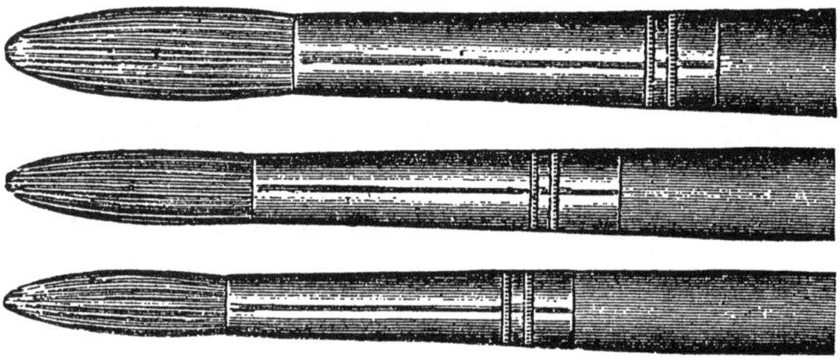

Here are three round brushes which, for all sorts of painting, will be of very general utility. For most of your brushes select the long and thin, rather than the short and thick ones. The stubby brush is a useless sort of thing for most work. There are men who use them and like them, but most painters prefer the more flexible and springy brush, if it is not weak. So, too, the brush should not be too thick. A thick brush takes up too much paint into itself, and does not change its tint so readily. For rubbing over large surfaces where a good deal of the same color is thickly spread on the canvas, the thick, strong brush is a very proper tool. But where there is to be any delicacy of tone, it is too clumsy; you want a more delicate instrument. The same proportions hold with large and small brushes, so these remarks apply to all.

Flat Brushes. — This is particularly applicable to the flat brushes, and the more that most of your brushes will be flat.

You should have both broad-ended and pointed brushes among your flat ones. For broad surfaces, such as backgrounds and skies, the broad ends come in well; and for the small ones there are many square touches where they are useful. The most practical sizes are those shown on page 28. But you will often need much larger brushes than the largest of these.

For the smaller brushes you will have to be very careful in your selections. For only the silkiest of bristle will do good work in a very small brush, and then the temptation is to use a sable, which should be resisted. Why you should avoid using the sable as a rule is that it will make the painting too "slick" and edgy. There is a looseness that is a quality to prize. All the hardness, flatness, and rigidity that are desirable you can get with the bristle brush. When you work too much with sables, the overworking brings a waxy and woodeny surface, which is against all the qualities

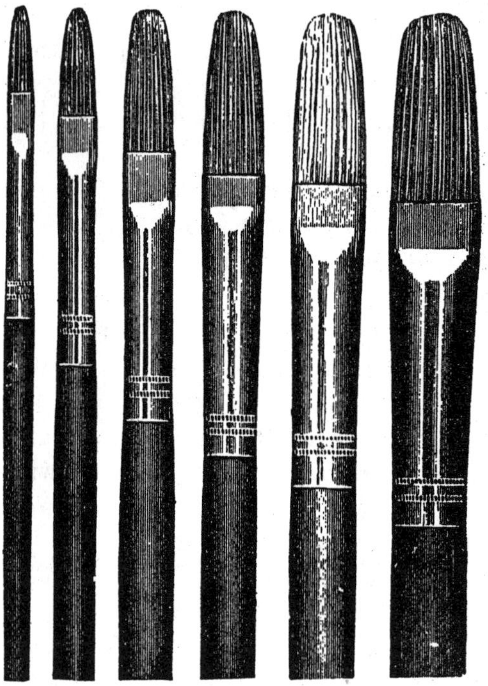

of atmosphere and luminosity, and of freshness and freedom of touch.

Some of the most useful sizes of the more pointed brushes are shown on opposite page.

There are, of course, sizes between these, and many larger; but these are what you will find the best. It would be better to have more of each size than to have more sizes. You should try to

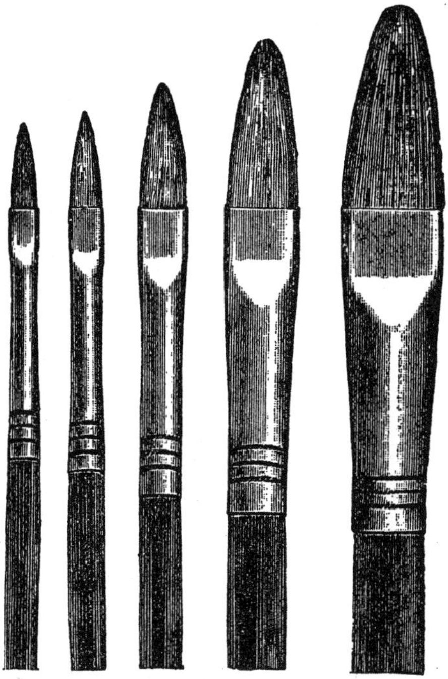

work with fewer rather than more sizes, and, as a rule, work more with the larger than with the smaller brush, even for fine work. You will work with more force and tend less to pettiness, if you learn to put in small touches with the largest brush that will do it. Breadth is not painting with a large brush; but the man who works always with a small brush instinctively looks for the things a small brush is adapted to, and will unconsciously drift into a little way of working.

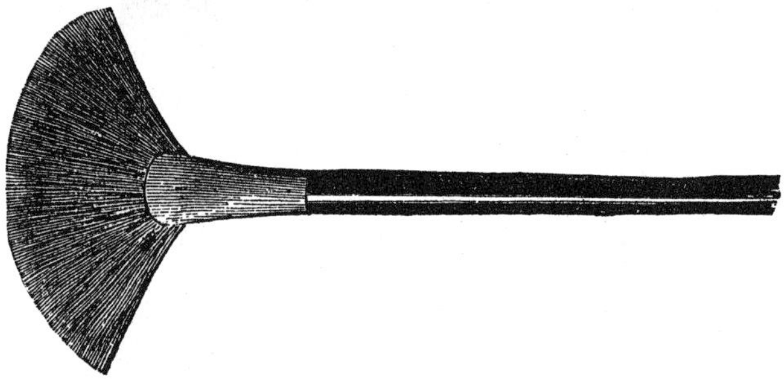

The fan brush, such as here illustrated, is a useful brush, not to paint with, but to flick or drag across an outline or other part of a painting when it is getting too hard and liney. You may not want it once a month, but it is very useful when you do want it.

Care of Brushes.—The best of economy in brushes lies in your care of them. You should never let the paint dry on them nor go too long without careful washing. It is not necessary to wash them every day with soap and water, but they would be the better for such treatment.

Quite often, once a week, say, you should wash your brushes carefully with soap and water. You may use warm water, but don't have it hot, as that may melt the glue which holds the bristles together in the ferrule. Use strong soap with plenty of lye in it — common bar soap, or better, the old-fashioned soft soap. Hold several brushes together in one hand so that the tips are all of a length, dip them together into or rub them onto the soap, and then rub them briskly in the palm of the other hand. When the paint is well worked into the lather, do the same with the other brushes, letting the first ones soak in the soap, but not in the water. Then rinse them, and carefully work them clean one by one, with the fingers. When you lay them aside to dry, see that the bristles are all straight and smooth, and they will be in perfect condition for next painting.

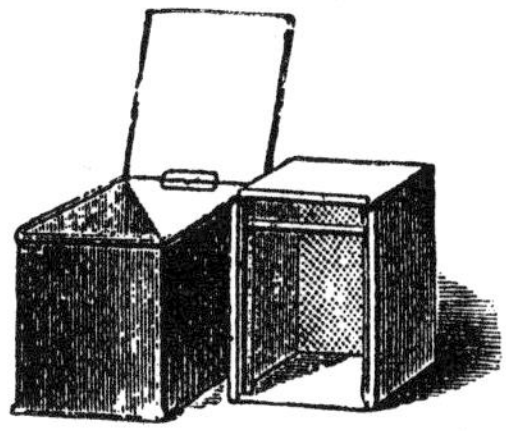

Cleaning. — But from day to day you need not take quite so much trouble as this. True, the brushes will keep in better condition if washed in soap and water every day, but it is not always convenient to do this. You may then use the brush-cleaner. This is a tin box with a false bottom of perforated tin or of wire netting about half-way down, which allows the liquid to stand a half-inch or so above it; so that when you put your brush in and rub it around, the paint is rinsed from it, and settles through the perforations to the bottom, leaving the liquid clear again above it. If you use this carefully, cleaning one brush at a time, not rubbing it too hard, and pulling the hairs straight by wiping them on a clean rag, you may keep your brushes in good condition quite easily. But they will need a careful soap-and-water washing every little while, besides. The liquid best for use in this cleaner is the common kerosene or coal oil. Never use turpentine to rinse your brushes. It will make them brittle and harsh; but the kerosene will remove all the paint, and will not affect the brush.

CHAPTER V

PAINTS

Of all your materials, it is on your paints that quality has the most vital effect. With bad paint your work is hopeless. You may get an effect that looks all right, but how long will it stand, and how much better may it not have been if your colors had been good? You can tell nothing about it. You may have luck, and your work hold; or you may not have luck, and in a month your picture is ruined. Don't trust to luck. Keep that element out as much as you can, always. But in the matter of paints, if you count on luck at all, remember that the chances are altogether against you. Don't let yourself be persuaded to indulge in experiments with colors which you have reason to think are of doubtful quality. Keep on the safe side, and use colors you are sure of, even if they do cost a little more — at first; for they are cheaper in the long-run. And even in the time of using of one tube, generally the good paint does enough more work to cover the difference of cost.

Bad Paints. — Suspect colors which are too cheap. Good work is expensive. Ability and skill and experience count in making artists' colors, and must be paid for. If you would get around the cost of first-class material you must mix it with inferior material.

The first effect you will notice in using poor colors is a certain hindrance to your facility, due to the fact that the color is weak — does not have the snap and strength in it that you expect. The paint has not a full color quality, but mixes dead and flat. This you will find particularly in the finer and lighter yellows. You need not fear much adulteration in those paints which are naturally cheap, of course. It is in those higher-priced colors, on which you must largely depend for the more sparkling qualities, that you will have most trouble.

Unevenness of working, and lack of covering or mixing power, you will find in poor paints also. They have no strength, and you must keep adding them more and more to other colors to get them to do their work. All these things are bothersome. They make you give more attention to the pigments while working than you ought to, and when all is done, your picture is weak and negative in color.

Another effect to be feared from bad colors is that your work will not stand; the colors fade or change, and the paint cracks. The former effect is from bad material, or bad combinations of them in the working, and the latter mainly from bad vehicles used in grinding them.

I have seen pictures go to pieces within a month of their painting — bad paint and bad combinations. Of course you can use good colors so that the picture will not stand. But that will be your own fault, and it is no excuse for the use of colors which you can by no possibility do good work with.

Good Paints. — The three things on which the quality of good paint depends are good pigment, good vehicles, and good preparation.

The pigments used are of mineral, chemical, and vegetable origin. The term *pigment* technically means the powdered substance which, when mixed with a vehicle, as oil, becomes *paint.* The most important pigments now used are artificial products, chiefly chemical compounds, including chemical preparations of natural mineral earths.

As a rule, the colors made from earths may be classed as all permanent; those from chemicals, permanent or not, as the case may be; and those of vegetable origin fugitive, with few exceptions. Some colors are good when used as water colors, and bad when used in oil. Further on I will speak of the fugitiveness and permanency of colors in detail. I wish here to emphasize the fact that the origin of the material of which the pigment is made has much to do with the sort of work that that pigment will do, and with the permanency of the effect which is produced; and therefore that while a paint may look like another, its working or its lasting qualities may be quite different.

The Vehicles. — The vehicles by which the pigment is made fluent and plastic are quite as important in their effects. They not only have to do with the business of drying, owing to the substances used as dryers, but they may have to do with the chemical action of one pigment on another.

The Preparation. — Finally, the preparation of the pigment demands the utmost skill and knowledge, if the colors are to be good. The paints used by the old masters were few and simple, and the fact that they prepared them themselves had much to do with the manner in which they kept their color. The paints used now are less simple. We do not prepare and grind them ourselves, and we could hardly do so if we wished to, so we are the more dependent on the integrity of the colorman who does it for us.

The preparation of the paint begins with the chemical or physical preparation of each pigment, and then comes the mixing of several to produce any particular color; and finally the mechanical process of grinding with the proper vehicle to bring it to the proper fineness and smoothness.

Grinding.—The color which the artist uses must be most evenly and perfectly ground. The grinding which will do for ordinary house paints will not do for the artist's colors. Neither will the chemical processes suitable for the one serve for the other. Not only must the machinery, but the experience, skill and care, be much greater for artist's colors. Therefore it is that the specialization of color-making is most important to good colors for the use of the artist.

Reliable Makers.—If you would work to the best advantage as far as your colors are concerned, both as to getting the best effects which pure pigments skilfully and honestly prepared will give you, and as to the permanency of those effects when you have gotten them, see to it that you get paint made by a thoroughly reliable colorman.

It is not my province to say whose colors you should use; doubtless there are many colormen who make artists' materials honestly and well. Nevertheless, I may mention that there are no colors which have been more thoroughly tested, both by the length of time they have been in the possession of painters, and by the number of painters who have used them, than those of Winsor and Newton of London. No colors have been so generally sold and for so long a time, particularly in this country, as these, and none are so well known for their evenness and excellence of quality.

I do not say that these manufacturers do not make any colors which should not go on the palette of the cautious artist — I believe that they do not make that claim themselves; but such colors as they do assert to be good, pure, and permanent, you may feel perfectly safe in using, and be sure that they are as well made as colors can be. This is as much as can be said of any paints, and more than can be said of most. I have used these colors for many years, and my own experience is that they have always been all that a painter need ask.

The fact that Winsor and Newton's colors can be found in any town where colors can be had at all, makes me the more free to recommend them, as you can always command them. This fact also speaks for the general approval of them.

Inasmuch as certain colors are not claimed to be permanent and others are, it is for you to compose your palette of those which will combine safely. This you can do with a little care. Some colors are permanent by themselves or with some colors, but not in combination with certain others. You should then take the trouble to consider these chemical relationships.

It is not necessary for you to study the chemistry of paints, but you may read what has been ascertained as to the effects of combinations, and act accordingly. There are practically duplications of color-quality in pigments which are bad, and in pigments which are good; so that you can use the good color instead of the bad one to do the same work. The good color will cost more, but there is no way of making the bad color good, so you must pay the difference due to the cost of the better material, or put up with the result of using bad colors.

Chemical Changes.—The causes of change of color in pigments are of four kinds, all of them chemical effects. 1, the action of light; 2, the action of the atmosphere; 3, the action of the medium; and 4, the action of the pigments themselves on each other. The action of light is to bring about or to assist in the decomposition of the pigment. It is less marked in oil than in water color, because the oil forms a sort of sheath for the color particles. The manner in which light does its deteriorating work is somewhat similar to that of heat. The action of light is very slow, but it seems to do the same thing in a long time that heat would do in a short time.

Some colors are unaffected or little affected by light, and of course you will use them in preference to all others. The atmosphere affects the paint because of certain chemical elements contained in it, which tend to cause new combinations with the materials which are already in combination in the pigment. The action of the oxygen in the air is the chief agent in affecting the pigment, and it is here particularly that light, and especially sunlight, assists in décomposition. The air of towns and cities generally contains sulphuric and sulphurous acids and sulphuretted hydrogen. This latter gas is most effective in changing oil paintings, because of its action in turning white lead dark; and as white lead is the basis of many qualities in painting, this gas may have a very general action.

Moisture in the atmosphere is also a cause of change, but there is little to be dreaded from this, as the oil protects the colors.

Oil absorbs oxygen in drying, and so is apt to have an effect on colors liable to change from that element, and many vehicles contain materials to hasten the drying which further aid in the deterioration of the pigment. Bad oil will tend to crack the picture also. The greatest care should be used in this direction, as the most permanent colors may be ruined by bad vehicles.

Pigments will not have a deteriorating effect on each other as long as they are solid. But if one of them is soluble in the medium, then chemical action commences; but as most pigments are somewhat soluble, there is always some danger in mixing them. The best we can do is, as I said before, to try to have on the palette, as far as possible, only colors which are friendly to each other.

As a student you should not be much occupied, however, with all this. You must expect that all color will change somewhat. But you need not use those which change immediately or markedly, and you may use them in a way which will tend to make them change as little as may be. Colors have stood for years, and what is practical permanence, not perfect permanence, is all you need look for. If you think too much of the permanence of your colors, it will interfere with the directness of your study. Therefore, decide on a palette which is as complete and safe as you can make it, excluding the notably bad pigments, and think no more about it.

When you need to add a new color to your palette, choose it with reference to those already on it, and go ahead. This is what the whole subject resolves itself to, practically, for you as a student.

Opaque and Transparent Colors. — Some colors, like the madders, have a jelly-like consistency when mixed with oil, others, the earths among them, are dense and opaque. We speak of them respectively as "transparent" and "solid" colors. These qualities, which divide the paints into two classes, have no relation to their permanency. As far as that is concerned you use them in the same way, as some transparent colors are safe and some fugitive; and the same with the opaque colors.

The only difference is in the fact that, as a rule, the solid colors are better dryers. But you will notice that while you may mix these colors together as though this difference between them did not exist, in certain processes you use them differently. So you will see, farther on, that for a "glaze" you can use only the transparent or semi-opaque colors, for a scumble you naturally use the solid ones. You should know, however, for the sake of clearness, just what is meant when "solid" or "body" or "opaque" color is spoken of, and what is meant by "transparent" color.

Safe and Unsafe Colors. — Beyond what has been said of the causes of change in colors it is not necessary that you should know the chemical constituents of them. If you want to look into the matter further there are books, such as "Field's Chromatography," which treat fully of the subject, and which you may study.

But practically you should know which colors are to be depended on and which not. Let us consider the principal colors in detail then, merely as to their actual stability. I will speak of them in connection with the plates of colors at the end of this book. I would like you to compare what is said of each color with the corresponding color in the plates. Those colors in the plates which are not spoken of here, you may consider as useful in showing you the character of different colors which are made, but which may or may not be used, according as you may need them. I shall not attempt to mention all the pigments that are in the market. You need never use more than fifteen or twenty all told. Many painters use more, it is true; but if you know how to make the best use of that number, you may safely wait till you "grow to them" before you bother with more. And I shall speak only of those which you will find essential or most generally useful, and those which should be particularly avoided.

Permanency. — It should be stated what is meant by a permanent color. There is no color which is not to be influenced in some way. The most sound of pigments will change if the conditions favor the change. When we speak of a permanent color, we mean only one which under the usual conditions will stand for an indefinite time. By which is meant ordinary diffused daylight, not direct sunlight, and the ordinary air under normal conditions. If there be direct sunlight, you may expect your picture to change sooner or later. But one does not hang his pictures where the sun's rays will fall on them. If there is any exceptional condition of moisture in the air, the picture may suffer. Or if from any cause unusual gases are in the atmosphere, or if the picture be too long in a dark, close place, the picture may smother for lack of fresh air, just as any other thing, plant or animal, which depends on normal conditions of atmosphere would do.

Let us say, then, that what we mean by a permanent color is one which will stand unchanged for an indefinite length of time in a room which is of the usual condition of temperature and freedom from moisture, and where the light is diffused, and such that the direct rays of the sun are not on the picture often, or to any great extent. Cold will not hurt a picture if the canvas is not disturbed in that condition, but to bend or roll it while it is very cold will of course crack it, and sudden and extreme changes of temperature may have the same effect. In other words, some care must be used with all pictures as a matter of course.

COLOR LIST

Whites. — *Zinc white* is the only permanent white, but it lacks body and is little used. The lead whites, *flake*, *silver*, *cremnitz*, will darken in time, and will turn yellow with oil, and may change with or affect change in other pigments. The zinc white is liable to crack. We have no perfect white, so practically you may consider the lead whites as permanent enough, as other painters do.

Yellows. — *Cadmium* is permanent in all three of its forms. It is a color the permanence of which is of great importance; for its brilliancy is quite essential to modern painting, and if it were not permanent, the picture would soon lose the very quality for which the color was used. *The chromes*, which are of similar color-quality, are less permanent, and are almost sure to turn to a horny sort of yellow; and a green, which by their use was bright and sparkling, will, in a few months, lose its freshness — this cadmium will not do. Cadmium is also to be preferred to chrome, because it is of a much finer tonality. Greens and yellows made by the admixture of chrome are apt to be crude as compared with those in which cadmium was used.

Strontian yellow is a permanent and most useful light yellow, much to be preferred to all other citron yellows except the pale cadmium, and can be used in place of that if necessary. They are both expensive colors of about the same cost.

Naples yellow was a very prominent pigment with the older painters. It is still very much used, but in the simplification of your palette you may as well leave it out, as you can get the same qualities with cadmium and white. It is durable and safe, but adds another tube to your palette which you can well dispense with.

The ochres are among the oldest and safest of

pigments. You can use them with any colors which are themselves permanent. There are several of them, —*yellow ochre, Roman ochre, transparent gold ochre*, and others. They are all native earths, and though they contain iron, they are sufficiently inert to be thoroughly sound colors.

The siennas, burnt and raw, are like the ochres, native earths, very old and permanent colors, and may be used anywhere.

The umbers are in the same class with the siennas and ochres. They should all rank among the yellows. The browns of umber and sienna will make greens with blues.

Indian yellow and yellow lake should both be avoided as fugitive.

Aureolin is a rich, warm golden yellow of the greatest permanence, and should be used when Indian yellow and yellow lake would be used if they were permanent.

Reds. — The *vermilions* are permanent when well made. They are of great body and power, as well as delicacy. They are of two kinds, — *Chinese*, which is bluish in tone, and *scarlet* and *orange vermilion*, which have the yellow quality. Both kinds are useful to the palette because of the practical necessities of mixing.

Light red is a deep, warm red earth, made by calcining ochre, and has the same permanence as the other ochres. It is a fine color, of especial value in painting flesh, and mixes with everything safely.

The madders — rose, pink, purple, and *madder carmine* — are the only transparent reds which are permanent. Whatever the name given them, they should not be confounded with the *lakes,* which are absolutely untrustworthy. By reference to the plates you will see that the madders are practically the same as the lakes in color when first used. But the lakes fade and the madders do not. The madders cost about twice as much as the lakes; but you must pay the difference, for the lakes cannot be made to stand, and you must have the color. There is nothing for it but to pay twice as much and buy the madders.

The lakes — scarlet, geranium, crimson, and *purple* — are all bad. The madders and lakes are all slow dryers; but unless carelessly used with other colors which are not yet dry they need not have a bad effect on the picture from cracking.

Distinguish the so-called *madder lakes* and the *lakes;* and between *carmine,* which is a lake, and *madder carmine,* which is a madder.

Blues. — The *ultramarine* of the old masters is practically unused to-day because of its cost. But the artificial ultramarines, while not quite of the same purity of color, are equally permanent, and are in every respect worthy to be used. Of these the *brilliant ultramarine* is the nearest in color to the real lapis lazuli. The *French ultramarine* is less clear and vivid, but is a splendid deep blue, and most useful. The so-called *permanent blue* is not quite so permanent as its name implies, but permanent enough for practical purposes.

Cobalt blue and *cerulean blue* are two pigments, one very light and clear, the other darker, which are made of the oxide of the metal cobalt. In oil they are permanent, and do not change when mixed with other colors. For delicate tints, when the tones are to be subtly gray yet full of the primary colors, the cobalts are indispensable. You should always have them on hand, and generally on your palette. Cerulean blue is of less importance than the other, but in very clear, delicate blue skies it is often the only color which will get the effect.

Prussian blue possesses a depth and power and a quality of color which make it unique. The greenish tone gives it great value in certain combinations *as far as its tinting effect is concerned.* But it is not reliable as a pigment. It changes under various conditions, and fades with the light. It is not to be depended upon. *Antwerp blue,* a weaker kind of Prussian blue, is even more fugitive. It is a pity that these colors will not stand, but as they will not, we must get along without them.

Indigo has a certain grayish quality which is useful sometimes, but it cannot be placed among the even moderately permanent colors.

The blacks may be classed as blues, because they will make green if mixed with yellow. Considered as blues, they are, of course, dense and negative, and should not be too freely used. But they are all permanent. The only ones we need speak of are *ivory black*, which has a reddish cast, and *blue black*, which is weaker, but lacks the purplish note, which is often an advantage.

Greens. — We need mention only a few greens. There are numerous greens, of various degrees of permanence, but it is not necessary to speak of all the colors on the market. You could not use them all if you had them, and we may as well confine ourselves to those we really need.

Veridian, or *emeraude green*, is the deepest and coldest of our greens, and is permanent. It is too cold, and looks even more so at night. In use it needs the addition of some yellow which holds its own at night, such as yellow ochre, or the painting will be impossible in gaslight, and even worse under electric light.

Emerald green is the same as the French *Veronese* green, and is generally permanent. It is said to turn dark, and does lose some of its brilliancy with time and the effect of impure air. But there are places where one needs it, especially in sketching, and it is well to use it sometimes. But bear in mind that it is not absolutely permanent, and as the quality that it gives, brilliant light green, is the very one it will lose should it change, don't expect too much of it.

Terre verte is a very weak color. But it is most tender in its quality, and is permanent to all intents and purposes. It may get slightly darker in time, but will not lose the qualities for which it will be used. It is very useful to use with ivory black or elsewhere, to slightly modify a reddish tendency, and is a fine glazing color.

The chrome greens, by whatever name, Brunswick green, or the better-known Cinnabar or Zinnober greens, are all bad. They are useful colors as color, but they will not stand, and you will even get better color by mixing certain yellows and blues than these will give you, so you had better lay them aside, tempting as they are.

Other Colors. — You will notice that I have said nothing about the various browns and olives and purples. It is simply because it is better for you to make all these colors than to get them in the tubes. The earths and the browns of madder are all good, and the mixing of madders and good blues will make all the shades of violet and purple you can possibly want in their purity.

Palettes. — We have, then, a number of pigments which are solid and safe, of each of the primary colors, and of such variety of qualities that the whole range of possible color is practicable with them in combination. To recapitulate, let us make a list of them.

THE PERMANENT COLORS.

Zinc white.
(Lead white enough so.)
Cadmium yellow.
Cadmium orange.
Cadmium yellow, pale.
Strontian yellow.
Yellow ochre.
Roman ochre.
Transparent gold ochre.
Raw sienna.
Burnt sienna.
Raw umber.
Aureolin.
Chinese vermilion.
Scarlet vermilion.
Orange vermilion.
Light red.
Rose madder.
Pink madder.
Purple madder.
Madder carmine.
Rubens madder.
Ultramarine blue brilliant.
Ultramarine blue French.
Permanent blue.
Cobalt.
Cerulean blue.
Ivory black.
Blue black.
Veridian.
Emerald green.
Terre verte.

Here is a list of colors which will work well together, and with which you can do as much as is possible with colors as far as our present materials go.

Most of these colors, I am aware, are among the more expensive ones. This I am sorry for, but cannot help. The good colors are at times the expensive ones, but as there are no cheaper ones which are permanent to take their places, it would be the falsest of economy to use others.

Palette Principles. — In making up your palette, you must so arrange it that you can get pure color when you want it. There is never any trouble to get the color negative; to get richness and balance is another matter. If you will refer to the color plates, you will see that in each of the three primary colors there are pigments which lean towards one or the other of the other two. The scarlet red is a yellow red. The Chinese vermilion and the rose madder are blue reds. The same holds with yellows and blues, as orange cadmium is a red yellow, and strontian yellow is a greenish yellow. This is, in practice, of the utmost importance in the absence of the ideal color, for when we deal with the practical side of pigment, we deal with very imperfect materials which will not follow in the lines of the scientific theory of color. If we would have the purest and richest secondary color, we must take two primaries, each of which partakes of the quality of the other. To make a pure orange, for instance, we must use a yellow red and a red yellow. If we used a bluish red and a bluish (greenish) yellow, the blue in both would give us a sort of tertiary in the form of a negative secondary instead of the pure rich orange we wanted. This latter fact is quite as useful in keeping colors gray without too much mixing when we want them so, but nevertheless we must know how to get pure color also.

These characteristics have a bearing on the setting of our palette, for we must have at least two of each of the three primary colors — red, yellow, and blue — and white. There may be as many more as you want, but there must be at least that number.

But the character of the work you are doing will also have an influence on the colors you use. You may not need the same palette for one sort of picture that is essential to another. You can have a palette which will do all sorts of work, but a change in the combinations may often be called for in accordance with the different color characteristics of your picture.

I will suggest several palettes of different combinations which will give you an idea of how you may compose a palette to suit an occasion. I do not say that you should confine yourself to any or all of these palettes, nor that they are the best possible. But they are safe and practical, and you may use them until you can find or compose one better suited to your purposes. They will all be made up from the colors we have in our list, and will all have the arrangement I called your attention to as to the use of two of each primary.

It would be well if you were to compare each of the colors with the corresponding one in the plates at the end of the book, and get acquainted with its characteristic look.

Expense. — I have several times referred to the relative expense of colors, and stated that when the good color was of greater cost than others, there was nothing for it but to get the best. I cannot modify that statement, but it is well to say that as a rule the expensive colors are not those that you use the most of, although some are used constantly. Vermilion is so

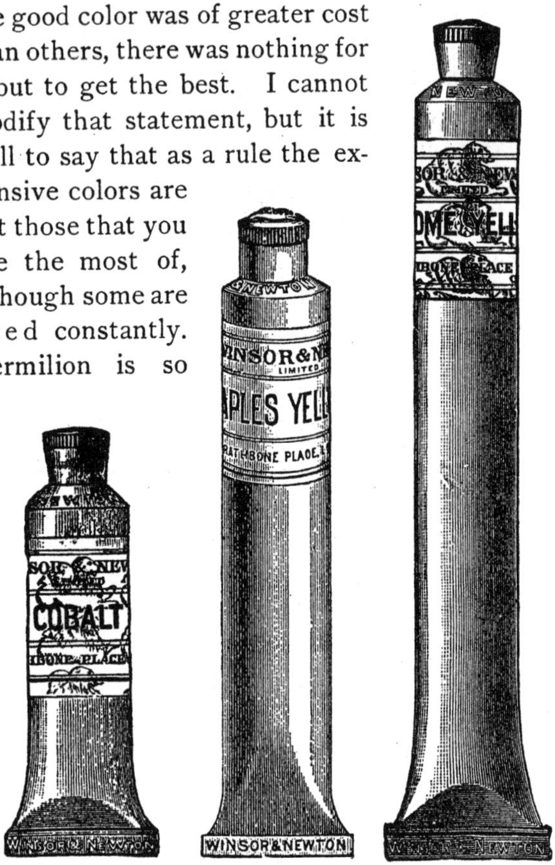

No. 1. No. 2. No. 3.

strong a color that the cost hardly matters. Of

the deep blues the same is true. But the light yellows, and the madders and cobalt, will often make you groan at the rapidity of their disappearance. But you can get more tubes of them, and their work remains, while were you to use the cheaper paints, the flight of the color from the canvas would make you groan more, and that disappearance could never be made good except by doing the work all over.

Sizes. — The cheapest colors come in the largest tubes. In the illustration, No. 3 represents the full size of the ordinary tube of the average cost. Some of the most commonly used colors come in larger tubes at corresponding price. Only professionals get these large sizes except in the case of white. You use so much of this color that it hardly pays to bother at all with the ordinary tube of it. Get the quadruple tube, which is nominally four times as large, but contains nearly five times as much.

No. 2 represents the actual size of the second size of tubes in which a few regular-priced colors come; while the smallest tube is the size of No. 1. In this sized tube all the high-priced colors are put up; the cadmiums, the madders, vermilions, and ultramarines and cobalts. The cheap colors are the ordinary earths, such as the ochres, umbers, siennas, the blacks and whites, and all sorts of greens and blues and lakes, which you had better have nothing to do with.

Arrangement. — In the following palettes I shall give the names of the colors, as you would look down upon them on your palette. The arrangement is that of a good many painters, and is a convenient one. It is as well to arrange them with white at the right, then the yellows, then the reds, the browns, blues, blacks, and greens. But I have found this as I give it, to be the best for use, simply because it keeps the proper colors together, and the white, which you use most, where it is most easily got at, and I think you will find it a good arrangement.

A Cheap Palette. — This palette I give so that you may see the range possible with absolutely sound colors which are all of the least price. You can get no high key with it. All the colors are low in tone. You could not paint the bright pitch of landscape with it, yet it is practically what they tried to paint landscape with a hundred years ago, and it accounts largely for the lack of bright greens in the landscapes of that date. But for all sorts of indoor work and for portraits you will find it possible to get most beautiful results. You will notice there is no bright yellow. That is because cadmium is expensive and chrome is not permanent. Vermilion is left out for the same reason. Add orange vermilion and cadmium yellow and orange cadmium, and you have a powerful palette of great range and absolute permanency.

White. Naples Yellow.
Venetian Red. Yellow Ochre.
Light Red. Roman Ochre.
Indian Red. Transparent Gold Ochre
Burnt Sienna.
Raw Umber.
Permanent Blue.
Ivory Black.
Terre Verte.

An All-Round Palette: —

White. Strontian Yellow.
Orange Vermilion. Cadmium Yellow.
Rose Madder. Orange Cadmium.
Burnt Sienna. Yellow Ochre.
Raw Umber.
Cobalt.
Ultramarine.
Ivory Black.
Terre Verte.

This palette is a pretty large one, and you can do almost anything with it. But for many things it is better to have more of certain kinds of colors and less of others. This is a good palette for all sorts of in-the-house work, and if you call it a still-life palette, it will name it very well. For a student it will do anything he is apt to be capable of for a good while.

A Rich Low-Keyed Portrait and Figure Palette: —

White. Cadmium.
Chinese Vermilion. Orange Cadmium.
Light Red. Yellow Ochre.
Rose Madder. Transparent Gold Ochre.
Raw Umber.
Cobalt.
Blue Black.
Terre Verte.

A Landscape Palette. — Landscape calls for pitch and vibration. You must have pure color and great luminosity, yet a range of color which will permit of all sorts of effects. The following will serve for everything out-of-doors, and I have seen it with practically no change in the hands of very powerful and exquisite painters. There are no browns and blacks in it because the colors which they would give are to be made by mixing the purer pigments, so as to give more life and vibration to the color. The blackest note may be gotten with ultramarine and rose madder with a little veridian if too purple; the result will be blacker than black, and have daylight in it. The ochre is needed more particularly to warm the veridian.

WHITE. STRONTIAN YELLOW.
ORANGE VERMILION. CADMIUM YELLOW.
PINK MADDER. ORANGE CADMIUM.
ROSE MADDER. YELLOW OCHRE.
COBALT.
ULTRAMARINE.
VERIDIAN.

If you paint figures out-of-doors you will need this same palette. Madder carmine or purple madder, and cerulean blue may also usefully added to this list.

A Flower Palette. — For painting flowers the colors should be capable of the most exquisite and delicate of tints. There should be no color on the palette which cannot be used in any part of the picture. The range need not be so great in some respects as in others, but the richness should be unlimited. In the matter of greens, it is true though hard to convince the amateur of, that if there were no green tube in your box, and you mixed all your greens from the yellows and blues, the picture would be the better. As to the browns, they will put your whole picture out of key. In this palette I am sure you will find every color which is needed. There are few greens, but those given can be used to gray a petal as well as to paint a leaf; therefore there is no likelihood of your using a color in a leaf which is not in tone with the flower.

I am calculating on your using all your ability in studying the influence of color on color, and in mixing pure colors to make gray. Here as elsewhere in these palettes I have in mind their use according to the principles of color and light and effect as laid down in the other parts of the book, which deal specially with those principles. If you do not understand just why I arrange these palettes as I do, turn to the chapters on color, and on the different kinds of painting, and I think you will see what I mean, and understand better what I say, about these combinations.

Of course you do not need all of these colors on your palette at the same time. Some are necessary to certain flowers whose richness and depth you could hardly get without them.

The secret of a palette, however, beyond a chemical harmony which ensures the permanency of its colors, is in knowing what each pigment will do, either alone, in tints with white or in shades with black, or in combination with one or more of the others. Whatever group of pigments you select then, experiment with; make tints and shades; make combinations; test and try them; learn to know your palette. You can never paint till you do.

CHAPTER VI

VEHICLES AND VARNISHES

A VEHICLE is any liquid which is mixed with the color to make it fluent. The vehicle may be ground with the pigment or mixed with it on the palette, or both. Oil colors are of course ground in oil as a vehicle; but it is often necessary or convenient to add to them, in working, such a vehicle as will thin them, or make them dry better. Those which thin or render more fluent the paint are oils and spirits; those which make them dry more quickly are "dryers" or "siccatives."

All vehicles must of necessity have an effect on the permanency of the pigments. Bad vehicles tend to deteriorate them; good ones preserve them.

Oils. — The most commonly used oils are linseed and poppy oil. They are neither of them quick dryers, and are usually mixed with sugar of lead, manganese, etc., to hasten the drying. These have a tendency to affect the colors; but if one will have recourse to none but the pure oils, he must be patient with the drying of his picture. For this reason it would be well to use vehicles with the colors on the palette as little as possible — and that is against thin and smooth painting.

Oil has the tendency to turn dark with time, thus turning the color dark also. The only way to reduce this tendency is to clarify the oil by long exposure to the sunlight. The early German painters used oil so clarified, and their pictures are the best preserved as to color of any that we have. But the drying is even slower with purified oil than with the ordinary oil.

It would be best, then, to use oil as little as may be in painting, and if you need a dryer, use it only as you actually need it in bad drying colors, and then very little of it.

The essences of turpentine and of petroleum may be used to thin the paint, and are preferable to oil, because they have less darkening tendency. They do not, however, bind the color so well, and the paint should not be put on too thinly with them. Usually there is enough oil ground with the pigment as it comes in the tubes to overcome any probability of the paint scaling or rubbing when thinned with turpentine, but in the slow-drying, transparent colors there will be a liability to crack. Moderation in the use of any and all vehicles is the best means of avoiding difficulty. Use vehicles only when you need them, not habitually, and then only as much as there is real need of. If you use oil, use the lighter oils, and expect some darkening in time. Prefer turpentine to oil, and expect your color to dry rather "dead," or without gloss, by its use. If you intend to varnish, this is all right. If you do not intend to varnish the picture, keep the color as near the pure tones as you can. The grayer the color, the more the "dead" or "flat" drying will make it look colorless.

Varnishes. — When the picture is done, after it is dry, varnishes are used to bring out the freshness of color, and to preserve the surface from outside influences of all sorts. A picture must be well dried before it is varnished, or it is likely to crack; six months is not too long to be safe. If you are in a hurry to varnish, use a temporary or retouching varnish.

The best varnish is necessary for use on pictures. Never use any except a varnish especially made for the purpose by a reliable colorman. Those made by Winsor and Newton may all be depended upon. Pay a good price for it, and don't use too much.

Mastic varnish is that which is most favorably known. Be sure you get a good and pure quality.

Varnishes are made from various gums or resins dissolved in a solvent such as alcohol, turpentine, or oil, as the case may be. The lighter gums are the best for pictures, because they do not affect the color of the picture. Much care should be used in putting on the varnish — that it is even and as thinly distributed as will serve the purpose. It should not be flowed on, but carefully worked out with a clean brush, and then kept from dirt and dust until dry.

The finer varnishes in oil or turpentine are best for ordinary use. Those in alcohol do not hold their freshness so well.

Varnishes are sometimes used as siccatives, and to mix with colors which are liable to affect other colors, or to lack consistency. Usually, however, they are not needed.

Permanency in painting depends 1st, on the pigment being chemically safe in itself and in combination with others; 2nd, in the composition of the sequent layers of pigment — if not used properly you get cracking; 3rd, the darkening of color through the action of time and light on the oil.

1. The chemical relation of the pigments has been elsewhere dealt with.

2. The secret of the avoidance of cracking is in never using a quick, hard drying layer over a slower soft drying one until the softer one is hard — after a year's drying at least: and this considers varnish a hard drying layer, of course. The more oil the slower drying, the softer and more flexible and the more slow drying the pigment; the more varnish, the quicker the harder and the more brittle it will dry. Paint the picture through, then

from the ground up to the finish with the same vehicle and don't varnish or even varnish out except with the same or until the picture is at least a year old. Or else begin with a varnish or siccative medium and finish and over paint with an oily one; oil out with oil or oil and turpentine, wiping off carefully excess of oil; and, again, don't varnish until a year has gone by.

The Medium.— Your vehicle is most important to your work in every way. It can be hard or soft, or fast or slow drying, as I have said. And you can easily infer how this will act in your painting, both as to its substance and its permanence: how it will work, that is, and whether it will crack or not. Varnish or siccative will make it set more quickly — make it "tacky" and stiff in a little while, and you will have to keep adding more juice. As to the oil, of course, that is the normal softener and binding substance. But don't forget that its tendency is to darken, and in oiling out if you do that too freely, as well as in making the paint too thin with it, don't be surprised if it turns dark. It will give a leathery sort of shiny surface also which is very disagreeable.

Turpentine or petroleum will make the paint set quickly and dry flat — without gloss — make it flow watery and run if you do not look out. But they facilitate the handling, thin it for rubbing in and are necessary to balance the otherwise too heavy and oily vehicle. Your best medium should contain all three of these elements, their proportion determining its character.

Linseed oil and turpentine, one to three, is a good all round medium. With mastic or amber varnish, or with siccative de Harlem (which I have used all my life) you can make this a strong hard vehicle which will work and dry well, will not crack nor scale, and will "lock up" the more fugitive colors — a most necessary power sometimes. This mixture should be about one part varnish to five or six of the turpentine and oil. Mix a quantity of each of these vehicles and keep them in bottles for regular use. But don't forget that one has varnish in it and the other is oil and a layer of the varnish over the oil will make your picture crack. Under paint with the varnish medium and over paint with the oil; or paint from start to finish with either of them and you are safe, so far at least as the vehicle goes.

CHAPTER VII

PALETTES

THE most important qualities in a palette are that it should be large enough, and that it should balance well on the thumb. Whether it is round or square is a slight matter. The oval palette is usually best for the studio because the corners are seldom of use, and add weight. But for sketching, the square palette fits the box best.

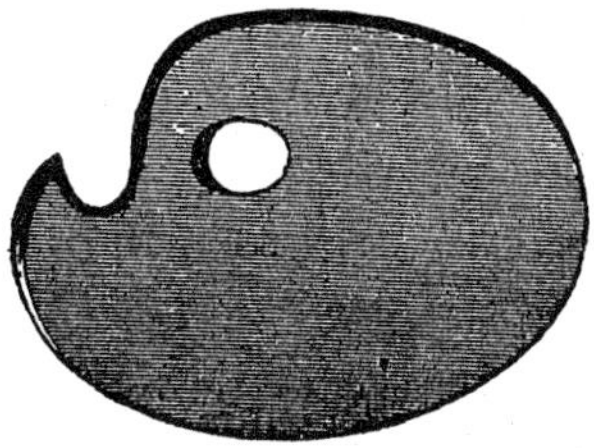

Oval Palette.

Get a palette much larger than you think you want. When you get it on your thumb the mixing-surface is much less than there seemed to be before it was set, for all the actual surface is between the row of colors and the thumb. If the palette is polished it is not essentially better; it is easier to keep clean, as far as looks go, but of no greater real service. If the choice is between a larger unpolished and a smaller polished one, the price being the consideration, get the larger one.

Get a light wood in preference to a dark wood for a choice of color, but not if there is better grain or lighter weight in the darker palette. It is an assistance in painting not to have to compare the tint you are mixing with too dark a surface, for the color looks lighter than it is ; so the light wood will help you to judge justly of the color while the palette is new. When it has been worked on a while it will come to have a sympathetic color anyway.

This bears on the cleanliness of your palette. It is a mistake to consider that cleanliness demands that the palette should be cleaned to the wood and polished after every painting. On the contrary, if a little of the paint is rubbed out over the palette every time it is cleaned, after a few weeks there will come a fine smooth polish of paint, which will have a delicate light gray color, which is a most friendly mixing surface.

Adapting. — When you get a new palette, before you use it take a little trouble to carve out the thumb-hole to fit your thumb. Make it large enough to go over the ball of the thumb, and set easily on the top of the hand. When the hole is too small the thumb gets numb after working a little while, which this will obviate.

Cleanliness. — The cleanliness of a palette consists in its being always in such a condition that you can handle it without getting dirty ; that the mixing-surface will not foul the freshly mixed paint; and that the paint around the edge is always so that you can pick up a fresh, clean brushful. If you try to clean off all your color every day and polish your palette nicely, you will not only take up more time with your palette than you do with your painting, but the fact that some left-over paint may be wasted will make you a little stingy in putting on fresh paint, which is one of the worst habits a beginner can fall into. You cannot paint well unless you have paint enough on your palette to use freely when you need it. It is all well enough to put on more, but nothing is more vexing than to have to squeeze out new paint at almost every brushful. You must have paint enough when you begin, to work with, or you waste too much time with these details.

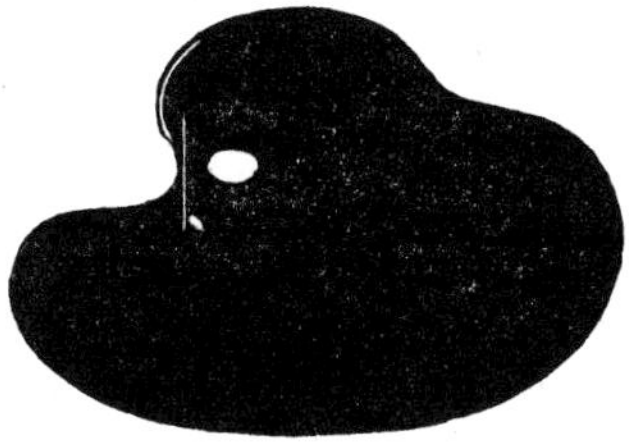

Arm Palette.

If you are painting every day, leave the good paint where it is at the end of your work, and scrape off all the muddy or half-used piles, and clean carefully all the palette except those places where the paint is still fresh and pure. Then, when you have to add more to that, clean that place with the palette-knife before squeezing out the new color. In this way the palette will not look like a centre-table, but it will be practically clean, have a good clear mixing-surface, and you will neither waste paint nor be stingy with it.

The Arm Palette. — For painting large canvases, where the largest-sized brushes are used and paint must be mixed in greater quantities, the arm palette is a most convenient thing if it is well balanced. It is in the way rather than otherwise for small pictures, and is useful only as it is particularly called for.

CHAPTER VIII

OTHER TOOLS

IT remains to speak of those tools which are not essentials, but conveniences, to painting. Even as conveniences, however, they are of importance enough to have an influence on your work. You can paint without them, but you will work more easily for the having of them; and something of the sort, although not necessarily of the same kind, you must have. You may improvise something, in other words, to take the place of these, but you would be wiser to get those which are made for the purpose.

The Box. — First, the box. You must keep your things together somehow, and it would be as well that you keep them in a box which is portable and suited to the purpose. When you sketch you must have a proper box, and why not have one which is equally serviceable in the house? Those most commonly sold to amateurs are of tin, and they are various in size and construction, and not too expensive. The only thing against them is the difficulty of adapting them to service different from that they were designed for; that is, if you want to put in a different sort of panel, or if you want to fix it in the cover for convenience, or anything like that, you cannot readily do it, because you cannot use tacks in them. This counts for more than would seem on a sketching trip. But the tin box is light, and is not easily broken, and while it is in shape is practical.

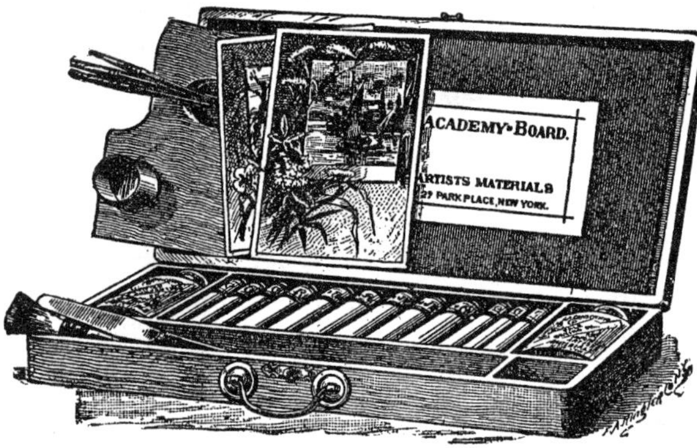

The Color Box.

The box to be most recommended is the wooden one. It costs more than the tin one, — about twice as much ; but you can always arrange it for an emergency very readily, and if it gets broken you can fix it yourself, or get any carpenter to do it for you, while you may be a good many miles from a tinner, who would be necessary to mend your tin box.

You had better not get too large a box. Get one long enough for the brushes; but if you are going to use it out-of-doors much, get a narrow one with a folding palette, so as to save weight. In this way you will get a larger palette than you could get in a smaller and wider box, which is an important consideration.

The Palette-Knife. — Of more immediate necessity to your painting is the palette-knife. You

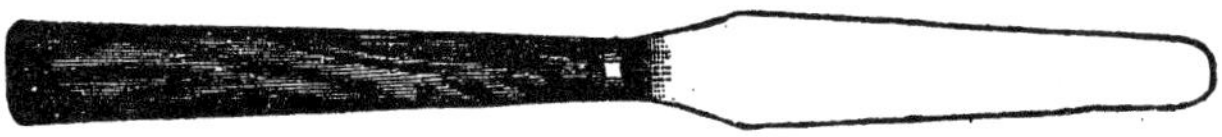

Palette Knife.

cannot keep the palette clean without it. Now and again you may want to mix colors, or even paint with it. But you constantly get rid of the too much mixed color on your palette with it, and this is essential to good painting. Take some care to select a good knife; have the blade long enough to be springy and flexible, but not too long. About five inches from the wood of the handle to the end of the blade is a good length. And see that it bends in a true curve from one end to the other, and is not stiff at the end and weak in the middle. It should have the same even elasticity that a brush should have.

For painting you need a "trowel palette-knife," which has a bent shank, making the blade and the handle on different levels, so that as you press the blade to the canvas, the fingers are kept away from the painted surface. The shank should be round, and the blade very fine and flexible. The knife should balance nicely in the hand, and turn freely in the fingers, so that you can paint with either face of the blade with equal balance. It takes some care to pick out a good trowel-knife, as a poor one is worse than none.

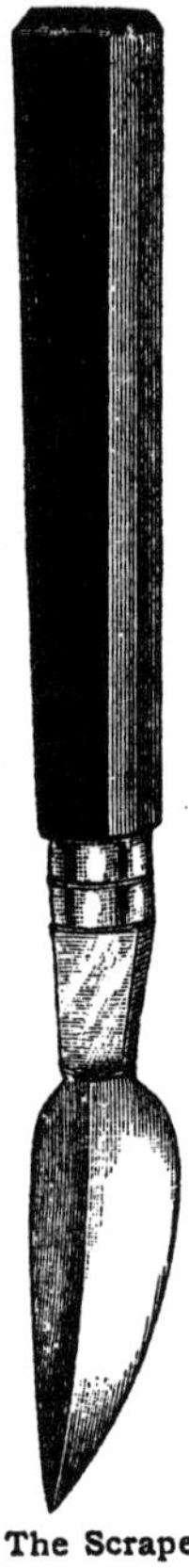

The Scraper.

The Scraper. — You frequently need to scrape rough paint from a canvas or a picture, and you need to scrape strongly to get a dirty palette clean. You can use an old razor for the first purpose, or a piece of broken glass, if you use it carefully, and any old knife can be used to clean your palette. But a regular tool is better than either. The scraper here shown is the best.

The Oil-Cup. — Do not use oils and vehicles very much. But when you need them you must have something to keep them in, convenient to the brush when working. It should have a spring to hold it on to the palette, and of such form that the contents are not easily spilled by the movement of the hand or the body when painting.

The form here illustrated is the best that has been brought out so far.

The Mahl-Stick. — Sometimes you want to rest

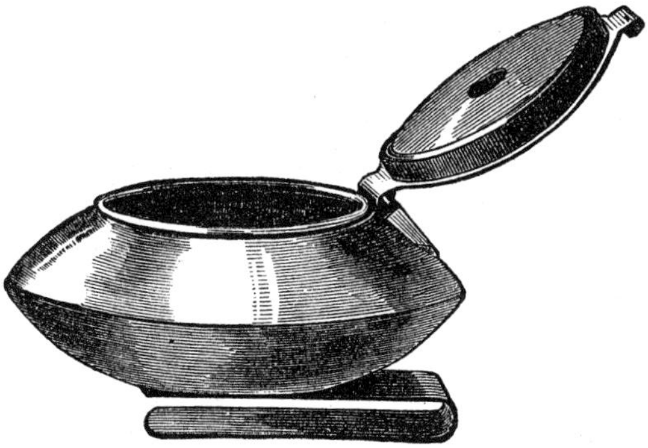

The Oil-Cup.

the hand when painting, for steadiness. The "mahl-" or rest-stick has a ball on the end, which one usually covers with a wad of rag, so that it can be placed against the canvas without injury, and the hand rested on it. It is so light that it

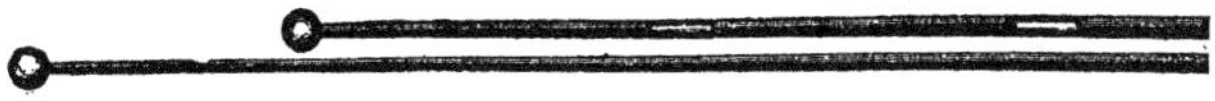

Mahl-Sticks.

can be held with the brushes in the palette hand, and stiff enough to support the brush-hand.

Sketching Adjuncts. — Out-of-doors you must have a seat, and you should have an umbrella. The best seat for a man, because it can be folded into so small a space, is the three-legged stool. This is not usually satisfactory for a woman, whose skirts tip it over. The better seat for her is shown below. The back is not very firm, but it does give support, and the whole is light and strong.

The umbrella

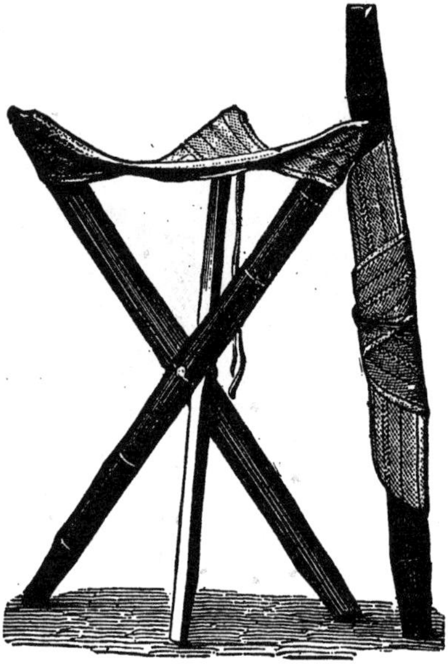

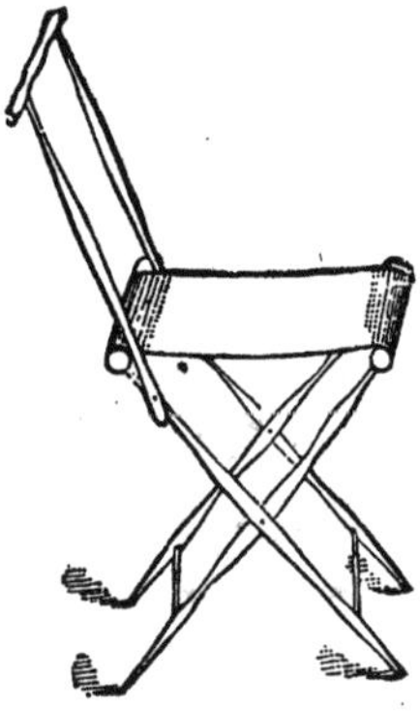

should be large and light, and one such as the illustration, with a valve in the top to let the wind and hot air through, will be found cooler and less easily blown over. You should have some strong rings sewed on to it, so that you can fasten it from four sides by strings, to keep it steady if the wind blows hard. The umbrella should be of light-colored material, preferably white; but if it is lined with black, the shade will be better, and give no false glow to the color.

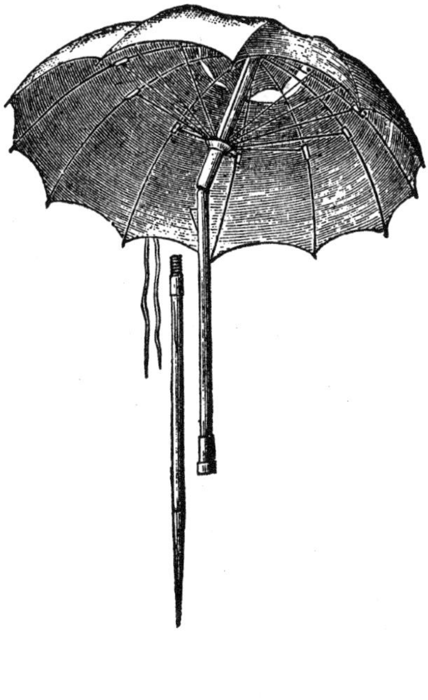

CHAPTER IX

STUDIOS

A PAINTING-ROOM is always a matter of serious consideration, and to the beginner one of difficulty. The arrangement of light is not easy, and a special window is almost always out of the question; yet in some way the light must be so managed that the canvas is not covered with reflected lights which prevent one from seeing what the paint is really like.

The North Light. — The first thing to be looked for is a steady light which will be always about the same, and not be sunny part of the time and in the shade the rest. A window looking to the north for this reason is generally selected. The sun does not come into it, and the light is diffused and regular. The effect of the light in the studio is cool, but colors are justly seen in it, and the light that falls on any object or model in it will be always the same. If there is to be a skylight, this should be arranged in the same way. The sash must not be flat, but must be nearly enough to the vertical to prevent the sun's direct rays from entering, and it must for that purpose face to the north. This makes the skylight practically a high north light in the roof or ceiling, and that is what it should be.

Whether the sash is above the ceiling or just below it, in the roof or in the wall, is of no particular importance. The thing to be seen to is that it is high enough for the light to enter above the head of the painter, and that it be so directed that only north light can come in.

The size of the window is also to be carefully considered. It should not be too large. Too much light will be sure to interfere with the proper control of light and shade on your model, and too little will make your painting too dark. The position of the window with reference to the shape of the room has to do with this. The most probable form of a room is long and narrow. For painting it is better that the window be in the middle of the end wall, high up, rather than in the middle of the side wall. You will find that you can more easily get distance from your model, and at the same time get the light both on him and on your canvas. But a painting-room should not be too narrow. About one-third longer than it is wide, with the window in one end, will give you a good light, and the further end of the room will not be too dark, as it would be apt to be if the room were longer. Preferably, too, the window should be to the left of the centre of the wall rather than to the right, as you face it; so that when you are as near the side wall as you can get, with the light over your left shoulder (as it should be), the light will strike on the canvas well, and not too directly on the front of the model. It will give you a better lateral position to the window, in other words. If you have to accept a window in a side wall, this is even more to be looked for. If the window is to the right of the centre, you will have a strong side-light on your model; but you will either have no light on your canvas, or you will have to turn so that the light falls on your canvas from the right, which is awkward, as the paint is in the shadow of the hand and brush which puts it on.

The height of the lower part of the window should be at least six feet from the floor, and for ordinary purposes the proportion of window space to floor space should be about one-tenth. It is impossible to give a rule; but if the floor is about twelve feet by sixteen, say, a window about five feet by four will be enough, or six and a half by three if it is placed horizontally. If you want intense light with strong contrast of light and shade on your model, have the window smaller and squarer, and place your easel just under it, where the light is good. The rest of the room will be dark. Better have the window large enough, and have it so curtained that you can cut off as much light as you need to. All this is if you are going to make yourself a window; in which case you will think well before you commit yourself. More probably you will have to get along as best you can with the ordinary room and the ordinary window. In which case get a high room with the window running up as close to the ceiling as possible, and facing north, then you can curtain it so as to control the light.

Arrangement of Ordinary Windows. — For a good working light you should have only one window in your room; for the light coming in from two openings will make a crossing of rays which will not only interfere with the simplicity of the effect of light and shade on your model, but will make a glare on your canvas. You can either close the light out of the right-hand window, or, better, arrange a curtain so the light from one window will not fall on the same place as that from the other.

When you are working from still life or from a model this is often an advantage, for you can have a strong side-light on the model, and a second light on the canvas. To arrange this, have a sort of crane made of iron, shaped like a carpenter's square, which will swing at right angles with the wall, the arm reaching, say, six feet into the room. Swing this by means of staples well up to the ceiling, so that the light cannot get over it, and near to the right-hand window. From this arm you can hang a thick, dark curtain, which will cover and shut out the light from the right-hand window when swung back over it. If you want to pose your model in the light of that window, while you paint in that of the other, swing the curtain out into the room at right angles to the wall, and it will prevent a cross light from the two windows; so that when the model is posed back of the curtain the light from that window will not fall on the canvas, nor the light from the other fall on the model.

The light will be best on your picture coming from well above you as you work. There will then be no reflections on the paint. You may find it necessary to cover entirely the lower half of the window which gives your painting-light. You will find it useful to have a shade of good solid holland, arranged with the roller at the bottom, and a string running up through a pulley at the top; so that you may pull the shade *up* from the bottom instead of *down* from the top, and so cut off as much of the lower part of the window as is necessary.

If you need the light from the lower part of the window, you may make a thin curtain of muslin to cover the lower sash, which will let the light through, but diffuse the rays and prevent reflection.

The Size of the Studio. — Of course a large studio is a good thing, but it is not always at one's command. But you should try to have the room large enough to let you work freely, and have distance enough from the model. The size that I have mentioned, twelve feet by sixteen, is as small as one should have, and one that you can almost always get. If the room is smaller than that, you cannot do much in it, and fifteen by twenty will give ample space.

PART II

GENERAL PRINCIPLES

CHAPTER X

MENTAL ATTITUDE

THERE is a theoretical and a practical side to art. The business of the student is with the practical. Theories are not a part of his work. Before any theoretical work is done there is the bald work of learning to see facts justly, in their proper degree of relative importance; and how to convey these facts visibly, so that they shall be recognizable to another person.

The ideals of art are for the artist; not for the student. The student's ideal should be only to see quickly and justly, and to render directly and frankly.

Technique is a word which includes all the material and educational resources of representation. The beginner need bother himself little with what is good and what is bad technique. Let him study facts and their representation only. Choice of means and materials implies a knowledge by which he can choose. The beginner can have no such knowledge. Choice, then, is not for him; but to work quite simply with whatever comes to hand, intent only on training the eye to see, the brain to judge, and the hand to execute. Later, with the gaining of experience and of knowledge, for both will surely come, the determination of what is best suited for the individual temperament or purpose will work itself out naturally.

The student should not allow the theoretical basis of art to interfere with the directness of his study of the material and the actual. Nevertheless, he should know the fact that there is something back of the material and the actual, as well as in a general way what that something is.

Because the student's business is with the practical is no reason why he should remain ignorant of everything else. It is important that he should think as a painter as well as work as a painter. If he has no thought of what all this practical is for, he will get a false idea of his craft. He will see, and think of, and believe in, nothing but the craftsmanship: that which every good workman respects as good and necessary, but which the wise workman knows is but the perfect means for the expression of thought.

Some consideration, then, of the theoretical side of art is necessary in a book of this kind. A number of considerations arise at the outset, about which you must make up your mind:—

Is judgment of a picture based on individual liking?

Can you hope to paint well by following your own liking only?

Is it worth your while to try to do good work?

Can you hope to do good work at all?

You must decide these questions for yourself, but you must remember that it depends upon how you decide them whether your work will be good or bad.

To take the last consideration first, you may be sure that it is worth while to try to do good work, and mainly because you may hope to do as good work as you want to do. That is, precisely as good work as you are willing to take the trouble to learn to do. Talent is only another name for love of a thing. If you love a thing enough to try to find out what is good, to train your judgment; and to train your abilities up to what that judgment tells you is good, the good work is only a matter of time.

You will notice that you must train your judgment as well as your ability; not all at once, of course. But how can you hope to do good work if you do not know what good work is when you see it? If you have no point of view, how can you tell what you are working for, what you are aiming at? And if you do not know what you are aiming at, are you likely to hit anything?

Train Your Judgment. — Let us say, then, that you must train your critical judgment. How are you to set about it?

In the first place, don't set up your own liking as a criterion. Make up your mind that when it comes to a choice between your personal taste and that of some one who may be supposed to know, between what you think and what has been consented to by all the men who have ever had an opinion worthy of respect, you may rest assured that you are wrong. And when you have made up your mind to that, when you have reached that mental attitude, you have taken a long step towards training your judgment; for you have admitted a standard outside of mere opinion.

Another attitude that you should place your mind in is one of catholicity — one of openness to the possibility of there being many ways of being right. Don't allow yourself to take it for granted that any one school or way of painting or looking at things is the only right one, and that all the other ways are wrong. That point of view may do for a man who has studied and thought, and finally arrived at that conclusion which suits his mind and his nature, — but it will not do for a student. Such an attitude is a sure bar to progress. It results in narrowness of idea, narrowness of perception, and narrowness of appreciation. You should try all things, and hold fast to that which is good. And having found what is good, and even while holding fast to it, you should remember that what is good and true for you is not necessarily the only good and true for some one else. You must not only hold to your own liberty of choice, but recognize the same right for others. If this is not recognized, what room has originality to work in?

The range of subject, of style, and of technical methods among acknowledged masters, should alone be proof of the fact that there is no one way which is the only good way; and if you would know how to judge and like a good picture, the study of really great pictures, without regard to school, is the way to learn.

How to Look at Pictures. — The study of pictures means something more than merely looking at them and counting the figures in them. It implies the study of the treatment of the subject in every way. The management of light and shade; the color; the composition and drawing; and finally those technical processes of brush-work by means of which the canvas gets covered, and the idea of the artist becomes visible. All these things are important in some degree; they all go to the making of the complete work of art: and you do not understand the picture, you do not really and fully judge it, unless you know how to appreciate the bearing on the result, of all the means which were used to bring it about. All this adds to your own technical knowledge as well as to your critical judgment, both of which ends are important to your becoming a good painter.

Why Paint Well. — You see I am assuming that you wish to be a good painter. There is no reason why you should be a bad painter because you are not a professional one. The better you paint the better your appreciation will be of all good work, the keener your appreciation of what is beautiful in nature, and the greater your satisfaction and pleasure in your own work. There are better reasons for painting than the desire to "make a picture." Painting implies making a picture, it is true; but it means also seeing and representing charming things, and working out problems of beauty in the expression of color and form: and this is something more than what is commonly meant by a picture. The picture comes, and is the result; but the making of it carries with it a pleasure and joy which are in exact proportion to the power of appreciation, perception, and expression of the painter. This is the real reason for painting, and it makes the desire and the attempt to paint well a matter of course.

Craftsmanship. — The mechanical side of painting naturally is an important part of your problem. You cannot be too catholic in your opinion with regard to it. It is vital that you be not narrowed by any prejudices as to the surface effect of paint. Whether the canvas be smooth or rough, the paint thick or thin, the details few or many, — the goodness or badness of the picture does not depend on any of these. They are or should be the result, the natural outcome because the natural means of expression, of the manner in which the picture is conceived. One picture may demand one way of painting and another demand a quite different way; and each way be the best possible for the thing expressed. It all depends on the man; the make-up of his mind; the way he sees things; the results he aims to attain, —all of them controlled more or less by temperament and idiosyncrasy. What would produce a perfect work for one man would not do at all for another. The works of the great masters offer the most marked contrasts of ideal and of treatment, and painters have varied greatly in their manner of some painting at different periods of their lives. Rembrandt, for instance, painted very thinly in his early years, with transparent shadows and carefully modelled, solidly loaded lights. Later in life he painted most roughly; and "The Syndics" was so heavily and roughly loaded that even now, after two hundred years, the paint stands out in lumps — and this is one of his masterpieces. So again, if you will compare the manipulation in the work of Raphael with that of Tintoretto, that of Rubens with that of Velasquez, or most markedly, the work of Frans Hals with that of Gerard

Dou, you will see that the greatest extremes of handling are consistent with equal greatness of result.

Finish. — From this you may conclude that what is generally understood by the word "finish" is not necessarily a thing to be sought for. The tendency of great painters is rather away from excessive smoothness and detail than towards it. While a picture may be a good one and be very minute and smooth, it by no means follows that a picture is bad because it is rough. The truth is that the test of a picture does not lie in the character of the pigment surface *in itself* at all, nor in whether it be full of detail or the reverse, but in the conception and in the harmonious relation of the technique to the manner in which the whole is conceived. The true "finish" is whatever surface the picture happens to have when the idea which is the purpose of the picture is fully expressed, with nothing lacking to make that expression more complete, nor with anything present which is not needed to that completeness. This too is the truth about "breadth," that much misunderstood word. Breadth is not merely breadth of brush stroke. It is breadth of idea, breadth of perception; the power of conceiving the picture as a whole, and the power of not putting in any details which will interfere with the unity of effect.

Intent. — In this connection it would be well to bear in mind the purpose of the work on which the painter may be engaged. A man would, and should, work very differently on canvases intended for a study, a sketch, and a picture. The study would contain many things which the other two would not need. It is the work in which and by which the painter informs himself. It is his way of acquiring facts, or of assuring himself of what he wants and how he wants it. And he may put into it all sorts of things for their value as facts which he may never care to use, but which he wishes to have at command in case he should want them.

The sketch, on the other hand, is a note of an effect merely, or of a general idea, and calls for only those qualities which most successfully show the central idea, which might sometime become a picture, or which suggests a scheme. A carefully worked-up sketch is a contradiction in terms, just as a careless study would be.

A picture might have more or less of the character of either of these two types, and yet belong to neither. It might have the sketch as its motive, and would use as much or as little of the material of the study as should be needed to make the result express exactly the idea the painter wished to impart, and no more and no less.

All these things should be borne in mind, as

you study the characteristics of paintings to learn what they can mean to you beyond the surface which is obvious to any one; or as you work on your own canvas to attain such power or proficiency, such cleverness or facility, as you may conclude it is worth your while to try for.

CHAPTER XI

TRADITION AND INDIVIDUALITY

A PICTURE is made up of many elements. Certain of them are essentially abstract. They must be thought out by a sort of *mental vision without words.* This is the most subtle and intimate part of the picture. These are the means by which the ideal is brought into the picture.

Line, Mass, and Color. — Such are the qualities of *line*, dissociated from representation; of *mass*, not as representing external forms; and *color*, considered as a *quality*, not as yet expressed visibly in pigment, nor representing the color of any *thing*. When these elements are combined they may make up such conceptions as proportion, rhythm, repetition, and balance, with all the modifications that may come from still further combination.

It is because these elements are qualities in themselves beautiful that actual objects not beautiful may be made so in a painting, by being treated as *color* or *line* or *mass*, and so given place on the canvas, rather than as being of themselves interesting. A face, for instance, may be ugly as a *face*, yet be beautiful as color or light and shade in the picture. These qualities, I say, do not represent — they do not necessarily even exist, except in the mind to which they are the terms of its thought. Nevertheless, they are the soul of the picture. For whatever the subject, or the objects chosen for representation, it is by working out combinations of these elements, through and by means of those objects, that the picture really is made.

The picture, *as a work of art*, is not the representation of objects making up a subject, but a fabric woven of color, line, and mass; of form, proportion, balance, rhythm, and movement, expressed through those actual objects in the picture which give it visible form.

I do not purpose to go deeply into these matters here. Elsewhere, as they bear practically on the subject in hand, as in the chapters on "Composition" and on "Color," I shall speak of them more fully. But I wish here to call attention to this abstract side of painting in order to show the relation between the two classes of things, the one abstract and the other concrete, which together are needed to make up a picture.

The concrete, or material, part of a picture includes all those things which you can look at or feel on the canvas; and by seeing which you can also see the abstract qualities, which do not *visibly* exist until made visible through the disposition of these tangible things, on the canvas.

Beyond this is included all the technical qualities of expression; form, as *drawing;* all representations of objects; the pigment by means of which color is seen; and all those technical processes which produce the various kinds of surface in the putting on of paint, and bring about the different effects of light and shade and color, form or accent.

In learning to paint, it is with these concrete things that you should concern yourself mainly. The science of painting consists in the knowledge of how to be the master of all the practical means of the craft. For it is with these that you must work, with these you must express yourself. These are the tools of your trade. They are the words of your art language — the language itself being the abstract elements — and the thoughts, the combinations which you may conceive in your brain by means of these abstract elements.

You must have absolute command of these *materials* of painting. No matter how ideal your thought may be, no matter how fine your feeling for line and color and composition, if you do not know how to handle the gross material which is the only medium by which this can all be made visible and recognizable to another person, you will fail of either expressing yourself, or of representing anything else.

Now you will see what I have been driving at

all this time; why I have been talking in terms which may well be called not practical. I want to fix your attention on the fact that there are two qualities in a picture: that one will be always within you, mainly, and will control the character of your picture, because it will be the expression of your mental self; and the other the practical part, which any one may, and all painters must learn, because it is the only means of getting the first into existence.

The one, the abstract part, no one can tell you how to cultivate nor how to use. If I tried to do so, it would be my idea and not yours which would result. I can only tell you that it is the *thought of art*, and you must think your own thoughts.

But the other, the material, the concrete, the practical, it is the purpose of this whole book to help you to understand and to acquire the mastery of, so far as may be done by words.

Teaching by words is difficult, and never completely satisfactory. But much may be done. If you will use your own brains, so that what does not seem clear at first may come to have a meaning because of your thinking about it, we may accomplish a great deal. I cannot make you paint. I cannot make you understand. I can give you the principles, but you must apply them and think them out.

Everything I say must be in a measure general; for the needs of every one are individual, and the requirement of each technical problem is individual. I must speak for all, and not to any one. Yet I shall state principles which can always be made to apply to each single need, and I will try to show how the application may be made.

Technique. — The science of painting consists of a variety of processes by means of which a canvas is covered with pigment, and various objects are represented thereon. The whole body of method and means is called technique; the several parts of technique are called by names of their own. That part which applies to the putting on of the paint may be generally called *handling*, although the word *painting* is sometimes restricted to this sense, and *brush-work* is often used for the same thing. The other technical means will be spoken of in their proper place. Let me say now a few words as to *handling* in general.

Where did all this technique come from?

From experiment.

Ever since art began, men have been searching for means of fixing ideas upon surfaces. But it is only within the last four hundred years that the processes of oil painting have been in existence — simply because they are peculiar to the use of pigments ground in oil as a vehicle, and the oil medium was not invented until the middle of the fifteenth century.

With the invention of this medium new possibilities came into the world, and a continual succession of painters have been inventing ways of putting on paint, the result being the stock of methods and processes of handling which are the groundwork of the art of painting to-day.

From time to time there have been groups of artists who have used common methods, and who have developed expression through those methods which became characteristic of their epoch; and because the resulting pictures were of a high degree of perfection, their methods of handling acquired an authority which had a very determining effect on different periods of painting.

In this way have come those ideas as to what kind of painting or what ways of putting paint on canvas should be accepted as "legitimate." And the methods accepted as legitimate or condemned as illegitimate have been varied from time to time — those condemned by one period being advocated by another; and the processes themselves have been almost as varied as the periods or groups of men using them.

In the long run, methods and processes have received such authoritative sanction from having been each and all used by undoubted masters, that they have become the traditional property of all art, which any one is free to use as he finds need of them. They have become the stock in trade of the craft.

The artist may use them as he will, provided only he will take the trouble to understand them. He must understand them, because the manipulations which make up these different processes accomplish different effects and different qualities; and as the painter aims at results, if he does not understand the result of a process when he uses it, he will get a different one from that which he intended.

The painter should not be hampered by process; he should not be controlled in the expression of himself by tradition. He should feel free to use any or all means to bring about the result he aims at, and he should allow no tradition or point of view to prevent him from selecting whichever means will most surely or satisfactorily bring about his true purpose.

Of course there are many ways of using paint which are unsafe. Some pigments are unsafe to use because they either do not hold their own color, or tend to destroy the color of others. You should always bear this in mind; and if you care for the permanence of your work, you should not use such materials or such processes as work against it. But beyond this, the whole range of the experience and experiment of the workers who have gone before you are at your command, to help you to express yourself most perfectly or completely; to represent whatever of visible beauty you may conceive or perceive.

And this is the whole aim of the painter; to stand for this is the whole purpose of the picture.

CHAPTER XII

ORIGINALITY

ORIGINALITY is not a thing to strive for. If it comes, it is not through striving. The search for originality seldom results in anything worth having. It is a quality inherent in the man; and the best way of being original in your work is to be natural. Perhaps the most useful advice which you could receive is that you be always natural. Never be artificial nor insincere; never copy another person's subject, manner, or method, with the intention of doing as he does. The most original things are often the most simple, because they have come naturally from a sincere desire to express what has been seen or felt, in the most direct way.

If every one were content to be himself, there would be no dearth of originality. No two people are alike, neither are any two painters alike; they could not be. They do not look alike, nor see alike, nor feel alike, nor think alike. How, then, should they paint alike? The attempt to do a thing because another has made a success of that sort of thing is the most fruitful source of the commonplace in painting.

Paint that which appeals to you most fully. Don't try to paint what appeals to some one else. If you like it, then do it; and do it in the most direct way you can find; only do it so as to fully and completely convey just what it is that *you* like, unaffected by anything else. And because you have seen or felt for yourself in your own way, and expressed that; and because you are not another, nor like any other that ever was, what you have done will not be like anything else that ever was — and that is originality.

But never imitate yourself, either. Be open. Be ready to receive impressions and emotions. And if you have done one thing well, accept that in itself as a reason for not doing it again. There are always plenty of things — ideas, impressions, conceptions, appreciations — waiting to be painted; and if you try to paint one twice, you fail once of freshness, and lose a chance of doing a new thing.

That is what a painter is for, not to cover a canvas with paint, hang it on a wall, and call it by a name. The painter is the eye of the people. He sees things which they have no time to look for, or looking, have not learned to see. The painter serves his purpose best when he recognizes the beautiful where it was not perceived before, and so sets it forth that it is recognized to be beautiful through his having seen it.

There is the difference between the artist and

the photograph, which sees only facts as facts; which while often distorting them does so mindlessly, and at best, when accurate, gives the bad with the good in unconscious impartiality. But back of the painter's eye which sees and distinguishes is the painter's brain which selects and arranges, using facts as material for the expression of beauties more important than the facts.

But what is a picture? I have met some strange though positive notions as to what is and what is not a picture. Some persons think that a certain (or uncertain) proportion of definite forms and objects are necessary to make canvas a picture; that it must contain some definite and tangible facts of the more obvious kind. I remember one man who asserted that a canvas in an exhibition was not a picture, but only a sketch, because it had nothing in it but an expanse of sea and sky. To make a picture of it there was needed at least a moon, and some birds, or better, a ship and some reflections. All this sort of thing is idle. A picture is not a picture because it has more of this or less of that; it is a picture because it is complete in the expression of the idea which is the cause of its existence. And that idea may be tangible or not. It may include many details or none. It is an idea which is best or only expressed by being made visible, and which is worthy of being expressed because of its beauty; and when that idea is wholly and fully visible on canvas or other surface, that surface is a picture. What the contents of a picture shall be is a matter personal to the painter of it. The manner in which it is conceived and produced is determined by his temperament and idiosyncrasy.

A picture is a visible idea expressed in terms of color, form, and line. It is the product of perception plus feeling, plus intent, plus knowledge, plus temperament, plus pigment. And as all these are differently proportioned in all persons, it is only a matter of being natural on the part of the painter that his picture should be original.

CHAPTER XIII

THE ARTIST AND THE STUDENT

IT is a mistake to make pictures too soon. The nearest a student is likely to get to a picture is a careful study, and he will be as successful with this, if he makes it for the study of it, as if he made it for the sake of making a picture — better probably. The making of a picture for the picture's sake is dangerous to the student. His is less likely to be sincere. He is apt to "idealize," to make up something according to some notion of how a picture should be, rather than from knowledge of how nature is. Real pictures grow from study of nature.

They are the outcome of maturity, not of the student stage. This implies something deeper than superficial facts, and a power of selection, — of choice and of purpose which must rest on a very broad and deep knowledge. The artist is always a student, of course; but he is not a student only. He is a student who knows what and why he wants to study; not one who is in process of finding out these things.

Aims. — It should be noted that the aim of the

student and the aim of the artist are essentially different. The student's first aim is to learn to see and represent nature's facts; to distinguish justly between relations. It is the training of the eye and the judgment. Imitation is not the highest art; but the highest art requires the ability to imitate as a mere power of representation. The mind must not be hampered in its expression by lack of knowledge and control of materials, and the painter who is constantly occupied with the problems he should have worked out in his student days, is just so far from being a master. He must have all his means perfectly at his command before he can freely express himself.

The acquirement of this mastery of means is the student's business. Everything he does which aids him in this makes him so much nearer to being a painter. But he must remember that he is still a student, and as he hopes to be a painter, must have patience with himself; must not hurry himself, must work as a student for the ends of a student.

All the facts of nature art uses. But she uses them as she needs them, simplifying, emphasizing, suppressing, combining as will best meet the necessities of the case in hand. All this requires the utmost knowledge, for it must be done in accordance not only with laws of art, but with the laws of nature.

There are changes which can be made, and be right — made as nature might make them. Other changes which would be false to nature's ways, and so false to art also. For art works through nature always, and in accordance with her. This is the aim of the painter, to express ideas through nature, not to express notions about nature.

The facts of nature are the material of art; the words of the language in which the ideas of art are to be conveyed. But there are truths more important than these facts. The underlying sentiment of which they are the external manifestation, and which is the vivifying spirit of them. This is the true fact of the picture.

It is more important to give the sentiment of the thing than to give the fact of it; not merely because it is more truly represented so, but because the beauty is shown in showing the character. For the character of the fact is the beauty of the fact.

To bring out the beauty which may lie in the fact is the aim of the artist; to acquire the ability to do this is the aim of the student.

CHAPTER XIV

HOW TO STUDY

THERE is a right and a wrong way to study, and it all centres around the fact that what you aim to learn is perception and expression. What you are to express you do not learn; you grow to that. But you must learn how to use all possible means; all the facts of visible nature, and all the characteristics of pigments. All qualities, color and form and texture, are but the means of your expression, and you must know how they may be used. Your perception and appreciation must be trained, and your mind stored with facts and relativities. Then you are ready to recognize and to convey the true inwardness you find in conditions commonplace to others.

You are to see where others see not; for it is marvellous how little the average eye sees of the really interesting things, how little of the visual facts, and how rarely it sees the picture before it is painted. All is material to the painter. It is not that "everything that is, is beautiful," but that everything that is has qualities and possibilities of beauty; and these, when expressed, make the picture, in spite of the superficial or obvious ugliness. In one sense nothing is commonplace, for everything exists visibly by means of light and color, and light and color are of the fundamental beauties. So arrange or look upon the commonplace that light and color are the most obvious qualities, and the commonplace sinks into the background — is lost. There is nothing like painting to make life fascinating; for there is nothing which brings so many charming combinations into your perception, as the habit of looking to find the possibilities of beauty in everything that comes within your view.

You must form the habit of looking always from the painter's point of view. The painter deals primarily with pigment, and what can be represented with pigment; chiefly color and light in the broadest sense, including form and composition, as things which give bodily presence and action to the possibilities of pigment. Shade, or shadow, of course, is an actuality in painting, because it is the foil of light and color, and furnishes the element of relation.

Methods. — Two general methods are at the command of the student from the first, — to study at once from nature, or to copy. I think I may safely claim to speak for the great body of teachers who are also professional artists, in saying that copying is a means of study rather for the advanced student than for the beginner. You cannot begin too soon to study nature with your own eyes, and to accumulate your own facts and observations and deductions. The use of copying is not to find out how to paint, but to see how many ways there are of painting. The great end of all study in painting is to train the eyes to see relations, to see them in nature. It is not to see that there are relations, but to see where they are; to recognize and to measure and to judge them. Painting is the art of perception before everything, and when you copy you only see, accept, what some one else has already perceived. Copying does not help you to *perceive*, it can only help to show you how something can be *expressed after* it has been perceived, and that is not the vital thing in the study of painting. Handling, composition, management of color, technique of the brush generally, may be studied by copying. These only — and for these things it is useful and wise. But the beginner is not ready for these, for they are not the alphabet, but the grammar of painting.

Danger. — The danger of too early copying is that the student learns to set too much value on surface qualities rather than those to which the surface is merely incidental. With this is the danger (a serious one, and one hard to overcome the results of) that the student becomes clever as a producer of pictures before he has trained his power to see. He becomes a student of pictures rather than a student of nature, and when in doubt will go to art rather than to nature for help and suggestion. Could anything be more fatal? Consider the things that student will have to unlearn before he can think a picture in terms of nature — the only healthy, the only prolific way of thinking. He sees always through other people's eyes, and thinks with other people's brains, and feels other people's emotions; that is not creation; that is the attitude for the spectator, not for the painter.

These things are all useful and good, but not for the beginner. Later, when you have found out something for yourself, when you have ground of your own to stand on, then you may not only without danger, but with benefit, go to the work of other men to see the range of possible point of view and expression, to see the scope of technical material and individual adaptation; and so broaden your own mental view and sympathy, possibly reform or educate your taste, and perhaps get some hints which will help you in the solving of some future problem.

But rather than the undue sophistication which can result from unwise copying, — the over-knowledge of process and surface, and under-knowledge of nature, — is to be preferred a frank crudeness of work which is the result of an honest going to nature for study. You should not expect a perfect eye for color and form too soon. Better a healthily youthful crudity of perception based on nature, and standing for what you have yourself studied and worked out, which represents your own attainment, than a greater show of knowledge which is insincere and superficial because it represents a mere acceptance of the facts set down by others; and not only that, but even with it an acceptance also of the actual terms used by those others.

Often copying is the most convenient way in which you can get help. There is really much to be learned from it, and you can make a picture serve as a criticism on your own work. Particularly in the matter of color or tone, as something to recognize the achievement of for its own sake. If you can recognize good color as such, aside from what it represents, if you can appreciate tone in a picture which is the work of some one else, you are so much the more likely to notice the lack of those qualities in your own work. So, too, there are qualities of brush-work which are always good, and some which are always bad. You can study the former positively, and the latter negatively, in studying and copying other pictures.

I have mentioned the training of your critical judgment as a necessity in your education. You can do it slowly in learning to paint, but you can facilitate that training by copying and studying really good pictures, if you do it in the right way.

The Right Way. — So if you do copy, do it in the right way, so as to get all the real help out of it, and not so as to have to unlearn the greater part of it. Don't copy "to get a picture." Don't make a copy which at a distance has a resemblance to the original, but which on a more careful study shows none of the qualities which make the original what it is. Not only see to it that the same subtleties of perception and representation are preserved in your copy, but that they are attained in the same way. Use the same brush-work or other execution. Use the same pigments in the same places, with the same vehicles ; study the original with your brain as well as with your eyes and hands ; try to see not only how the painter did a certain thing but why. So that as you work, you follow him in the working out of his problem, and make it your problem also. In this way you will get some real good from his picture, and not a mere canvas which has been of no use to you, nor can be of any satisfaction to any one else who knows a good picture (copy or original) when he sees it.

Why Copy. — There are only two good reasons for making a copy, — to study the original as a problem, and to have something to serve as an example of the master on a work which you like. And in either case such a sincere manner of copying as I urge is the only possible way to get what you want. To "get a picture," regardless of whether it really does justice to the original, is the wrong way, and this leads always through bad copying to bad painting, and you are fortunate if you escape an entire perversion of your point of view.

You may be able to make some money now and again by doing this sort of thing, but you will never learn anything from it. On the contrary, it is the surest way you could find of closing your eyes to all that is worth seeing.

Get to Nature. — If you would really learn to paint, to see for yourself, to represent what you see in your own way, you cannot get to nature too soon. Don't bother about what the thing is, so long as it is nature herself. By nature I mean anything, absolutely anything which exists of itself, not painted. Whether it be the living figure, or a cast, or a bit of landscape, or a room interior — all things which actually exist must show themselves by the facts of light falling upon them: the relation of color, and the contrasts of light and dark. Whatever you see is useful to you in this way, for these bring about all the qualities and conditions which you most need to study. But models are not always at command, interiors do not easily stay a long time at your disposal, and bits of landscape which interest you are not always easy to get at; for a student is apt to be either far advanced or unusually ardent who will find interest in the first combination which falls under his eye. Therefore the most practically useful material for study, which is always "nature," is what we call "still life," — "*morte*" *nature*, dead nature is the better or more descriptive name the French give to it. By this is meant any and all combinations of objects and backgrounds grouped arbitrarily for representation. Bottles and jugs and fruits, books and bric-a-brac; all sorts of things lend themselves readily and interestingly to this use.

The great value of still life for the student lies in the variety of combinations of color and form, of light and shade and texture, that he can always command. There is practically no problem possible to in-the-house light which may not be worked out by means of still life. The training in perception and representation, in composition and arrangement, and in technique, which it will give you is invaluable; and most important of all, while you can always make such arrangements as will interest you, because you need place only such things or colors as you like, you are really studying nature herself, you are looking at the things themselves, and the result you get is the product of your own eyes and brain. The problem is entirely your own, both in the stating and the solving, and what you learn is well learned, and represents a definite progress along the right line.

You have worked for the sake of the working, and there is nothing which you have got from it that may not be applicable to any future work you may do, that does not directly lead to the great object you have in view, — to learn how to paint well.

Be Sincere. — But, above all, be sincere with yourself; don't do anything to be clever, nor because it pleases some one else. Painting is difficult enough at best. You need all the interest and fascination that the most charming thing can have for you to help you to do it so that it is worth the trouble. Don't take away the whole life of it by insincerity. A very thoughtful painter said to me once that he believed that all really good pictures could be shown to be good by the sole criterion of conviction. Can you think of any painting being good without it? Can you think of any amount of cleverness and ability making a picture good without that. And it is quite as important in study as elsewhere. Never do anything except seriously; take yourself and your work seriously; only by serious work can serious results come.

Joy in Your Work. — Do it because you like to. But like good work and hate bad work; and, above all, hate half-way work. Understand yourself: what you want to do and why you want to do it, and then be honest enough with yourself to work till you have honestly done what you wanted to do, and as you wanted to do it.

PART III

TECHNICAL PRINCIPLES

CHAPTER XV

TECHNICAL PRELIMINARIES

Reasons. — Painting is something more than laying on paint. It implies a certain amount of knowledge of necessary preliminaries — techinal matters which are not strictly painting, but without which good painting is impossible.

It is all well enough to put paint on canvas, but there must be a knowledge on which to base the where and the why of laying it on, as well as the knowledge of how to lay it on. If anything, the where and why are more important than the how. There are almost infinite methods and processes of getting the paint onto the surface. Every painter may select or invent his own way, and provided it accomplishes the main purpose — the bringing about of combinations of form, relative color and pitch, the expression of an idea — it is all right. But there are laws which govern the positions of the different spots of paint, and the reasons for placing them in certain relations. These laws are back of personal idiosyncrasy. They are a part of the laws which control all material things. The painter may no more go contrary to them in painting than he may go contrary to physical laws in any of the practical matters of life. If pigments are not used in accordance with the laws governing their chemical composition, they will not stand. If the laws of proportion are not observed in composition, the picture will not balance. The laws of color harmony are as mathematically fixed as the law of gravity. So, too, the relations of size, which give the impression of nearness or distance to objects, rest on the laws of optics. You have infinite scope for individual expression inside of those laws, but you cannot go outside of them.

Scientific Knowledge not Necessary.—It is not necessary that you should have any special knowledge of all these laws nor even of the application of them; but you must recognize their existence, and have some practical notions about them and their effect on your work.

You can of course carry the study as far as you are interested to go. The farther the better. The more you study them the more you will find them interesting, and the easier will it be for you to work freely within their limitations. But this is not the place for special study. There are books which treat particularly of these things, and you must go to them.

But a superficial consideration of these subjects cannot be left out of any book which would be really helpful to the student of painting. I can go into the theory of things only so far as to give you that amount of practical knowledge which is absolutely necessary to you as a painter. What I shall give is given only because it cannot be wisely left out, and the form of it as well as the substance and quantity are determined by the same reason.

As you hope to become a painter, then, do not neglect to study and think of this part of the book, not merely as a preliminary to the process of painting, but as containing matter which is continually essential to it — which is part and parcel of it.

Another reason for the careful reading of these chapters is that any discussion of the art of painting necessarily demands the use of words or phrases which must be understood. To speak of technical things presupposes the use of technical phrases, and without a knowledge of the words there can be no comprehension of the thought.

CHAPTER XVI

DRAWING

DRAWING is basic to painting. Good painting cannot exist without it. I do not mean that there must be always the outline felt or seen, but that the understanding of relative position, size, and form must be felt; and that is drawing. Drawing is not merely form, but implies these other things, and painting is not legible without them. They go to the completeness of expression. Movement, and action, as well as composition and all that it implies or includes, depend upon drawing, and they are vital to a painting.

Importance of Drawing. — Much has been said and written of drawing as being the most important thing in a picture; so much so, as to excuse all sorts of shortcomings in other directions. This is a mistake. Drawing is essential because you cannot lay on color to express anything without the colors taking shape, and this is drawing. But still the color itself, and other characteristics which are not strictly a part of drawing, are quite as important to painting, simply because the thing without them could not be a painting at all: it would be a drawing.

All painters fall into two classes, — those who are most sensitive to the refinements of form, and those most sensitive to refinements of color and tone. But the great colorists, the painters *par excellence*, the workers in pigment before everything else, those who find their sentiment mainly there, these are the men who have made painting what it is, and who have brought out its possibilities. And looking at painting from their point of view, drawing cannot be more important than other qualities.

Neglect of Drawing. — Great artists have sometimes not been perfect draughtsmen. They have been careless of exactness of form. But they have always been strong in the great essentials of drawing, and they have made up for such deficiencies as they showed, by their greatness in other directions. Delacroix, for instance, sometimes let his temperament run him into carelessness of form in his hurry to express his temperamental richness of color. These things are superficial to the greater ends he had in view, but we have to distinctly forgive it in accepting the picture. And a great colorist may be so forgiven; he makes up for his fault by other things. But there is no forgiveness for the student or the painter who is simply a poor draughtsman.

The effect of neglect of drawing is to make a weak picture. A painter, who was also an exceptionally fine draughtsman, once spoke of work weak in drawing as resembling "boned turkey." Lack of firmness, indecision, characterize the painter who cannot draw. Those firm, simple, but effective touches which are evident somewhere in the work of all good painters, are impossible without draughtsmanship. They mean precision. Precision means position. Position means drawing.

Proportions. — All good work is from the general to the particular, from the mass to the detail. Keep that in mind as a fundamental principle in good work, whatever the kind. You should never place a detail till you have placed your larger masses. The relative importance of things depends on the consideration of those most important first. Let this be your first rule in drawing.

Proportions next. Largest proportions, then exactness of relative proportions. Study first in masses. See nothing at first but the large planes. As Hunt said, "Hang the nose on to the head, not the head on to the nose." In getting proportions of the great masses, let no small variations of line or form break into your study of the whole. Therefore, see outlines first in straight lines and angles. If you cannot see them at first, study to find them; look at the long lines of movement; mass several curves into one line representing the general direction of them. Train yourself to look at things in this way. There is nothing which will not fall into position so. This will not be easy at first. The training of a quick perception of these things is a part of your training in drawing—the first essential. It is not that the straight lines are to be sought for themselves, but that they simplify the first breaking up of the whole into its parts, and so makes more easy the study of proportion. The accuracy of the general masses makes possible a greater accuracy of the lesser proportions which come within them.

You see form more truly also, when the perception of it is founded on a mass or a line indicating the larger character of it. It saves time for you, too. You do not have to rub out so much. The great lines and planes once established, everything else falls naturally into place. Spend much time over this part of a drawing. Cut the time you give to a drawing into parts, and let the part given to the laying in of larger proportions be from a third to a half of the whole time, and study and correct these until they are right.

Once these are right a very slight accent tells for twice what it would otherwise, and so you need much less detail to give the effect.

Modelling.—In the same way that you have laid out the proportions in mass, lay out your proportions of light and shade. Model your drawing by avoiding the small until the large variations of shade are in place. Avoid seeing curves in relief as you have avoided curves of outline. Try to analyze the modelling into flat planes, each one large enough to give a definite mass of relief. Don't be afraid of an edge in doing this. Let your flat tone come frankly up to the next tone and stop. This again is not for any effect in itself, but only for facility and exactness. Later you can loose it as much as you see fit in breaking up the drawing into the more delicate planes, and these again into the most subtle.

Study first the outline and then the planes. Constantly compare them as to relation; you will find it suggestive. Remember that your aim is to produce a whole, not a lot of parts, and although a whole includes the parts, the parts are incidental.

Measurements. — You will always have to use measurements for the sake of accuracy. Probably you will never be able to dispense with them. The best way would be to take them as a matter of course, and get so that you make them almost mechanically, without thinking of it. You will save yourself an immense deal of time and trouble by accepting this at once; for accuracy is impossible without measurements, and the habit of accuracy is the greatest time-saver.

Hold your charcoal in your hand freely, so that your thumb can slip along it and mark off parts of the object when you sight at them across the coal. Measure horizontal and vertical proportions into themselves and into each other. Height and breadth are checks to each other. If the height is a certain proportion of the breadth, then the smaller proportions of height must have equivalent proportions to each other *as well as to breadth.* Measure these and you are sure of being right.

Steps. — Divide your drawing into steps or stages of work. You will find it a helpful thing in studying. You will do it quite naturally later. Do it deliberately at first, as a matter of training.

First step. — Measure the extreme height and breadth of the whole group or object of your drawing, with accuracy, and mark each extreme.

Second step. — Outline the great mass of it with the simplest lines possible. Give the general shape of the whole. This blocks it in.

Third step. — Measure each of the objects in the group, or the parts most prominent, if it be a single object. Measure its height and breadth, both in its own proportion and in proportion to the dimensions of the other parts and of the whole. Enclose it in straight lines as you did with the whole mass.

Fourth step. — Find the more important of the lesser proportions in each object, and block them out also. This should map out your drawing exactly and with some completeness.

Fifth step. — Lay in simple flat tones to fill in

these outlines, and keep the relations of light and dark very carefully as you do so.

Sixth step. — This should leave your paper with a few large masses of dark and light, which can now be cut into again with the next smaller masses, giving more refinement to the whole. This also should so break up the edges as to get rid of any feeling of squareness or edginess.

Seventh step. — Put in such accents of dark, or take out such of light, as will give necessary character and force to the drawing.

I do not say that this method produces the most finished drawing; but it is a most excellent way to study drawing, and, more or less modified, is practically the basis of all methods. In practised hands it allows of any amount of exactness or freedom of execution. I have seen most beautiful work done in this way.

Home Study. — It is not necessary to have a teacher in order to draw well; but it is necessary to find out what are the essentials of good drawing, and to work definitely and acquire them.

Good drawing is a combination of exactness and freedom; and the exactness must come first. The structure of the thing must be shown without unnecessary detail. You should always look at any really good drawing you can come at, and try to see what there may be in it of helpful suggestion to you.

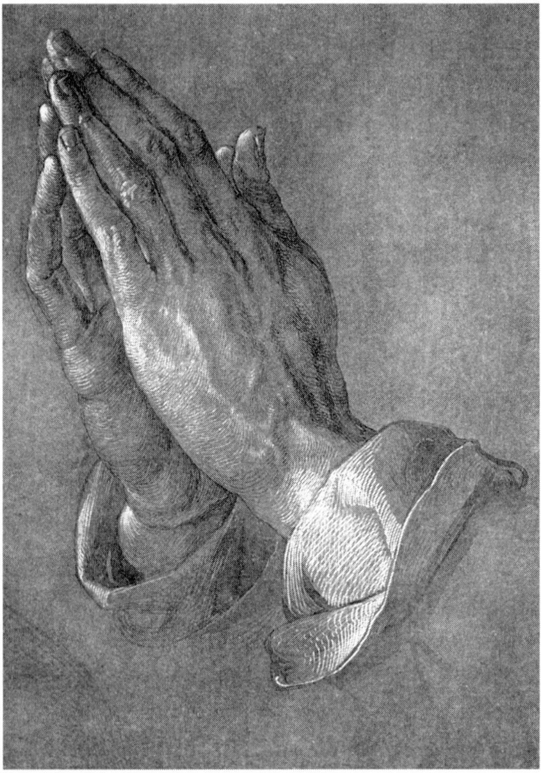

Drawing of Hands. *Dürer.*

Study the Masters. — Get photographs of drawings by the masters of drawing, and study them. See how they searched their model for form and character. Do not make so much of the actual stroke as the manner in which it is made to express and lend itself to the meaning.

In this drawing by Albrecht Dürer you have a splendid example of exactness and feeling for character. You could have no better type of what to look for and how to express it. Although it is not important that you should lay on the lines of shading just as this is done, it is important to notice how naturally they follow, and conform to, the character of the surface — which is one of the ways in which the point helps to search out the modelling.

This drawing is made with a black and a white chalk on a gray ground; a very good way to study.

A good hint is also offered in this drawing, of the modesty of the old masters, in subject. A hand or part of any object is enough to study from. There is no need to always demand a picture in everything you do.

Materials. — For all purposes which come in the range of the painter you should use charcoal. For purposes of study it is the most satisfactory of materials; it is sensitive, easily controlled, and easily corrected. For sketching or preliminary drawing on the canvas it is equally good.

You should have also a plumb-line with which to test vertical positions of parts in relation to each other, and this, with the pencil held horizontally for other relative positions, gives you all you need in that direction.

In drawing on the canvas it is not often necessary to do more than place the various objects and draw their outlines carefully and accurately. Sometimes, however, as in faces, or in pictures which include important figures, you will need a shaded drawing, and this can be done perfectly with charcoal, and fixed with fixative afterwards.

Imitation. — Perfect drawing, in the sense of exact drawing, is not the most important thing. A drawing may be exact, and yet not be the truer for it. It may be inexact, and yet be true to the greater character. So, too, the drawing may have to change an accidental fact which is not worth the trouble of expression or which will injure the whole. There is something more important than detail, and the essential characteristics can be expressed sometimes only by a drawing which is deliberately false in certain things in order to be the more true to the larger fact.

Then, too, there is an individuality which the artist has to express through his representation of the external; and he is justified in altering or slighting facts in order to bring about that more important self-expression. Of course the self must be worth expressing. There is no excuse for mere falsification nor for mere inability. But a good workman will not be guilty of that, and the complete picture in its unity will be his justification for whatever means he has taken.

Feeling. — Drawing must be a matter of feeling. A perception of essential truth of a thing, as much as of trained observation of the facts. The good draughtsman becomes so by training his observation of facts first, always searching for those most important, and emphasizing those; and with the power which will come in time to his eye and hand easily and quickly to grasp and express facts, will come also the power of mind to grasp the essential characteristics. And the trained hand and eye will permit the most perfect freedom of expression. This is the desideratum of the student; this is the end to be aimed at, — the perfect union of the trained eye and hand to see and do, and the trained mind to feel and select, and the freedom of expression which comes of that perfect union.

CHAPTER XVII

VALUES

The Term. — The word "values" is seldom understood by the average individual, yet it should not be difficult to take in. It means simply the relation between degrees of strength of light and dark, and of color considered as light and dark. Translate the word into "importance," and think what it means. The relative importance, strength, force, power, value, of a touch of color to make itself felt in the whole — that is its value. A weak value is a note which does not make itself felt; a strong value is one which does. A false value is a touch of color which has not its proper relation to the other spots or masses of color in the picture, *considered* as *light and dark* — *not as color per se.*

Importance. — As soon as you grasp this idea you see at once how important values must be to the whole picture. It is not possible to do any good work, either in black and white or color, without it. In one sense it is incidental to drawing. When you consider drawing as the expression of modelling, the relative roundness of parts, and of relief, as well as outline, values come into play to give the relations of planes of light and dark in black and white. In this it becomes part of drawing.

Values and Color. — As soon, however, as color becomes a part of the picture, values become the basis of modern painting as distinguished from the painting of previous centuries. Values, of course, always existed wherever good painting existed, because you cannot paint without recognizing the relations, the relative pitch and relative strength of tones. But the word is never heard in relation to old masters. It is apparently of quite modern coinage and use, and it probably was coined because of a new and greater importance of the fact which it represents.

The older painters in painting a picture kept parts of a whole object—a head or a figure, say—in relation to itself; and that was values—but restricted values. The whole picture was arranged on the basis of arbitrary lighting, which entered into the scheme of composition of that picture. This is not values, but what is generally understood by the older writers when they speak of "chiaroscuro." The modern painter deals little with chiaroscuro. It is almost obsolete as a technical word. Arbitrary arrangement of light and shade in a picture is not usual nowadays, and consequently the word which expressed it has dropped somewhat into disuse.

Basis of Modern Painting. — Instead of the old composition in arbitrary light and shade, the modern painter accepts the actual arrangement of light as the basis of his picture, and spreads the values over the whole canvas. In this way the quality of "value" becomes the very foundation of the modern picture. For you cannot accept the ordinary or actual condition of light, as governing the light and shade of your picture, without extending the same scheme of relations over the whole canvas. Every most insignificant spot of light and shade and color, as well as the most significant, must keep its place, must hold its true relation to every other spot and to all the rest. Each value must keep its place according to the laws of fact, or it is out of touch with the whole. The whole picture must be either on a scheme of general fact, or a scheme of general arbitrary arrangement. Any one piece of arbitrary arrangement in this connection must be backed up by other pieces of arbitrary arrangement, or else there must be no arbitrary arrangement at all. The modern painter accepts the former; and the importance of "values" is the result.

Absolute and Relative Values. — We may speak of values as absolute or relative. This relates to the key or pitch of a painting. It is the contribution to the art of painting which was made by the French painter, Manet. You may paint a picture in the same pitch as nature, or you may transpose it to a higher or a lower pitch.

The relations of the different values of the picture will hold the same relation to each other as the values of nature do to each other. But the actual pitch of each, the relation of each to an absolute light or an absolute dark, will be higher or lower than in nature. This would be relative values.

Or the pitch, relation to absolute light and dark, of each value may be the same, value for value, as in nature. This would be absolute values.

The attempt at absolute values was not made at all before Manet's time. A landscape was frankly painted down, or darker, from the pitch of nature, and an interor as frankly painted up, or lighter. In both cases the values had to be condensed, — telescoped, so to speak, — because pigment would not express the highest light nor the lowest dark in nature; and to have the same number of gradations between the highest and lowest notes in the picture, the amount of difference between each value had to be diminished — but *relatively* they were the same. The degree of variation from the actual was the same all through.

With absolute values the painter aims at giving the *just note,* — the exact equivalent in value that he finds in nature. He tries to paint up to outdoor light or paint down to in-door light.

Close Values. — This naturally calls for a fine distinction of tones — the utmost subtlety of perception of values. To paint a picture in which the highest light may not be white nor the lowest dark black, and yet give a great range and variety to the values all through the picture, the values must be *close;* must be studied so closely as to take cognizance of the slightest possible distinction, and to justly express it. This sort of thing was not thought of by the older painters. It is the distinguishing characteristic of modern painting. It is a substitution of the study of *relation* for the study of *contrast.*

Study of Values. — You see at once how important, how vital, the study of values is to painting. Even if you paint with arbitrary lighting, as is still done by many painters, especially in portraits, you have to consider and study them as they apply to *parts* of your picture. You will find no good painter of old time who did not study relations. If you look at a Velasquez, you will find that he knew values, even though he did not use the word.

But if you are in touch with your century, if you would paint to express the suggestion you receive from the nature you study, or if you would convey the idea of truth to the world around you, as that world exists, frankly accepting the conditions of it, you will have to make the study of values fundamental to your work.

"The Fourth Dimension." — You study values with your eyes only, but you cannot *measure* values. Length, breadth, and thickness you can measure; but values constitute what might be called a "*Fourth Dimension*," and you must measure it by your eye, and without any mechanical aid. Your eye must be trained to distinguish and judge differences of value.

Helps. — There are, however, several things which you can use to help you in training your eye to distinguish values. When you look for values you do not wish to see details nor things, you wish to see only masses and relations. You must *unfocus* your eye. The focussed eye sees the fact, and not the relation. Anything which will help you to see outlines and details less distinctly will help you to see the values more distinctly.

Half-closed Eyes. — The most common way is to half close the eyes, which shuts out details, but permits you to see the values. Some painters think this falsifies pitch, and prefer to keep the eyes wide open, but to focus them on some point *beyond* the values they are studying. This is not so easy to do as to half close the eyes, but becomes less difficult with practice.

The Blur Glass. — An ordinary magnifying-glass of about 15-inch focus, which you can get at an optician's for fifteen or twenty cents, will blur the details, and help you to see the values, because it makes everything vague except the masses. You can frame it for use by putting it between two pieces of cardboard with a hole in them, or you can do the same with two pieces of leather sewed around the edge. Of course the glass itself is all you need, but it will be easily broken if unprotected.

Do not try to look *through* the glass at your subject, but *at* the glass and the image on it.

The Claude Loraine Mirror. — This is a curved mirror with a black reflecting surface. The object is reflected on it, *reduced* both in size and pitch. It concentrates the masses and the color, and so helps to distinguish the relative values.

You can make a mirror of this sort for yourself by painting the back of a piece of plate glass black. The real Claude Loraine mirror is expensive.

The Common Mirror is also very helpful in distinguishing values. It reduces the size of things, and reverses the drawing so that you see your subject under different conditions, and a fresh eye is the result. Place the group and your painting side by side, if you are painting still life, and look at both at the same time in the mirror. Do the same with a portrait and the sitter.

Diminishing Glass.— Much the same effect can be had by using a double concave lens. The picture is not reversed, but it is reduced, and the details eliminated.

In using any of these means you must remember that it is always the relations and not the things you are studying; and the most useful of these aids is the blur glass, because you cannot possibly see anything in it but the values and color masses, everything else being blurred.

CHAPTER XVIII

PERSPECTIVE

There are two kinds of perspective, linear and aërial. The former has to do with the manner in which horizontal lines appear to converge as they recede from the foreground, and so produce the effect of distance. The latter has to do with the effect of distance, which is due to the successive gradations of gray in color noticeable in objects farther and farther away from the observer.

Aërial Perspective. — To the student, aërial is *color* perspective, because of the modifications which colors undergo when removed to a distance. Modifications of tone are largely due to varying distance, and so aërial perspective is largely a matter of *values*. That they are due to the greater or less thickness of the atmosphere is only a matter of interest, not of importance, to the artist; the important thing to him is that the careful study of values is necessary to relief, perspective, and particularly, atmosphere and envelopment in a picture.

To the student, aërial perspective should be only a matter of observation and of the study of relations of color and value. There are no rules. The effect depends on greater or less density of atmosphere. Near objects are seen through a thin stratum of air, and farther objects through a thicker one. All you have to do to express it is to recognize the relative tones of color. Paint the colors as they are, as you see them in nature, and you need have no trouble with aërial perspective.

But though I say "this is all you have to do," don't imagine that I mean that it is always easy, or that it can be done without thought and study. You will have to use all your powers of perception if you wish to do good work in this direction. Especially on clear days, or in those climates where the air is so rare that objects at great distances seem near, you will find that atmospheric perspective is simply another name for close values. And close values, you remember, are the most subtle of relations of light and shade and color.

The only rule for aërial perspective is to use your eyes, and do nothing without a previous careful study of nature.

Linear Perspective. — For most kinds of painting, a technical knowledge of linear perspective is not necessary, although every painter should understand the general principles of it. In most cases all the exactness needed can be obtained by comparing all lines carefully with the pencil or brush handle held horizontally or vertically, and studying the angle any line makes with it. Appy to all objects in perspective the same observation that you do in any other kind of drawing, and you will have little trouble, as long as you are drawing from an object before you. But if you go into perspective at all, go into it thoroughly. A little perspective is a dangerous thing, and more likely to mix you up by suggesting all sorts of half-understood things than to be of any real help.

There are some kinds of subjects, however, which require a complete knowledge of all the rules and processes of perspective. Whenever you have to construct a picture from details stated but not seen; when you have a complicated architectural interior or exterior; when figures are to be placed at certain distances or in definite positions, and they are too numerous or the conditions are otherwise such that you cannot pose your models for this purpose; then you may have to make most elaborate perspective plans, and lay out your picture with great exactness, or the drawing which is fundamental to such a picture will not be true.

Such men as Gérôme and Alma-Tadema plan their pictures most carefully, and so did Paul Veronese, and it requires a thorough and practical knowledge of perspective.

But this is not the place to teach you perspective. It is a subject which requires special study, and whole volumes are given to the elucidation of it. In a work of this kind anything more than a mention of the bearings of perspective on painting would be out of place. If you do not care to take up seriously the study of perspective, avoid attempting to paint any subjects which call for it; or, if you do care to study it, get a special work on that subject, give plenty of time to it, and study it thoroughly.

Foreshortening. — In this connection I may speak of something which is akin to perspective, yet the very reverse of it. As its name implies, foreshortening means the way in which anything seems shortened or in modified drawing as it projects towards you; while perspective is the manner in which lines appear as they recede from you. Like aërial perspective, the best way to study foreshortening is to study nature, not rules.

Perspective can be worked out by rule, foreshortening cannot. Pose your model, or if it be a branch of a tree, or anything of that sort, place yourself in the proper position with reference to it, and then study the drawing *as it appears*, thinking nothing of *how it is;* make your measurements, and place your lines as if there were no problem of foreshortening at all, but study the relations of lines, of size, and of values, and the foreshortening will take care of itself.

After all, foreshortening is only good drawing, and a good draughtsman will foreshorten well, while a bad draughtsman will not. Therefore, learn to draw, and don't worry about the foreshortening.

CHAPTER XIX

LIGHT AND SHADE

Chiaroscuro. — A few words about chiaroscuro will be useful. This is a term of great importance and frequent use with artists and writers up to within the last thirty or forty years. It has of late become almost unused. The reason for this was explained in the chapter on "Values." Nevertheless, it is well that the student should know what the word meant, and still means. Although he may hear and use it less frequently than if he had lived earlier in the century, the pictures, certain qualities of which no other word expresses, still exist, and are probably as immortal as anything in this world can be. He should know what those qualities are, and he should understand their relation to the work of to-day.

Chiaroscuro is described by an old writer as suggesting "a theme which is the most interesting, perhaps, in the whole range of the art of painting. Of vast importance, great extent, and extreme intricacy. Chiaroscuro is an Italian compound word whose two parts, *chiar* and *oscuro*, signify simply *bright* and *obscure*, or *light* and *dark*.

Hence the art or branch of art that bears the name regards all the relations of light and shade, and this independently of coloring, notwithstanding that in painting, coloring and the clair-obscure are of their very nature inseparable. The art of clair-obscure, therefore, teaches the painter the disposition and arrangement in general of his lights and darks, with all their degrees, extreme and intermediate, of tint and shade, both in single objects, as the parts of a picture, and in combination as one whole, so as to produce the best representation possible in the best manner possible; that is, *so as to produce the most desirable effect upon the senses and spirit of the observers.* In a word, its end and aim are fidelity and beauty of imitation; its means, every effect of light; chromatic harmonies and contrasts; chromatic values, reflections; the degradations of atmospheric perspective, etc." The italics are mine.

You see at once that this covers a pretty wide field. But it is to be again noted that the use of chiaroscuro by the old painters meant not only the expression of the light and shade of nature, but the so arranging of the objects and the way that the light was permitted to fall on them, that certain parts of the picture became shadow, while the light was concentrated in some other part or parts. In this way the arrangement of the light and shade of a picture became a distinct element of composition, and a very important one. The *quality* of "light" was something to be emphasized by contrast. It is stated (whether truly or not) that the proportion of light to dark was according to a definite rule or principle with certain painters, some permitting more, and some less, space of canvas to be proportioned to light and to dark. The gradations of light and dark were studied of course; but the quantity of light spread over the canvas was calculated upon, so that the less space of light and the greater the space of dark, the more brilliant would be the main spot of light in the picture. They wrought with the *quality of light and shade* as an *element*, just as they would with the quality of line or of color, considered apart from objects or facts they might represent.

Arbitrary Lighting. — This is the arbitrary light and shade spoken of in the chapter on "Values"; and although the older painters included what we now call values in their word chiaroscuro, it is this fact of arbitrary lighting as opposed to accepting the light as it does fall, or selecting those places or times where it does naturally fall as we would like it to, that makes the difference between modern painting generally and the older method, and has made chiaroscuro as a word and as a quality of painting so much a thing of the past.

Light and Shade. — But we may use the old word

with a more restricted meaning. If we use it to mean literally light and shade, the way light falls on objects and the relief due to the light side and the shadow side of them, we get a use which implies a very important and practical matter for present study.

Objects Visible by Light and Shadow. — If you will put a white egg on a piece of white paper, with

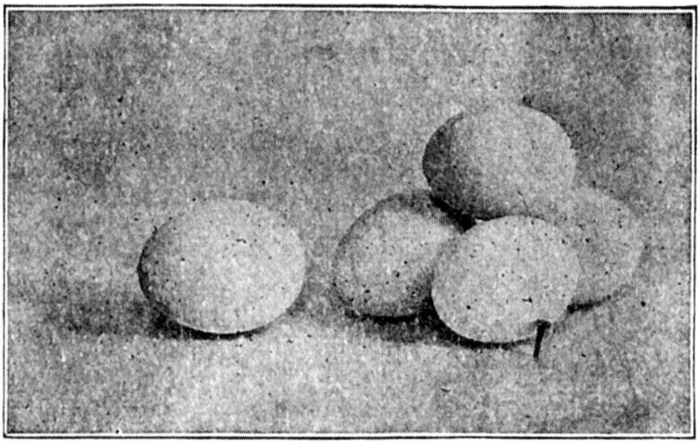

Eggs. White against White.

another white paper back of it, you will see that it is only because the egg obstructs the light, the side of it towards the light preventing the light rays from touching the other side, and so casting a shadow on itself and on the paper, that the egg is visible. You will also see, if you manipulate the egg, that according as the light is concentrated or diffused, or according to the sharpness of the shadow and light, is the egg more or less distinct.

Contrast. — Apply these facts to other objects, and you will see how important the principle of contrast is to the representation of nature. Not only contrast of light and shade, but contrast of color. And you should make a study, both by setting up groups of objects in different lights, and by studying effects of lights wherever you are, of the possibilities and combinations of light and shadow.

Constant Observation. — The painter is constantly studying with his eyes. It is not necessary always to have the brush in your hand in order to be always studying. Keep your brain active in making observations and considering the relations in nature around you. The amount of material you can store up in this way is immense, to say nothing of the training it gives you in the use of your eyes, and in the practice of selection of motives for work. Schemes of color or composition are not usually deliberately invented within the painter's brain. They are in most cases the result of some suggestion from a chance effect noticed and remembered or jotted down, and afterwards worked out. Nature is the great suggester. It is the artist's business to catch the suggestion and make it his own. For nature seldom works out her own suggestions. The effect as nature gives it is either not complete, or is so evanescent as to be uncopyable. But the habit of constant receptivity on the part of the artist makes nature an infinite mine of possibilities to him.

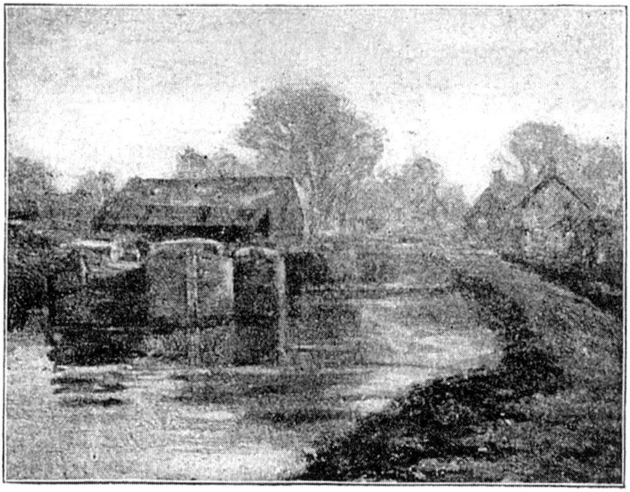

The Canal. *Burleigh Parkhurst.*

Effect of diffused out-door light to be compared with effect of studio light in "Bohemian Woman," and artificial light in "Woman Sewing by Lamplight."

Perception. — Only by continually observing and judging of contrasts and relations can the eye be trained to perceive subtle distinctions; yet it must be so trained, for all good work is dependent on these distinctions.

Effects of Light. — It is important to study the different qualities of light. Take, for instance, the difference of character on a sunny day and on a gray day. On the former, fine distinctions of color are less pronounced; they are lost in the contrasts of sunlight and shadow. On a gray day the light is diffused; contrast is less, but the finer distinctions are more marked. For the study of the subtleties of color choose a gray day.

So, too, is the difference marked between the general light of out-doors and the more concentrated light of the house. The pitch is different. Outside, even in a dark day, the general character of light is clearer, more full, than in-doors.

There is nothing possible under the open sky like the strong contrasts you get from a single window in an otherwise unlighted room.

Compare, for instance, the character of the light and shade as shown in the illustrations on pages 156 and 159. The one is the diffused, out-of-door light, the other that from a studio window. The character of the subject has nothing to do with this quality. The head would have less of sharpness and contrast in the open air, and more reflected light.

Other differences to be studied as to quality of the light in the manner of its contrast, and also for its color quality, are to be seen in moonlight or nightlight as compared with daylight. Artificial light, such as lamp- and candle-light, gives marked effects also, which may be compared with daylight both as it is out-of-doors and in its more concentrated effects in the studio. Compare the picture of the "Woman Sewing by Lamplight," by Millet, with the "Canal" and the "Bohemian Woman" given above. The effects of gas and electric light also should be studied. Their characteristics both of contrast and, particularly, of color are worth your attention as a student, inasmuch as the essence of some pictures lies in these qualities.

Another matter of great importance to the student, and one which the same three illustrations just referred to may serve to show, is the effect on objects of the position of the point of entrance of the light with reference to them and to the observer. The simplest light is the side-light from a single window. This gives broad, sharp masses of light and shade, and makes the study of drawing and painting more simple. With the observer in the same relative position to the subject, as the light swings round towards a point back of him the contrasts become less, the relations more subtle and difficult of recognition, and naturally the study of them more difficult. In this position of light the values become "close." To make the object seen at all, it is necessary that the finest distinctions shall be observed.

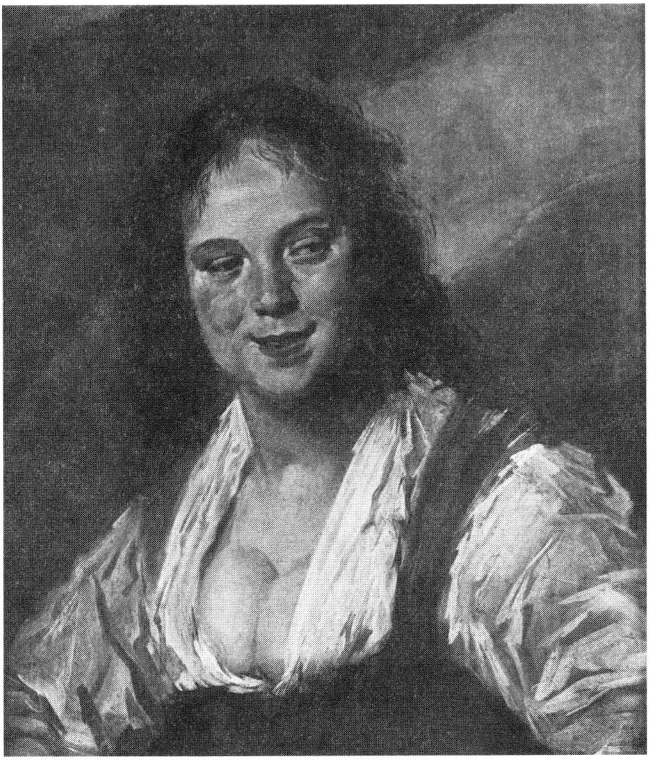

Bohemian Woman. *Frans Hals.*

Effect of contrast of light and shade in studio to be compared with diffused light of open air in the "Canal," and artificial light in "Woman Sewing by Lamplight."

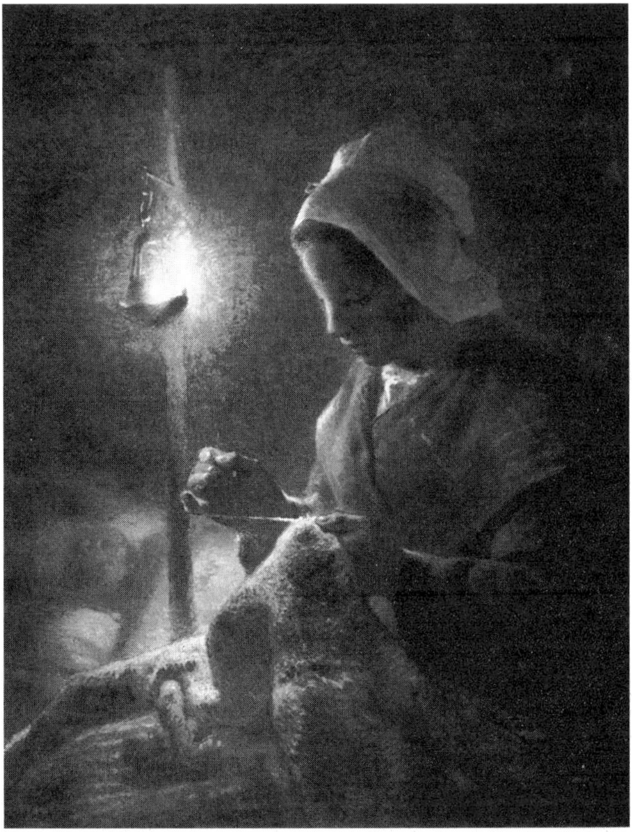

Sewing by Lamplight. *Millet.*

Effect of artificial light contrast to be compared with natural light in illustrations of " Canal " and " Bohemian Woman."

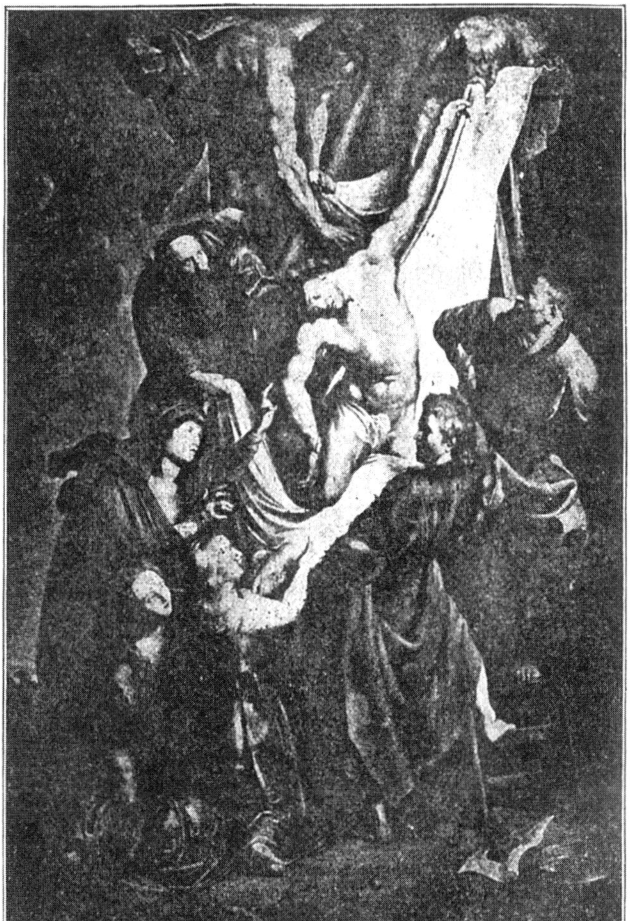

Descent from the Cross.

Portrait painters have always been fond of a top light, which gives a direct concentrated light descending on the sitter, very similar in character to the side-light, but more favorable to the expression and drawing of the face.

Cross Lights. — The most confusing and difficult of study and representation are the "*cross lights.*" If there are several windows or other points for the admission of light, and the sitter or object painted is between them, the light comes from all sides, so that the rays cross each other and there is no single scheme of light and shade. The rays from one side modify the shadows cast from the other side, and a perplexing and involved arrangement of values is the result. This is a favorite technical problem with painters, and its solution is splendid training; but the student who can successfully solve it is not far from the end of his "student days."

CHAPTER XX

COMPOSITION

Importance. — Composition is of the utmost importance. It is impossible that a picture should be good without it. You may define it as that study by means of which the balance of the picture comes about. But you must understand the word balance in its broadest sense. There is nothing in the planning of the picture which has not to be considered in making the picture balance.

The arrangement of the lines, of the forms, of the masses, and of the colors must all be right if the composition be right. Composition is the planning of the picture; and it is more or less complicated, more or less to be carefully studied beforehand in exact accordance with the simplicity or complication of the scheme of the picture. You may not need more than the consideration of a few main facts. It may almost be done by a few moments' deliberation in some simple studies or even pictures. But even then there is possible the most subtle discrimination of selection, and a perfect gem of composition may be found in the arrangement of a picture having the simplest and fewest elements. The more complicated the materials which are to be worked into a picture, the more careful must be the previous planning; but, for all that, the genius will find scope for his utmost powers in a simple figure, just because the fewer the means, the more each single thing can interfere with the balance of the whole, and the more a fine choice will tell.

The Æsthetic. — I have already mentioned briefly the æsthetic elements of a picture. I have called to your attention that back of the obvious facts of a subject and the objects in the picture, and the theme which the painter makes his picture represent; back of the technical processes and management of concrete material which make painting possible, is the æsthetic purpose of the work of art; without this it could not be a work of art at all: it would be merely a more or less exact representation of something, a mere prosaic description, the interest in which would lie wholly in the *fact*, and would perish whenever interest in the fact should cease. It is not the *fact*, nor even the able expression of the fact, which makes a work of art a thing of interest and delight centuries after the bearing of the fact has been forgotten. The perennial interest of a work of art lies in the way in which the artist has used his ostensible theme, and all the facts and objects appertaining to it, as a part of the material with which he expresses those ideas which are purely æsthetic; which do not rest on material things. These have to do with material things only by rendering them beautiful, giving to them an interest which they themselves could not otherwise have.

Theory. — Does this sound unpractical? Well, it is unpractical. Does it seem mere theory? It is theory. I want to impress it on you that it is theory. For it is the theory which underlies art, and if you do not understand it, you only understand art from the outside. Consciously or unconsciously every artist works to express these purely æsthetic qualities, and to a greater or less extent he expresses himself through them.

Art for Art's Sake. — This is the real meaning of the much-debated phrase, "Art for art's sake." The mistake which leads to the misconception and most of the discussion about it, is in confounding "art for art's sake" with "technique for technique's sake," which is a very different thing. Certainly every painter will work to attain the most perfect technique he is capable of. But not for the sake of the technique, but for what it will do. The better the technique the better the control of all the means to expression. If you take technique to mean only the understanding and knowledge of all the manipulations of art, technique is only a means, and it is so that I mean it to be understood here. If you broaden its meaning to include all the *mental* conceptions and means, that is another thing, and one likely to lead to confusion of idea. So I use the word technique in its strictest sense.

The Æsthetic Elements. — What, then, are these æsthetic qualities I have spoken of? Will you consider the quality of "line"? Not *a* line, but line as an element, excluding all the possible things which may be done with lines in different relations to themselves and to other elements. Now will you consider also the other elements, "mass" and "color"? Do you see that here are three terms which suggest possibilities of combination of infinite scope? and they are purely intellectual. What may be done with them may be done, primarily, without taking into consideration the representation of any material fact whatsoever. Take as the type, conventional ornament. You can make the most exquisite combinations, in which the only interest and charm lies in the fact of those combinations in line and mass and color.

Take architecture. Quite aside from the use of the building is the æsthetic resultant from combinations of line and mass and color.

And so in the picture the question of *art*, the question of æsthetic entity, lies in the intellectual qualities of combinations of line and mass and color which permeate through and through the technical and material structure that you call the picture, and give it whatever universal and permanent value it has, and which make it immortal, if immortal it ever can be.

Composition. — The bearing of all this on composition should be obvious, for composition is the technique of combination. In the composition of a picture all the elements come into play. It is in composition that the management of the abstract results in the concrete.

Let us look at it from a more practical side. Frankly, there are qualities, which you always look for in a picture, — good drawing, of course, and good color. But there are such things as these: Harmony, Balance, Rhythm, Grace, Impressiveness, Force, Dignity. Where do they come from? Must not every good picture have them, or some of them, to some extent? How are you going to get them? If you have fifteen or twenty square feet or square yards of surface, you will not get them onto it by unaided inspiration. Inspiration is, like any other intellectual quality, quite logical, only it acts more quickly and takes longer steps between conclusions perhaps. You will get these qualities onto your canvas only by so arranging all the objects which make up the body of your picture that these qualities shall be the result. It is arrangement then.

Arrangement. — But arrangement of what? how? The objects. But on some principle back of them. Consider another set of qualities: proportion, i.e., relative size; arrangement, relative position; contrast; accent, — these are what you manipulate your objects with, and your objects themselves are only line and mass and color in the concrete. Objects, figures, bric-a-brac, draperies, houses and trees, skies and mountains, and every and any other natural fact, you may consider as so many bits of form and color with which you may work out a scheme on canvas; and how you do it is to consider them as pawns in your game of æsthetics.

With these as materials, what you really do is to combine mass and line and color by means of proportion, arrangement, contrast, and accent, that a beautiful entity of harmony, balance, rhythm, grace, dignity, and force may result. And this is composition.

No Rules. — Naturally in dealing with a thing like this, which is the very essence of art, rules are of very little use. Ability in composition may be acquired when it is not natural, but it calls for a continuous training of the sense of proportion and arrangement, just as the development of any other ability calls for training.

The best thing that you can do is to study good examples and try to appreciate, not only their beauty, but how and why they are beautiful. Cultivate your taste in that direction; and with the taste to like good and dislike bad composition will come the feeling which tells you when it is good and when it is bad, and this feeling you can apply to your own work, and by experiment you will gain knowledge and skill.

Rules are not possible simply because they are limitations, and the true composer will always overstep a limitation of that kind, and with a successful result.

Principles of composition, too, must be variously adapted, according to the kind of picture you have in hand. The principles are the same, of course; but as the materials differ in a figure painting and a landscape, for instance, you must apply them to meet that difference.

Suggestions. — The first suggestion that might be made as a help to the study of composition is to consider your picture as a whole always. No matter how many figures, no matter how many groups, they must all be considered as parts of a *whole*, which must have no effect of being too much broken up.

If the figures are scattered, they must be scattered in such a way that they suggest a logical connection between them as individuals in each group, and groups in a whole. There should usually be a main mass, and the others subsidiary masses. There should be a centre of interest of some sort, whether it be a color, a mass, or a thing; and this centre should be the point to which all the other parts balance.

Simplicity is a good word to have in mind. However complicated the composition may seem superficially, you may treat it simply. You will control it by not considering any part as of any importance in itself, but only as it helps the whole; and you may strengthen or weaken that part as you need to. Don't cut the thing up too much. Let a half a dozen objects count as one in the whole. Mass things, simplify the masses, and make the elements of the masses hold as only parts of those masses.

Study placing of things in different sizes relative to the size of the canvas. Make sketches which take no note of anything but the largest masses or the most important lines, and change them about till they seem right; then break them up in the same way into their details. Apply the *steps* suggested for drawing to the study of composition, searching for balance chiefly, or for some other quality which is proper to composition.

Line.—Each of the main elements of composition can be used as a problem of arrangement. You can study *composition* in line, in mass, or in color.

"The Golden Stairs," by Burne-Jones, is almost purely an arrangement in *line*, and beautifully illus-

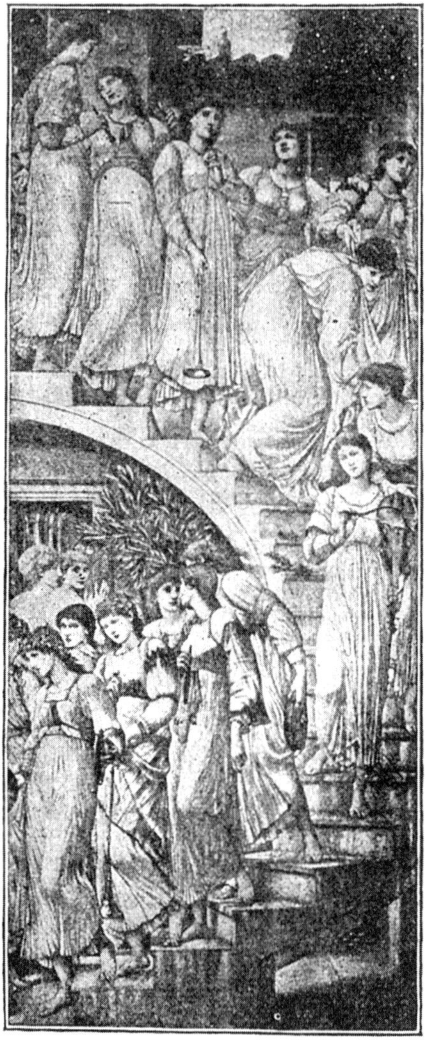

trates the use of this element as the main æsthetic motive in a picture.

Compare this composition in line with the "Descent from the Cross," in which the *line* is equally marked, but more complicated, and used in connection with *mass* to a much greater extent, and involved with interrelations of chiaroscuro and color. Consider the effect which each picture

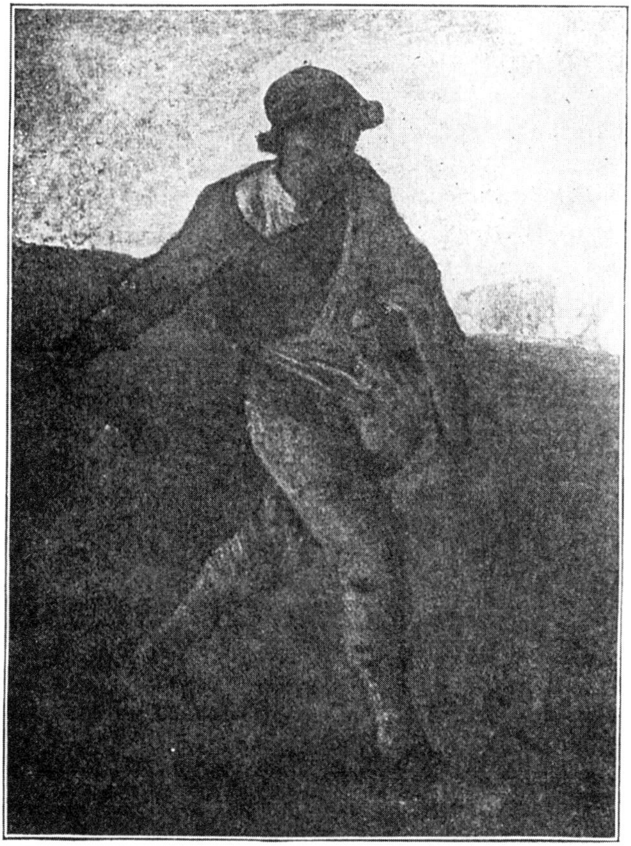

The Sower. *Millet.*

To show arrangement in mass and line, in which the mass gives weight and dignity without weakening the emphasis of rhythm in the line.

derives as a whole from this management of these elements. The one emphasizing that of line, with the resultant of rhythm and grace; the other balancing the elements, and so gaining power and impressiveness.

Often the whole composition should be a balancing of the elements, as in this case. But the emphasizing of one element will always emphasize the characteristics to which those elements tend as the main characteristic of the picture.

Grace, rhythm, movement, come most naturally from arrangement chiefly in *line*. If *mass* comes into the picture, the masses may be arranged to help the *line*, or to modify it. In "The Sower" the management of mass is such as to give great dignity, and almost solemnity, to the picture, yet not to take away from the rhythmic swing and action of the figure which comes from line, but even to emphasize it. Compare this in these respects with the lighter grace of "The Golden Stairs" and the less unified movement, but greater activity, of the "Descent from the Cross."

Of course masses will come into the picture; but either the masses themselves can be arranged into line, or there can be emphasis given to lines which break up or modify the masses, so that the character of the picture is governed by them.

Mass. — In the arrangement of mass, light and shade and color are effective. Smaller groups may be made into a larger one, and individual objects also brought together, by grouping them in light or in shade, or by giving them a common color.

Weight, dignity, the statuesque, scale, are char-

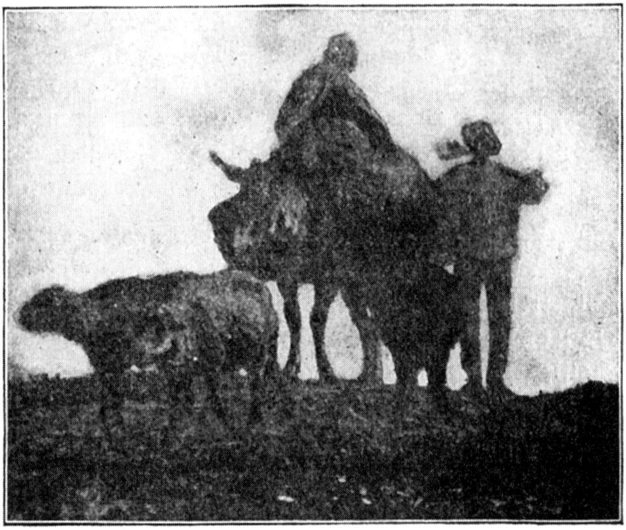

Return to the Farm. *Millet.*

To show the effect of mass in giving qualities of "scale" and "the statuesque."

acteristics of *mass*. Line in this connection only takes from the brusqueness that mass alone would have, or helps to break up any tendency to monotony. The "Return to the Farm," by Millet, shows this combination, the reverse of "The

Sower." In this, the *line* is used to enrich the repose and weight, the statuesque of the *mass*. In the other, the *mass* gives dignity and impressiveness to the grace and rhythm of the *line*.

The color scheme of course will have an equal effect in the emphasizing or modifying of the motive of line or mass. Color will not only have an effect on it, but must be in sympathy with it, or the balance will be lost.

Color. — This is mainly where composition in color will come in. Light and shade or chiaroscuro, as I explained in the last chapter, are necessarily intimately connected with composition here. And you never work in color or mass without working in light and shade also. Of color itself I shall speak in the next chapter. It is only necessary to point out the fact of connection here. Of course in painting, all the elements are most closely related. Although it is necessary to speak of them separately in the actual working out, you keep them all in mind together, and so make them continually help and modify each other.

A Principle. — There is a well-established principle in architecture, that you must never try to emphasize two proportions in one structure. A hall may be long and narrow, but not both long and wide; in which case the proportions would neutralize each other — you would have a simple square, characterless. You may emphasize height or breadth — not both, or you get the same negative character.

So you may apply this principle more or less exactly to the composition of a picture. Don't try to express too many things in one picture, or if you do, let some one be the main thing, and all the rest be subordinate to it. There is perhaps no law more rigid than the one which denies success to any attempt to scatter force, effect, and purpose. One main idea in each picture, and everything subordinated to lend itself to the strengthening of that.

To a certain extent this will apply to line and mass, though not absolutely. As a rule, line or mass, one or the other, must be the main element.

Leverage. — I have often thought that much insight into the principles of balance of masses, and of mass and line, could be gained by thinking of it analogously to equilibrium in leverage. A small mass, or a simple line or accent, may be made to balance a very much greater mass. The greater part of a canvas may be one mass, and be balanced by quite a small spot. But leverage must come in to help. Somewhere in the picture will be the point of support, the fulcrum. And the large mass and the small one will have an obvious relation with reference to that point. Or the element of apparent density will come in. The large mass will be the least dense, the small one the most dense, and the equilibrium is established. For composition is but the equilibrium of the picture, and equilibrium the picture must have.

There are many rules as to placing of mass and arrangement of line, but they are all more or less arbitrary and limiting in influence. Individuality must and will ignore such rules, just because composition deals chiefly with the abstract qualities rules will not help. A fine feeling or perception of what is right is the only law, and the trained eye is the only measure. As in values, so in composition you must study relations in nature, and results in the work of the masters, to train your eye to see; and you must sketch and block in all sorts of combinations with your own hand, to give you practical experience.

Scale.—One point of great importance should be noticed. That is the effect on the observer of the size of any main mass or object with reference to the size of the canvas. This is analogous to what is called *scale* in architecture.

If the mass or object is justly proportioned to the whole surface of the canvas, and is treated in accordance with it, it will impose its own scale on all other objects. You can make a figure impress the observer as being life size, although it may really be only a few inches long. A house or castle coming into the picture may be made to give its scale to the surroundings, and make them seem small instead of itself seeming merely an object in a picture. This will be due to the *placing* of it on the canvas, largely, and more in this than in anything else. The manner of painting will also lend importantly to it; for an object to appear big must not be drawn nor painted in a little manner.

The placing of objects of a known size near, to give scale, is a useless expedient in such a case. At times it may be successful, often of use; but if the scale of the main object is false, the other object of known size, instead of giving size to the main one, as it is intended to do, will be itself dwarfed by it.

Placing. — This matter of placing is one which you should constantly practise. Make it a regular study when you are sketching from nature. Try to concentrate in your sketches so as to help your study of composition. In making a sketch, look for one main effect, and often have that effect the importance of some object, studying to give it *scale* by the placing and the treatment of it, and its relation to the things surrounding it in nature and on the canvas. In this way you will be studying composition in a most practical way.

Still Life. — For practical study of composition, the most useful materials you can have are to be found in still life. Nowhere can you have so great freedom of arrangement in the concrete. You can take as many actual objects as you please, and place them in all sorts of relations to each other, studying their effect as to grouping ; and so study most tangibly the principles as well as the practice of bringing together line and mass and color as elements, through the means of actual objects. This you should constantly do, till composition is no more an abstract thing, but a practical study in which you may work out freely and visibly intellectual æsthetic ideas almost unconsciously, and train your eye to see instinctively the possibilities of all sorts of compositions, and to correct the falsities of accidental combinations.

Don't Attempt too much. — Don't be too ambitious. Begin with simple arrangements, and add to them, studying the structure of each new combination and grouping. When you are going to paint, remember that too much of an undertaking will not give you any more beauty in the picture, and may lead to discouragement.

In the Chapter on "Still Life" I will explain more practically the means you may take, and how you may take them, to the end of making composition a practical study to you.

CHAPTER XXI

COLOR

THE subject of color naturally divides, for the painter, into two branches, — color as a *quality*, and color as *material*. Considered in the former class, it divides into an abstract a theoretical and a scientific subject; considered in the latter, it is a material and technical one. The material and technical side has been treated of in the Chapter on "Pigments." In this chapter we will have to do with color considered as an æsthetic element.

The Abstract. — The quality of *color* is the third of the great elements or qualities, through the management of which the painter works æsthetically.

Just as he uses all the material elements of his picture as the means of making concrete and visible those combinations of line and mass which go to the making of the æsthetic structure, so he uses these in the expression of the ideal in combinations of color. In this relation nothing stands to him for what it is, but for what it may be made to do for the color-scheme of his picture. If he wants a certain red in a certain place, he wants it because it is red, and it makes little difference to him, *thinking in color,* whether that red note is actually made by a file of red-coated soldiers, by a scarlet ribbon, or by a lobster. The scarlet spot is what he is thinking of, and what object most naturally and rightly gives it to him is a matter to be decided by the demands of the subject of the picture; and its fitness as to that is the only thing which has any influence beyond the main fact that red color is needed at that point. If he were a designer of conventional ornament, the color problem would be the same. At that point a spot of red would be needed, and a spot of paint would do it. The painter thinks in color the same way, but he expresses himself in different materials.

The Ideal.—This is the reason that a still-life painting is as interesting to a painter as a subject which to another finds its great interest in the telling of a story. To the painter the story, or the objects which tell it, are of minor importance. That the picture is beautiful in color is what moves him. As composition and color the thing is an admirable piece of æsthetic thinking and æsthetic expression, and so gives him a purely æsthetic delight; and the technical process is secondary with him, interesting only because he is a technician. The representation of the objects incidental to the subject is as incidental to his interest, as it is to the picture considered as an æsthetic thought.

This is what the layman finds it so impossible to take into his mental consciousness. And it is probable that many painters do not so distinguish their artistic point of view from their human point of view. But consciously or unconsciously the painter does think in these terms of color, line, and mass when he is working out his picture; and whether he admits it to himself or not, these characteristics are the great influencing facts in his judgment of pictures, as well as in the growth and permanency of his own fame. That is why a great popular reputation dies so rapidly in many instances. The æsthetic qualities of the man's work are the only ones which can insure a permanent reputation for that work; for the art of painting is fundamentally æsthetic, and nothing external to that can give it an artistic value. Without that its popularity and fame are only matters of accidental coincidence with popular taste.

If a painter is really great in the power of conception and of expression of any of the great æsthetic elements, his work will be permanently great. It will be acknowledged to be so by the consensus of the world's opinion in the long run; nothing else can make it so, and nothing but obliteration can prevent it.

I am explicit in stating these ideas, not because I expect that you will learn from this book to be a great master of the æsthetic, but because I am assured that you can never be a painter unless you understand a painter's true problems. You must be able to know a good picture in order to make a good picture, and however little you try for, your work will be the better for having a painter's way of looking at a painter's work. The technical problems are the control of the materials of expression. The painter must have that control. The student's business is to attain that control, and then he has the means to convey his ideas. But those ideas, if he be a true painter, are not ideas of history or of fiction, but ideas of line and mass and color, and of their combinations.

The Color Sense. — Therefore color is a thing to be striven for for its own sake. Good color is a value in itself. You may not have the genius to be a good colorist, but you need not be a bad one; for the color sense can be definitely acquired. I will not say that color initiative can always be acquired; but the power to perceive and to judge good color can be, and it will go far towards the making of a good painter, even of a great one.

I knew one painter who came near to greatness, and near to greatness as a colorist, who in twelve years trained his eye and feeling from a very inferior perception of color to the power which, as I say, came near to greatness. He was an able painter and a well-trained one before that; but in this direction he was deficient, and he deliberately set about it to educate that side of himself, with the result I have stated. How did he do it? Simply by recognizing where he needed training, and working constantly from nature to perceive fine distinctions of tone; and by careful and severe self-criticism. Summer after summer he went outdoors and worked with colors and canvas to study out certain problems. Every year he set himself mainly one problem to solve. This year it might be luminosity; next it might be the domination of a certain color; another year the just discrimination of tones — and he became a most exquisite colorist.

So, as I knew his work before and after this self-training, and as I know personally of the means he took to attain his purpose, I think I can speak positively of the fact that such development of the color sense is possible.

Taste. — It is well to remember that taste in color is not dependent on personal judgment alone; that what is good and what is bad in color does not rest on mere opinion. That a good colorist's idea of color does not agree with your own is not a matter of mere whim or liking, in which you have quite as good a right to your opinion as he has to his. The colorist, it is true, does not produce or judge of color by rule. He works from his feeling of what is right. But there is a law back of his taste and feeling. The laws of color harmony are definite, and have been definitely studied and definitely calculated. Color depends for its existence on waves of vibration of rays of light, just as sound is dependent on sound waves.

Color Waves.—These waves of light give sensations of color which vary with the rapidity or length of the wave, and certain combinations of wave lengths will be harmonious (beautiful), and others will not be. This is a matter of scientific fact; it is not a notion. The mathematical relations of color waves have been calculated as accurately as the relations of sound waves have been. It is possible to make combinations of mathematical figures which shall represent a series of harmonious color waves. And it is possible to measure the waves radiated from a piece of bad coloring and prove them, *mathematically*, to be bad color.

It is a satisfaction to the artist to know that this is so; because although he will never compose color-schemes by the aid of mathematics, it gives him solid ground to stand on, and it diminishes the assurance of the man who claims the right to assert his opinion on color because "one man's taste is as good as another's." It is also encouraging to the student to know it, because he then knows that there is a definite knowledge, and not a personal idiosyncrasy, on which he can found his attempts to cultivate this side of his artistic life.

Color Composition.—The artist's problem in color

composition is analagous to that of line and mass, but is of course governed by conditions peculiar to it. The qualities which derive from line and mass are emphasized or modified by the management of color in relation to them. The painter in this direction uses the three elements together. Contrast and accent are attributes of color. Dignity and weight, as well as certain emotional qualities, such as vivacity and sombreness, may give the key to the picture in accordance with the arrangement of its color-scheme.

The mass may be simplified and strengthened, or broken up and lightened, by the color of the forms in it. By massing groups of objects in the same color, or by introducing different colors in the different forms in the same group, the mass is emphasized or weakened. So in line, the same color in repetition will carry the line through a series of otherwise isolated forms, and effect the emphasis of line. Masses can be strung into line, like beads, on a thread of color. In the great compositions of the old Venetian painters this marshalling of color groups constituted a principal element. The decorative unity of these great canvases could have been possible in no other way.

As I have said, the key of the color-scheme has a direct emotional effect, so adding to the power and dignity or the grace and lightsomeness of the composition. The analogy between color and imagination is marked. Certain temperaments instinctively express their ideals through color. To the painter color may be an all-influencing power; it is the glory of painting.

Drawing appeals to the intellect, but color speaks directly to the emotions, and conveys at a glance the idea which is re-enforced through the slower intellectual perception of the meaning of forms. In some unexplained way it expresses to the observer the temperamental mood; the joyousness, the severity or agitation which was the cause of its conception. In this strange but direct manner the color note aids the expression by line and mass of the æsthetic emotion which is the meaning of the painter's thought.

Key. — The key, then, is an important part of the picture. The very terms *warm* and *cold* applied to colors suggest what may be done by color arrangement. The *pitch* of the picture places it, in the emotional scale.

Tone. — Tone is harmony; the perfect balance of color in all parts of the picture. Fine color always means the presence, in all the color of the picture, of all the three primaries in greater or less proportion. Leave one color out in some proportion, and you have just so much less of a balance. I do not mean that some touch may not be pure color. On the contrary, the whole picture may be built up of touches of pure color. But the balance of color must be made then by touches of the different colors balancing each other, not only all over the picture, but in each part of it, to avoid crudity or over-proportion of any color. Generally the color scheme is dominated by some one color: which means that every touch of color on the canvas is modified to some extent by the presence of that color, keeping the whole in key. Each color retains its personal quality, but the quality of the dominant color is felt in it.

False Tone. — This is not to be attained by painting the picture regardless of color relations, and then glazing or scumbling some color all over the whole. This is the false tone of some of the older historical painters, particularly of the English school of the earlier part of this century. They "painted" the picture, and then just before exhibiting it "toned" it by glazing it all over with a large brush and some transparent pigment, generally bitumen. This did, in fact, bring the picture in tone after a fashion. But it is not a colorist's method. It is the rule of thumb method of a false technique and a vicious color sense. True tone is not something put onto the picture after it is painted. It is an inherent part of its color conception, and is worked into it while the picture is being painted, and grows to perfection with the growth of the picture. It is of the very essence of the picture. It is the dominant balance of color qualities; the result of a perfect appreciation of the value of every color spot which goes to the expression of the artist's thought.

In one sense it is the same as *atmosphere* in that the tonality of the picture is the atmosphere which pervades it. It may perhaps be best described by saying that it is that combination of color which gives to the picture the effect of every object and part in it having been seen under the same conditions of atmosphere; having been seen at the same time, with the same modification, and with the same degree and quality of light vibration. Tone is *color value* as distinguished from value as degree of power as light and shade; and in this is the perfection of subtlety of color feeling.

Tone Painters and Colorists. — Some painters have been called "tone painters," while others have been called "colorists;" not that tone painters are not colorists, but that there is a difference. It is a difference of aim, a difference of desire. Those painters who are usually called colorists, like Titian and Rubens, are in love with the richness and power of the color gamut. They are full of the splendor of color. They paint in full key, however balanced the canvas. Each note of color tells for its full power. Their stop is the open diapason, and their harmony is the harmony of large intervals and full chords.

The tone painter deals with close intervals. He is in love with subtle harmonies. What he loves is the essence of the color quality, and not its splendor. With the closest range he can give all possible half-tones and shades and modulations of color, yet never exceed the gray note perhaps; never once go to the full extent of his palette-power.

The utmost delicacy of perception and feeling, and the most perfect command of materials and of values, are necessary to such a painter. Above all, is he the "painter's painter," for the infinite subtlety and the exquisiteness of power are his. And yet this is the thing least appreciated by the lay mind, the most difficult to encompass, and requiring the most knowledge to appreciate.

Scientific Color.—To the scientist color is simply the irritation of the nerves of the retina of the eye by the waves of light. Different wave lengths give different color sensations. It is the generally accepted theory now that there are three primary sensations; that is, that the eye is sensitive to three kinds of color, and that all other shades and varieties of color are the results of mingling or overlapping of the waves which produce those three colors, and irritating more or less the nerves sensitive to each color simultaneously. These three primary colors are now stated to be red, blue, and *green*. The older idea was that they were red, blue, and *yellow;* and was based on experiments with pigments. Pigments do give these results; for a mixture of blue and yellow *pigment* will give green, and a mixture of red and green *pigment* will not give yellow, while the reverse is the fact with *light.*

White light is composed of all the colors. And the white light may be broken up (separated by refraction or the turning aside of light rays from their true course) into the colors of the rainbow, which is itself only this same decomposition of light by atmospheric refraction. Black is the absence of light, and consequently of color. This is not the case with pigment, for pure pigment has never been produced. The pigment simply reflects light rays which fall on it; that is, pigments have the power of absorbing, and so rendering invisible, certain of the rays which, combined, make up the white light which illumines them; and of transmitting others to the eye by reflection. We see, that is, our nerves of sight are irritated by, those rays which are not absorbed, but which are reflected.

All pigment is more or less absorbent of color rays, and more or less reflective of them; certain color rays being absorbed by a pigment, and certain other rays being reflected by it. The pigment is named according to those rays which it reflects. As a color-producing substance, then, the pigment is practically a mirror reflecting color rays. But a true mirror would reflect all rays unmodified. If we could paint with mirrors, each of which would reflect its own color *unsullied,* we could do what the scientist does with light; but the painter deals with an imperfect mirror which gives no color rays back unsullied by rays of another class, and so our results cannot be the same as the scientist's. So that just in accordance with the degree of purity of transmitting power of a pigment will be the purity of the color which we get by its use. But absolute purity of pigment we cannot get, so we cannot deal with it as we do with light, and we deal with a practical fact rather than a scientific fact, as painters.

Primaries and Secondaries. — As all the other shades of color are produced by the combinations (overlappings) of the waves or vibrations in the light rays from the primary colors, we have a series of colors called secondaries, because they are made up of the rays of any two of the three primaries: as purple, which is a combination of blue and red. When dealing with *light* the secondaries are: shades of violet and purple from red and blue; shades of orange red, orange, orange yellow, yellow, and yellowish green from red and green; and bluish green and greenish blue from blue and green — the character of the color being decided by the proportions of the primaries in the mixture.

These conclusions have been reached mainly through experiments in white light. The primaries so obtained do not hold good with pigment, as I have stated, but the principles do. It will avoid confusion if I speak hereafter of the combinations as they occur with pigment, it being borne in mind that it is a practical fact that we are dealing with rather than a scientific one.

In dealing with *pigment* the primaries are red, blue, and *yellow*, not *green*. Of course the secondaries are also changed; and we have purple and violet shades from red and blue, orange from red and *yellow*, and green from blue and yellow — all of which vary in shade with the proportion of the mixture of the primaries, as is the case with light.

Tertiaries. — Another class of shades or colors is called *tertiary*, or third; for they are mixtures of all the three primaries, or of a primary with a secondary which does not result from mixture with that primary. Tertiaries are all *grays*, and grays are practically always tertiaries. If you keep this in mind as a technical fact, it will help you in management of color. Grays are, to the painter, always combinations of color which include the three primaries. The usual idea is that gray is more or less of a negation of color. This is not so. Gray is the balancing of all color, so that any true harmony of color, however rich it may be, is always quiet in effect as a whole; that is, grayish —good color is never garish. It is very important that the painter should understand this characteristic of color. You cannot be too familiar with the management of grays. If you try to make your grays with negative colors, you will not produce harmonious color, but negative color, and negative color is only a shirking of the true problem. Grays made of mixtures of pure colors, balancings of primaries and secondaries, that is, modifications of the tertiaries, are quite as quiet in effect and quite as beautiful as any, but they are also more luminous; they are *live* color instead of *dead* color. Grays made by mixing black with everything are the reverse, and should not be used except when you use black as a color (which it is in *pigment*), giving a certain color quality to the gray that results from it.

Complementary Colors. — Two colors are said to be complementary to each other when they together contain the three primaries in equal strength. Green, for instance, is the complementary of red, for it contains yellow and blue; orange (yellow and red) is complementary to blue; and purple (red and blue) is complementary to yellow.

The knowledge of complements of colors is very important to the painter, for all the effects of color contrast and color harmony are due to this. Complementary colors, in mass, side by side, contrast.

The greatest possible contrast is that of the complementaries.

Complementary colors mixed, or so placed that small portions of them are side by side, as in hatching or stippling, give the tertiaries or grays by the mixing of the rays.

The Law of Color Contrast. — "When two dissimilar colors are placed in contiguity, they are always modified in such a manner as to increase their dissimilarity."

Warm and Cold Colors. — Red and yellow are called warm colors, and blue is called a cold color. This is not that the color is really cold or warm, of course, but that they convey the impression of warmth and coldness. It is mainly due to association probably, for those things which are warm contain a large proportion of yellow or red, and those which are cold contain more blue. There is a predominance of cold color in winter and of the warm colors in summer.

From the primaries various degrees of warmth and coldness characterize the secondaries and tertiaries, as they contain more or less proportionately of the warm or cold primaries.

In contrasting colors these qualities have great effect.

Color Juxtaposition. — In studying the facts of color contrast and color juxtaposition you will find that two pigments, if mixed in the ordinary way, will have one effect; and the same pigments in the same proportions, mixed not by stirring them into one mass, but by laying separate spots or lines of the pigment side by side, produce quite another. The gain in brilliancy by the latter mode of mixing is great, because you have mixed the *color rays* which are really light rays, instead of mixing the *pigment* as in the usual way. You have really mixed the color by mixing *light* as far as it is possible to do it with pigment. You have taken advantage of all the light reflecting power of the pigment on which the color effect depends. Each pigment, being nearly pure, reflects the rays of color peculiar to it, unaffected by the neutralizing effect of another color mixed with it; while the neutralizing power of the other color being side by side with it, the waves or vibrations of the color rays blend by overlapping as they come side by side to the eye; and so the color, made up of the two waves as they blend, is so much more vibrant and full of life.

"Yellow and Purple."—It is this principle which is the cause of the peculiarity in the technique of certain "Impressionist" painters. The "yellow lights and purple shadows" is only placing by the side of a color that color which will be most effective in forcing its note.

Brilliancy is what these men are after, and they get it by the study of the law of color contrast and color juxtaposition. The effect of complementaries in color contrast is what you must study for this, for the theory of it. For the practice of it, study carefully and faithfully the actual colors in nature, and try to see what are the real notes, what the really component colors, of any color contrast or light contrast which you see. Purple shadows and yellow light re-enforcing each other you will find to exist constantly in nature. Refine your color perception, and you will be able to get the result without the obviousness of the means which has brought down the condemnation on it. Closer study of the relations is the way to find the art of concealing art.

But yellow and purple are not the only complementaries. All through the range of color, the secondaries and tertiaries as well as the primaries, this principle of complement plays a part. There is no color effect you can use in painting which does not have to do, more or less, with the placing of the complementary color in mass, to emphasize; or mixed through to neutralize, the force of it. Train your eyes to see what the color is which makes the effect. Analyze it, see the parts in the thing, so that you may get the thing in the same way, if you would get it of the same force as in nature.

Practical Color. — All these theoretical ideas as to color have their relation to the actual handling of pigment, which is the craft of the painter. The facts of contrasting and harmonizing color relation have a practical bearing on the painter's work, both in what he is to express and how he is to do it; as to his conception of a picture and his representation of facts. In his conception he must deal with the possibilities of effect of color on color. The power of one color to strengthen the personal hue of another, or its power to modify that hue, is a fact bearing on whether the color in the picture is the true image of the color he has seen in his mind. In the same degree must this possibility affect his representation of actual objects.

The greatest possibilities of luminosity in sunlight or atmospheric effects come from the power to produce vibration by cool contrasted with warm color. You will find that a red is not so rich in any position as when you place its complementary near it. At times you will find it impossible to get the snap and sparkle to a scarlet — cannot make it carry, cannot make it felt in your picture as you want it without placing a touch of purple, perhaps, just beside it; to place near by a darker note will not have the same effect. It is the contrast of color vibration, not the contrast of light and shade, which gives the life. And at the same time that you enhance the brilliancy of the several notes of color in the picture, you harmonize the whole. For the mosaic of color spots all over the canvas brings about the balance of color in the composition, and harmony is the result.

Study Relations. — You must constantly study the actual relations of color in nature. You will find, if you look for it, that always, just where in art you would need a touch of the complementary for strength or for harmony, nature has put it there. She does it so subtly that only a close observer would suspect it. But the thing is there, and it is your business to be the close observer who sees it, both for your training as a colorist, and your use as an interpreter of nature's beauties. It is your business to see subtly, for nature uses colors subtly. The note sparkles in nature, but you do not notice the complementary color near it. Can you not also place the complementary color so that it is not seen, but its influence on the important color is felt? It is by searching out these *finesses* of nature that you train your eye. You must actually see these colors. At first you may only know that they must be there because the effect is there. But your eye is capable of actually recognizing them themselves, and you are no painter till it can. The theoretical knowledge is and should be a help to you, but the actual power of sight is most important. A painter may use theoretical knowledge to help his self-training, but power of eye he must have as the result of that training. The instantaneous recognition of facts and relations, the immediate and perfect union of eye and thought, are what make that intuitive perception which is the true feeling of the artist.

Work this out with eye and palette. Study the color and its relation in nature, and study its analogy in the pigment touches on the canvas.

The Palette. — You try to attain nature's effects of light with pigment. Pigment is less pure than light. You cannot have the same scale, the same range, but you must do the best you can, and the arrangement of your palette will help you. As you have not a perfect blue, a perfect red, and a perfect yellow, you must have two colors for one. Your paints will always be more or less impurely primary. No one red will make a pure purple with blue, and an equally pure orange with yellow. Yet pure purple and pure orange you must be able to make. Have, then, both a yellowish or orange red and a bluish or purplish red on your palette. Do the same with blue and yellow. In this way you can not only get approximately pure secondaries when you need them, but the primaries themselves lean somewhat towards the secondaries, so that you can make very delicate combinations with pure colors. A bluish yellow and a yellowish blue, for instance, will make a rather positive green. By using a reddish yellow and a bluish or purplish red, you practically bring in the red note, and make a grayer green while still using only two pigments.

So, too, you get similar control of effects by the use of opaque or transparent pigments, the transparent ones tending to richness, the opaque to dulness of color. Various processes in the manner of laying on paint bring about these different qualities, and will be spoken of in the chapter on "Processes."

Classify your pigments in your mind in accordance with these characteristics. Think of the ochres, for instance, as mainly opaque, and as yellows tending to the reddish. With any blue they make gray greens because of the latter quality, and they make gray oranges with red because of the dulness of their opacity and body. For richer greens think of the lighter chromes and cadmium yellows or citrons; and for the richer oranges, the deeper cadmiums and chromes. With reds, work the same way, scarlet or orange vermilions for one side of the scale, and the Chinese or bluish vermilion on the other side. The deeper and heavier reds fall in line the same way. Indian red is bluish, light red and venetian red are yellowish.

PART IV

PRACTICAL APPLICATION

CHAPTER XXII

REPRESENTATION

ALTHOUGH much has been said about the theoretical and abstract side of painting, and the importance of the æsthetic elements in art have been insisted upon, it is not to be supposed for a moment that painting does not deal with actual things. All painting which is not purely conventional must deal with and represent nature and natural facts. These are the body of the picture; the æsthetic elements are the heart of it. I believe that it is important that you should know that there is that side to painting, and should have some insight into it; that you should see that there is something else to think of than the imitation of natural objects. I would have you think more nobly of painting than to believe that "the greatest imitation is the greatest art." Beneath the imitation of the obvious facts of nature are the deeper facts and truths, and in and through these may you express those qualities of intellectual creation by means of which only, painting is not a craft, but an art.

But for all that, painting does, and always must,

deal with those obvious facts; and however much you may give your mind to the problems of composition and color, you must base it on a foundation of ability to represent what you see. Represent well the external objects, and you are in a position to interpret the spirit of them. For as nature only manifests her inner spirit through her outward forms and facts, you must be able to paint these well before you can do anything else.

The intellectual action which perceives and constructs is the art, the skill which represents and reproduces is the science, of painting.

Painting is the art of expression in color. The fact of color rather than form is the fundamental characteristic of it. The use of pigment rather than other materials is implied in its name. Therefore the science of painting deals with the materials with which to produce on canvas all manner of visible color combinations; and those processes of manipulation which make possible the representation of all the facts of color and light, of substance and texture, through which nature manifests herself.

It is not enough to have the pigment, nor even that it should get itself onto the canvas. Different characteristics call for different management of paint. Luminosity of light and sombreness of shadow will not be expressed by the same color, put on in the same way. Different forms and surfaces and objects demand different treatment. The science of painting must deal with all these.

It has been said that there are as many ways of painting as there are painters. Certainly there are as many ways as there are men of any originality. For however a painter has been trained, whatever the methods which he has been taught to use, he will always change them, more or less, in adapting them to his own purposes. And as the main intent of the art of an epoch or period differs from that of a previous one, so the manner of laying on paint will change to meet the needs of that difference. The manner of painting to-day is very different from that of other times. Some of the old processes are looked upon by the modern man as quite beneath his recognition. Yet these same methods are necessary to certain qualities, and if the modern man does not use or approve of those methods, it is because he is not especially interested in the qualities which they are necessary to.

There is probably no one statement which all fair-minded painters will more willingly acquiesce in, than one which affirms that the method by which the result is attained is unimportant, provided that the result *is* attained, and that it is one worth attaining. Every man will, whether it is right or not, use those methods which most surely and completely bring about the expression of the thing he wishes to express. In the face of this fact, and of the many acknowledged masterpieces, every one of which was painted in defiance of some rule some time or other alleged to be the only right one, it is not possible to prescribe or proscribe anything in the direction of the manipulation of colors. The result *must* be right, and if it is, it justifies the means. If it be not right, the thing is worthless, no matter how perfectly according to rule the process may be. As Hunt said, "What do I care about the grammar if you've got something to say?" The important thing is to say something, and if you do really say something, and do really completely and precisely express it, as far as a painter is concerned it will be grammatical. If not to-day, the grammar will come round to it to-morrow. Henry Ward Beecher is reported to have answered to a criticism on grammatical slips in the heat of eloquence, "Young man, if the English language gets in the way of the expression of my thought, so much the worse for the English language!" In painting, at any rate, the *complete* expression of thought *is* grammatical, and if not, so much the worse for the grammarians.

Try Everything. — Know, then, all you can about all the ways of manipulating paint that have ever been used. Use any or all of those ways as you find them needful or helpful. There is none which has not the authority of a master behind it, and though another master may decry it, it is because, being a master, he claims the very right he denies to you.

Experiment with all; but never use any method for the sake of the method, but only for what it is capable of doing for you in helping expression.

Safety. — The only real rule as to what to use and what not, applies to the effect on the permanence of your canvas. Never use pigments which will fade; nor in such a way that they will cause others to fade. Avoid all such using of materials as you know will make your picture crack, or in any other way bring about its deterioration.

Good Painting. — But for all I have just said, there is an acknowledged basis of what is good painting. If any man or school lays on paint in a frank, direct way, getting the effect by sheer force of putting on the right color in just the right place, with no tricks nor affectations, that is good painting; and the more simple, direct, and frank the manner of handling, the better the painting.

Let us understand what direct painting is first, and then consider varieties of handling. For whatever may be the subsequent manipulations, the picture is generally "laid in" with the most direct possible manner of laying on paint, and the other processes are mainly to modify or to further and strengthen the effect suggested in the first painting. And generally, also, in all sketches and studies which are preliminary preparations for the picture, the most direct painting is used, and the various processes are reserved for working out more subtle effects on the final canvas.

Old Dutch Painting. — Probably there are no better examples of frank painting than the works of the old Dutchmen. You should study them whenever you have a chance. Waiving all discussion as to the æsthetic qualities of their work, — as *painters*, as masters of the craft of laying on paint, they are unexcelled. And in most cases, too, they possessed the art of concealing their art. You will have to use the closest observation to discover the exact means they used to get the subtle tones and atmospheric effects.

The only obvious quality is the perfect understanding and skill of their brush-work. In the smoothest as well as in the roughest of their work, you can note how perfectly the brush searches the modelling, and with the most exquisite expressiveness and perfect frankness, follows the structural lines. No doubt there were over-paintings, glazings, and scumblings ; but they always furthered the meaning of the first painting, and never in the least interfered with or obscured the effect of *naïveté*, of candor of workmanship.

It is, however, this simple and sincere brush-work that you should strive to attain as the basis of your painting. Learn to express drawing with your brush, and to place at once and without indecision or timidity the exact tone and value of the color you see in nature at that point. Until you are enough of a master of your brush to get an effect in this way, do not meddle with the more complex methods of after-painting. You will never do good work by subsequent manipulation, if you have a groundwork of feebleness and indecision. Direct painting is the fundamental process of all good painting.

Let me take the type of old Dutch painting to represent to you this quality of direct painting. First of all notice a basis of perfect drawing, — a knowledge, exactness, and precision which admits of no fumbling, no vagueness, but only of a concise and direct recognition of structure. Note that this drawing is as characteristic of the brush-work as of the drawing which is under it. Observe that the handling of the whole school, from the least to the greatest, is founded on a similar and perfect craftsmanship, — the same use of materials; the same deliberateness; the same simple yet ample palette; the same use of solid color candidly expressing the planes of modelling, freely following the lines of structure; the absence of affectation or invention of individual means. Whatever the individuality of the artist, it rests on something else than difference of technique. From the freest and most direct of painters, Frans Hals, to the most smooth and detailed, Gerard Dou, the directness and ingenuousness of means to ends is the same, and founded on the same technical basis of color manipulation. The one is more eager, terse, the other more deliberate and complete; but both use the same pigments, both use the same solid color, are simple, lucid, both occupied solely with the thing to be expressed, and the least degree in the world with the manner of it. That manner comes from the same previous technical training which each uses in the most matter-of-course way, with only such change from the type, as his temperament unconsciously imposes on him.

There is nothing like it elsewhere. Study it; notice the unaffectedness of brush-stroke in Rembrandt. See how it is the same as Hals, but less perfunctory. See how the brush piles up paint again and again along the same ridge of flesh, taking no notice of its revelation of the insistence of attempt at the right value, nor of its roughness of surface. To get that drawing and that color in the freeest, frankest, most direct way: that is the aim. The absolute conviction of it: that is the essence of this technique of the old Dutch masters. And whatever else it may have or may not have, you will find in it all that you can find anywhere of suggestion of direct and frank and sincere painting, and nothing I can say will give you

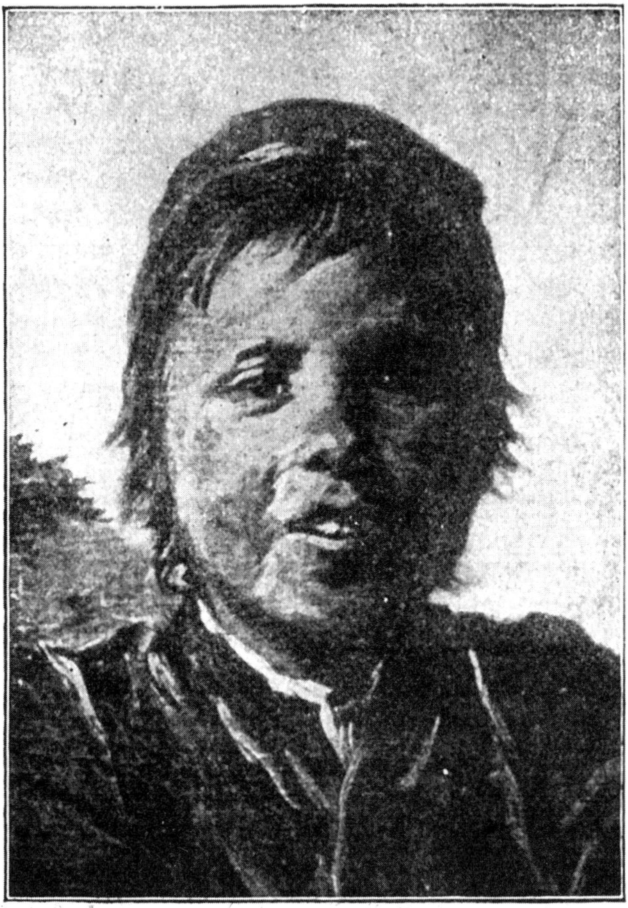

The Fisher Boy. *Frans Hals.*

To show the directness and sureness of brush-stroke, and candor and simplicity of means, always present in Dutch work, though never so free as with Hals.

any such clear idea of what you should strive for as the basis of all the different sorts of brush-work necessary or useful in the production of an oil painting.

Detail. — The question of detail may well come in here. How far are you to carry detail in your painting? The Dutch painters went to both extremes. Gerard Dou worked two weeks on a broom-handle, and hoped to finish it in a few days more. Frans Hals would paint a head in an hour. The French painter Meissonier paints the high light on every button of a trooper's coat, and De Neuville barely paints the button at all. What way are you to turn? Which are you to choose? We have a great deal said nowadays against detail in painting. Much is said of breadth and broad painting. Which is right?

True Breadth. — The answer lies in the central idea of the picture. There are times when detail may be very minute, and times when the greatest freedom is essential. True breadth is compatible with much even minute detail in the same canvas. For breadth does not mean merely a large brush. It never means slap-dash. It is the just conception of the amount of detail necessary (and the amount necessary to be left out) in order that the idea of the picture may be best expressed.

Detail is out of place in a large canvas always, and in proportion to its size it is allowable. A decorative canvas, a picture which is to be seen from a distance, or is to fill a wall space, wants effect, much justness of composition and color. Largeness of conception and execution, and only so much detail as shall be necessary to the best expression compatible with that largeness. On the other hand, a "cabinet picture," a small panel, will admit of microscopic detail if it be not so painted that the detail is all you can see. And just here is the heart of the whole matter. Whether you use much or little detail, it is not for the sake of the detail, not for any interest which lies in the detail itself, but for what power of expression may lie in it. If the picture, large or small, be largely conceived, and its main idea as to subject and those qualities of æsthetic meaning I have spoken of are always kept in view, and never allowed to lose themselves in the search for minuteness, then any amount of detail will take its place in true relation to the whole picture. If it does not do this it is bad.

The relations of parts to the whole are the key to the situation always.

Nothing is right which interferes with the true relations in the picture. This is where the working for detail is most likely to lead you astray. It takes great ability and power to keep detail where it belongs. Detail is always the search for small things, and they are almost sure to obtrude them-

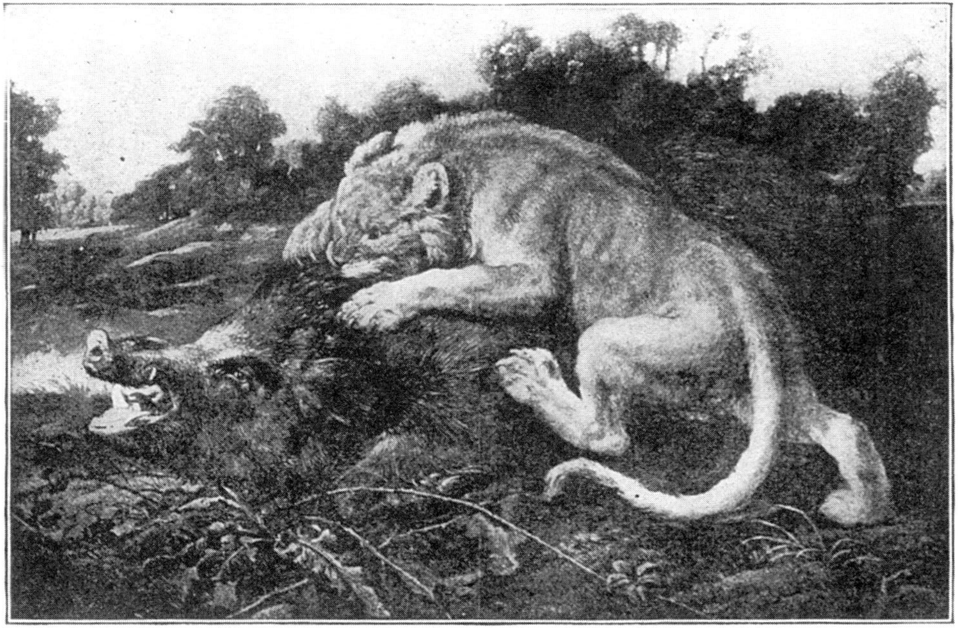

Boar-Hunt. *Snyders.*

To show relation of detail to the whole picture. The detail is carried far, yet does not interfere with emphasis of action and life. The picture is broad in spirit and effect if detailed in execution.

selves to the neglecting of the more important things. Details which do not stay in their places had better be left out of the picture. There is such a thing as *values* in *facts* as well as other parts of your work. And this applies to breadth as well as to detail.

Gerard Dou remains a great painter, and even a broad painter, strange as it may sound, in spite of his microscopic work. But only because of his breadth of eye. The detail is not the most important thing with him. It is in the picture, and you can see it when you look for it. But as you look at the picture it is not peppered all over with pin-points of detail, until the picture itself cannot be seen. Every detail stays back as it would in nature; loses itself in the part to which it belongs; modestly waits to be sought out; is not seen until it is looked for. This is broad painting, because the main things are emphasized; and if the details are painted they are seen in their true relations, and the power of the whole is not sacrificed to them.

With much or little detail, this is what is to be aimed at. Whether with big brushes or little ones, the expression of the main idea, of the important, the vital things, — this is broad painting, and this only.

CHAPTER XXIII

MANIPULATION

Premier Coup. — Something similar to what I have spoken of as "direct painting" has long been a much-advocated manner of painting in France, under the name of *Premier Coup;* which means, translated literally, "first stroke."

It is taught that the painter should use no after or overworkings at all; but that he should carefully and deliberately select the color for his brush-stroke, and then lay it on the canvas at one stroke, each after-stroke being laid beside some previous one, until the canvas has been covered by a mosaic of color each shade representing a single "first-stroke," with no after-stroke laid over it to modify its effect. Such a process tends to great deliberation of work and exactness of study. Probably no better thing was ever devised for the training of the eye and hand. But it has its limits, and is not often rigidly adhered to in the painting of pictures; although the fresh, direct effect of this sort of work is preserved as far as possible in much modern French work, and that quality is held in great esteem.

This manner of painting is especially useful in the making of sketches and studies, and leads to a strong control of the brush and the resources of the palette.

In all painting of this character the color should have body. Transparent color should not be used alone, but only to modify the tint of the more solid pigments; for the transparent colors used indiscriminately are apt to crack, which characteristic is avoided when the heavier color forms the body of the paint.

Solid Painting. — In most cases solid painting is the safest, — the least likely to crack, and the most safely cleaned from varnish and dirt without injury to the paint itself. It is firmer in character too, and gives more solidity of effect to the picture.

Mixing. — In mixing colors you should be careful not to over mix. Don't stir your paint. Too much mixing takes the life out of the color. Particles of the pure color not too much broken up by mixing are valuable to your work, giving vibration and brilliancy to it. The reverse is muddiness, which is sure to come from too much fussing and overworking of wet paint. Don't use more than three pigments in one tint if you can help it, and mix them loosely. If you must use more colors, mix still more loosely. Put all the colors together, one beside the other, drag them together with the brush, scoop them up loosely on the end of it, and lay the tint on freely and frankly. Never muddle the color on the canvas. Don't put one color over another more than you can help; you will only get a thick mass of paint of one kind mixing with a mass of another, and the result will be dirty color, which of all things in painting is most useless.

Keep the color clean and fresh, and have your brush-strokes firm and free. Never tap, tap, tap, your paint; make up your mind what the color is, and mix it as you want it. Decide just where the touch is to go, and lay it on frankly and fairly, and leave it. If it isn't right, daubing into it or pat-patting it won't help it. Either leave it, or mix a new color, and lay it on after having scraped this one off.

Don't try to economize on your mixing. A color mixed for one place will never do for another, so don't try to paint another place with it. Have the patience to proceed slowly, and mix the color specially for each brush-stroke. On the other hand, don't be niggardly with your paint. Don't use less paint than you need. Mix an ample brushful and put it on; then mix another, and use judgment as to how much you should use each time. The variety of tone and value which comes of mixing new color for every touch of the brush is in itself a charm in a painting, aside from the greater truth you are likely to get by it.

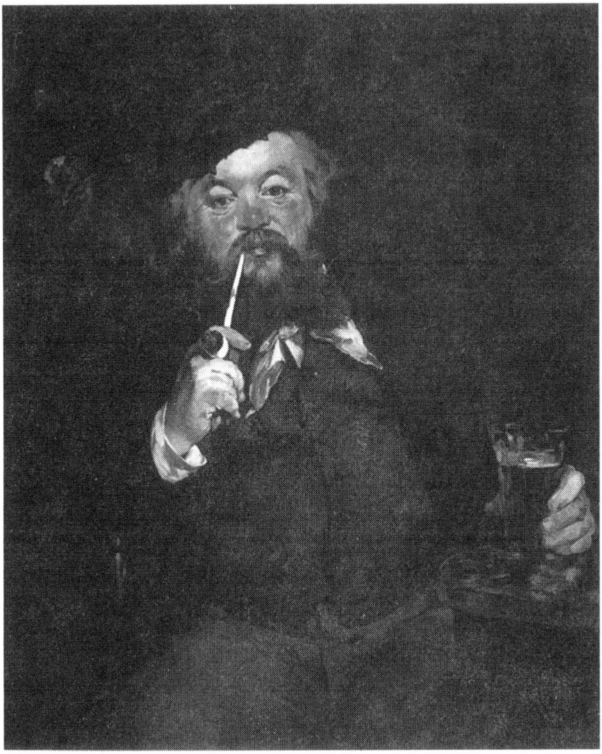

Good Bock. *Manet.*

To illustrate direct and solid painting.

Corrections. — As far as you can, make corrections by over-painting when the paint is dry, or nearly so. When I say don't work into wet color to correct, I do not mean that you are never to do so, but that to do it too much is likely to get your work muddy and pasty. Of course it is almost impossible to avoid doing so sometimes, but when you do, do it with deliberation. Don't lose your head and pile wet paint on wet paint in the vain hope of getting the color by force of piling it on. You will only get it worse and worse. Get it as nearly right as you can. If it is hopeless, scrape it off clean, and mix a fresh tint. If it is as near right as you can see to mix it now, go ahead; and put a better color on that place to-morrow when it is dry, if you can.

Keep at it. — But above all don't be permanently satisfied with the almost. Don't be afraid to put paint over dry paint till it is right. Work at it day after day. Let the paint get thick if it will, if only you get the thing right. The secret of getting it right is to keep at it, and be satisfied with nothing less than the best you can do. When you can see nothing wrong you can do no better. But as long as your eye will recognize a difference between what is on the canvas and what ought to be there, you have not done your best, and you are shirking if you stop. Never call a thing done as long as you can see something wrong about it. No matter what any one else says, your work must come up *at least* to the standard of what you yourself can see.

Loose Painting. — Sometimes it is necessary to lay on paint very loosely in order to get vibration of warm and cool color or of pure pigment in the same brush-stroke, or to let the under paint show somewhat through the loose texture of the paint over it. Too much of this sort of thing is not to be desired, but its effect in the right place is not to be obtained in any other way. The paint may be dragged over the canvas with a long brush charged with color more or less thoroughly mixed, as seems most effectual, or it may be flipped into its place, or it may be hatched on with parallel strokes. All these ways will be spoken of as they suggest themselves in other chapters. Solid color, generally, is used in this manner, and the effect of body is rather strengthened by it than the reverse.

Scumbling. — Another means of modifying the color and effect of a painting has perhaps always been more or less commonly in use. This is called *scumbling*, and may be considered under the head of solid painting, as it is always done with body, and never with transparent, color. The process consists of rubbing a mixture of body color, without thinning, over a surface previously painted and dried. Generally this *scumble* is of a lighter color than the under-painting, and is rubbed on with a stubby brush slightly charged with the paint. As much surface as is desired may be covered in this way, and the result is to give a hazy effect to that part, and to reduce any sharpness of color or of drawing. Often the effect is very successfully obtained. Distant effects may be painted solidly and rather frankly, and then brought into a general indefiniteness by scumbling. Too much scumbling will make a picture vague and soft, and after a scumble it is best to paint into it with firm color to avoid this.

The scumble may be used with the richer and darker colors, too, to modify towards richness the tone of parts of the picture, or to darken the value. Most often, however, its value lies in its use to bring harsher and sharper parts together, and to give the hazy effect when it is needed.

Scumbling will not have a good effect when it is not intended to varnish the picture afterwards; for the oil in the paint is absorbed immediately, and the rubbing of color gives a dead look to the canvas which is very unpleasant, and decidedly the reverse of artistic.

Glazing. — A very valuable process, the reverse of scumbling, is glazing. It has always been in use since the invention of the oil medium. All the Italian painters used it; it is an essential part of their system of coloring. The rich, deep color of Titian, the warm flesh of Raphael, and the jewel-like quality of the early German painters are impossible without some form of glaze. The Germans perhaps made glazes with white of egg before oil was used as a vehicle. But to glaze is the only way to get the fullest effect of the quality characteristic of the transparent paints.

A glaze is a thin wash of transparent color flowed over an under-painting to modify its tone or to add to its effect. It is not always transparent color, but usually it is. Sometimes opaque or semi-opaque color may be used, and it is a glaze by virtue of the fact that it is thinned with a vehicle either oil or varnish, and *flowed* on. A scumble is *rubbed* on, and is never pure transparent color.

Advantages of Glazing. — The advantages are the gain in harmony, in force, in brilliancy; you may correct a color when it is wrong, or perfect it when it is not possible to get the force or richness required without it. These are the qualities which have made it used by all schools more or less.

Disadvantages. — There are, however, quite as evident and marked disadvantages. The free use of oil as a thinning vehicle, although it makes possible a greater degree of richness of color, is very likely to turn the picture brown in time. Oil will always eventually have a browning effect on all paints, even when mixed with them as little as is absolutely necessary. If you make a tinted varnish of oil (which is practically what a glaze is), you add so much, to the surely darkening action of the oil on the picture.

If, again, you depend upon a glaze for the richness of color for your picture, and you use a color which is not permanent, your glaze fades, and your color is not there. A glaze is particularly liable to be injured by the cleaner if it ever gets into his hands. He works down to fresh color, and what with the browning of the glaze and the fact that the cleaner is more anxious that the picture should be cleaned than that its color should be fine, he will, in nine cases out of ten, *clean* off the glaze which may be the final and most expensive color the painter has put on it.

Glazing is little used nowadays, compared with what it once was. But there are times when you cannot get what you want in any other way, and when you are sure that glazing is the only thing which will give you your result, the only law for the painter comes in, — get your result.

Precautions. — If you do glaze, however, there is a right and a wrong way. You should not use a glaze as a last resort. It is better to calculate on it beforehand; for you always glaze with a darker tint upon a lighter one, so that if you have not allowed for this, you will get your picture too low in tone before you know it.

If you want to make your picture, or a part of it,

brighter and lighter, bring it up in pitch with body color first, with solid painting, and then glaze it.

Do not glaze on color which is not well dried. The drying of the under color and the drying of the glaze are apt to be different in point of time, and the picture will crack. If the vehicle is the same as was used in the under-painting, and the drying qualities of both paintings are the same, there is no danger. But when color dries, it shrinks and flattens, and two kinds of colors shrinking differently are sure to pull apart, and that causes cracking. If the under-painting is well dry, but not hard and glossy on the surface, and is capable of still absorbing enough of the new color's vehicle to bind the coats together, your glaze will stand. But rather than have it too soft, have the under-painting too hard, and then before you glaze go over it with a little thin, quick-drying varnish, and glaze into that. The varnish will hold the two coats of paint together.

Glazing, as well as scumbling, implies the obligation to varnish your picture. Whenever you use oil freely you will have to varnish your picture to keep it bright and fresh in color.

It would be wise never to use a glaze as a final process. Glaze to get the tone or to modify it, but paint into the glaze with body color, and you keep the advantage of the glaze without many of the disadvantages of it, and the picture has a more solid effect of painting.

Frottée. — Closely akin to the glaze in manner, but very different in use, is the *frottée*, or "rubbing." This is generally used on the fresh surface of the canvas, to "rub in" the light and shade or the first coloring of the picture after the drawing is done. It is one of the safest and wisest ways of beginning your picture. You can either rub in the picture with a *frottée* of one color, as sienna or umber, or you can use all the colors in their proper places, only using very little vehicle, and making something very thin in tint, somewhat between a glaze and a scumble. You can make a complete drawing in monochrome in this way, or you can lay in all the ground colors of the picture till it has much the effect of a complete painting. Then, as you paint and carry the picture forward, every color you put on will be surrounded with approximately the true relations, instead of being contrasted by a glare of white canvas.

A *frottée* is a most sympathetic ground to paint over.

CHAPTER XXIV

COPYING

Copying may well be spoken of here, as it is in a sense a kind of manipulation. It is a means of study to the student, and a useful, sometimes necessary process to the painter. In the transferring of the results of his sketches and studies to the final canvas, the painter must be able to copy, and to know all the conveniences of it. Before the painting begins on a picture, the main figures in it must be placed and drawn on the canvas with reference to the plan of it, and their relation to that plan. This calls for some method of exact reproduction of the facts stored in the artist's studies for that purpose. The process of copying is that method.

From the side of study, the copy gives the student the most practical means of understanding the intent and the expression of the painter whose work he wishes to know. There is no way of understanding the why and the how of technical expression so sure and complete as to study with the brush and paint, following the same method and processes as the master you copy, and trying to comprehend the meaning and the expression at the same time.

This is not the best means of study for a beginner, as I have said before. It trains the understanding of processes rather than the eye; and the training of the power of perception rather than the understanding of methods is what the young student needs. The processes with which he may put on canvas the effect he sees in nature are secondary matters to him. Let him really see the thing and find his own way of expressing it, clumsily, rudely most probably, it is still the best thing for him. He may take such help as he can find, as he needs it; get such suggestions as the work of good painters can give to him, when he cannot see his own way. But the searching of nature should come first. The *seeing* of what is must precede the *stating* of it.

But when you do undertake to make a copy, there is something more to be tried for than an approximation of the right colors in the right places.

Certainly to get out of copying all there is to get, one must try for something more than a recognizable picture. When a serious student makes a copy, he not only tries to get it like in color and drawing, but also in manner of treatment, peculiarities of technique, and whatever there may be that goes to make up the "manner" of the original.

This is not only for the sake of the copy, for the sake of really having a picture which is more than superficially like the original; but in this way can be gained much real knowledge of technique which cannot be gotten so easily otherwise.

Study your original carefully before and while working on your own canvas. See how it was done if you can (and you can), and do it in the same way, touch for touch, stroke for stroke, color for color. Use a large brush when he used a large brush; if the original was done with a palétte-knife, use yours; and particularly never use a smaller brush than the painter used on the picture you are copying.

The same thing holds as to processes. If your original was painted solidly, with full body of color, do so on your copy. Never glaze nor scumble because *you* can't get the colors without. Your business is to try to get the same qualities *in the same way.* And any other manipulation is not only getting a different thing, but shirking the problem. Because, if you can't get the effect in the way he did, you certainly won't get the *same one* any other way. You are not originating, you are not painting a picture, you are copying another man's work; and common honesty to him, as well as what you are trying to learn, demands that you shall not belie him by stating on your canvas implicitly, that he did the thing one way, when as a matter of fact his canvas shows that he did it another way.

This may seem commonplace, because one would think that as a matter of course any one would naturally make a copy this way. But this is precisely what the average person does not do when copying, and I have found it constantly necessary to insist upon these very points even to advanced students.

So in the pigments, the vehicles, the tools, and even the canvas if you can, as well as in the handling of the paint and the processes used, follow absolutely and humbly, but intelligently, the workmanship of the picture you copy, if it is worth your while to do it at all.

In making copies it is not usual to make the preliminary drawing freehand. It takes time that may better be given to something else, and often it is not exact enough. When a painter has made careful studies which he wishes to transfer to his canvas, they may have qualities of line or movement, or of emphasis or character which the model may not have had. These studies, probably, are much smaller than they will be in the picture. The same things may be true of the characteristics of the sketches. These are problems which have been worked out, and to copy them freehand makes the work to be done over again on a larger scale on the canvas of the picture. This would not only take too much time, but the same result might not follow. For this purpose a more mechanical process is commonly made use of, which combines the qualities of exactness with a certain freedom of hand, without which the work would be too rigid and hard.

"Squaring up." — This process is called "squaring-up," and consists of making a network of squares which cut up the study, and map out its lines and proportions, and make it possible to be sure that any part of the original will come in the same relative place in the copy no matter what the size may be, and at the same time leaves the actual laying out of the thing to freehand drawing.

The process is a very simple one. You mark off a number of points horizontally and vertically on the study. Make as many as you think best — if there are too few, you will have too much of the study in one part; if too many, it makes you more trouble. It is not necessary that there be as many points one way as the other; make the number to suit the lines of the study.

Draw straight lines across the study from each of the points, keeping them carefully parallel, and seeing to it that the horizontal lines cross the vertical ones exactly at right angles. These lines cut the study into right-angled parallelograms, which may be squares or not according as the vertical lines are the same distance from each other that the horizontal ones are, or not.

Number the spaces between the lines at the top, 1, 2, 3, etc., and at one side the same.

Now if you square off a part of your canvas with the same number of spaces at the top and the same number at the side as you have done with the study, and keep the relation of the spaces the same, you can make it as large or as small as you please, and you can draw the outlines within those squares as they fall in the study, and they will be the same in proportion without your having the trouble of working to scale. The squares furnish the scale for you, and the proportion is not of the study to the picture, but as the vertical spaces are to the horizontal, in both the study and the picture.

By numbering the squares on the canvas to correspond with those on the study, and noticing in which square, and in what part of it, any line or part of a line comes, you can, by drawing that line in the same part of the corresponding square on the canvas, repeat the line in the same relation and with exactness, while still leaving the hand free to modify it, or correct it.

In this way the simplest or the most complex, the largest or the smallest study sketch or drawing may be accurately transferred to any surface you please.

CHAPTER XXV

KINDS OF PAINTING

WHY not recognize that conviction, intense personal attraction to a certain sort of thing is the life of all art. How else can life get into art than through the love of what you paint? A man may understand what he does not love, but he will never infuse with life that which he does not love. Understand it he should, if he would express it; but love it he must, if he would have others love it.

You see it is not the thing, but the manner; not the fact, but what you can find in it; not the object, but what you can express by it. "*Un chef d'œuvre vaut un chef d'œuvre*," because perfect delight in loveliness found in a small thing is as perfect as perfect delight in loveliness found in a great thing. And still life uninteresting as a fact, may be fascinating if "seen through the medium of a temperament."

Don't let the idea get into your head that one thing is easier to do than another thing. Perhaps it is, but it is a bad mental attitude to think so. And even then, you may find that when you have worked out all that its easiness shows you, some one with better knowledge or insight may come along and point out undreamed-of beauties and subtleties. And are they easy? To see and express the possibilities in easy things is the hardest of all.

Classification. — Divide paintings into two classes, — those representing objects seen out-of-doors, and those representing objects in-doors. This is the most fundamental of all classifications, and it is one which belongs practically to this century. Before this century it was hardly thought of to distinguish out-door light from in-door light.

Some of the Dutchmen did it. But it is only in this century that the principle has made itself felt. It is this which makes the difference of pitch or key so marked between the modern and the ancient pictures. It has changed the whole color-scheme.

An out-door picture may be still painted in the studio, but it must be painted from studies made out-doors. It is no longer possible to pose a model in a studio-light and paint her so into a landscape. It was right to do it when it was done frankly, when the world had not waked up to the fact that things look different in diffused and in concentrated lights. It is not right now. You cannot go back of your century. To be born too late is more fatal than to be born too soon.

Whatever kind of picture you take in hand, remember that what distinguishes the treatment of it from that of other pictures depends on the inherent character of it. That the difficulties as well as the facilities in the working of it are due to the fact that it demands a different application of the universal principles. Don't think that landscape drawing is easier than that of the figure because smudges of green and blue and brown can be accepted as a landscape, while a smudge of pink will not do duty for the nude figure. It is only that the drawing of the figure is more obvious, and variations from the more obvious right are more easily seen.

You must study the necessities, the demands of treatment of the different sorts of subjects — see what is peculiar to each, and what common to all. You must find to what æsthetic qualities each most readily lends itself, what are the subtleties to be sought for, and what are the problems they offer.

CHAPTER XXVI

THE SKETCH

THE sketch is the germ of the picture. It contains the idea which may later become the finished work. In your sketches you gather effects and suggestions of possibilities, of all kinds. You do not work long over a sketch, nor do you work perfunctorily. You do not make it because you ought to, but because you see something in nature which charms you; or because you have found an idea you wish to make a note of.

Understand thoroughly the use and meaning of sketches, and you will get more good from the making of them. For your sketching is an important matter to your painting. You do not learn how to paint by sketching; but you can learn a great many things, and some of them you can learn no other way. A sketch is not a picture; neither is it a study. Each of these things has its special purpose and function, and its proper character.

A sketch is always a note of an idea — an idea seen or conceived. Everything is sacrificed in the sketch to thc noting of that idea. One idea only, in one sketch; more ideas, more sketches.

There are two kinds of sketches: those made from nature to seize an effect of some sort; and those made to work out or express tersely some composition or scheme of color which you have

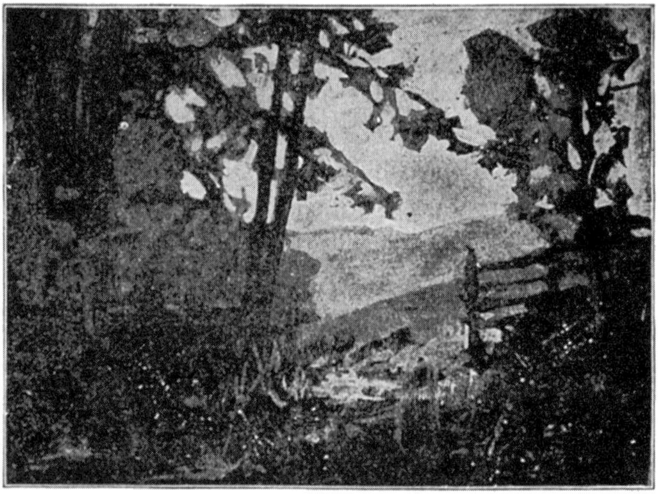

Sketch of a Hillside blocked in from Nature, First Suggestion of Composition, etc.

in your mind. Both are of great use to the student as well as essential to the work of the artist.

The first conception of a picture is always embodied in the form of a sketch, and the artist will make as many sketches as he thinks of changes in his original idea. It is in this form that he works out his picture problem. He is troubled here by nothing but the one thing he has in mind at this time. It may be an arrangement of line or of mass. He changes and rearranges it as he pleases, not troubling himself in the least with exactness of drawing, of modelling, of color, nor of anything but that one of composition. It may be a scheme of color, and here again the spots of pigment only vaguely resemble the things they will later represent; now they are only composition of color to the painter, and everything bends to that. When this has been decided on, has been successfully worked out, then it is time enough to think of other things. And think of other things he does, before he makes his picture; but not in this sketch; in another sketch or other sketches, each with its own problem, or in studies which will furnish more material to be used later; or in the picture itself, where the problem is the unity of the various ideas within the great whole in the completed painting.

It is the sketch on which the picture rests for its singleness of purpose. No picture but begins in this way, whether it is afterwards built up on the same canvas or not. The sketch points the way. But all the preliminary sketches of a painting are not problems of composition or color; are not conceptions of the brain. There are suggestions received from nature which the painter perceives rather than conceives. Possibilities show themselves in these, but it is in the sketch that they first become tangible and stable. This is the sketch from nature, always the record of an impression, the note of an idea hinted by one fact or condition seen more sharply or clearly than any or all of the thousands which surrounded it at the moment.

The painter must always sketch from nature. Only by so doing can he be constantly in touch with her, and receive her suggestions unaffected by multitudinous facts. The sketch preserves for him the evanescent effects of nature, which the study would not so entirely, because not so simply, grasp. The sudden storm approaches; the fleeting cloud shadow; or the last gleam of afterglow; these, as well as the more permanent, but equally charming effects of mass against mass of wood and sky, or of meadow and hill, he can only store up for future use or reference in his sketches.

Main Idea Only. — In the making of the sketch, then, no problem should come in but that of the expression of the main idea, — no problem of drawing or of manipulation of color. To get the idea expressed in the most direct and immediate and convenient way, anything will do to sketch on or with; that which presents the least difficulty is the best. The matter of temperament, of course, comes in largely, and technical facility. That which you can use most freely, use in your sketching, and keep for other occasions the new means or medium. Use freely, if you can, black and white for whatever black and white will express, and pigment for all color effects. Oil for greatest certainty and facility of correction.

Quick Work. — Make your sketch at one sitting, or you will have something which is not a sketch. Work long enough, and it may be a study; but more than one sitting makes it neither one thing nor the other. To say nothing of the fact that the conditions are unlikely to be exactly the same again, you are almost sure on the second working to have lost the first impression, — the freshness and directness of purpose which the first impress gives; and this is the very heart of a sketch. You must never lose sight of what was the original purpose of it; never forget what it was which first made you want to paint it. No matter what else you get or do not get, if you lose this you lose all that can give it life or reality.

The very fact that you have limited yourself to one working makes you concentrate on that which first caught your attention, and that is what you want to seize.

Overworkings and after-paintings will only interfere with the dircctness and force with which this is expressed.

Remember that nature is never at rest. You must catch her on the wing, and the more quickly you do it the more vivid will be the effect.

"Nature is economical. She puts her lights and darks only where she needs them." Do the

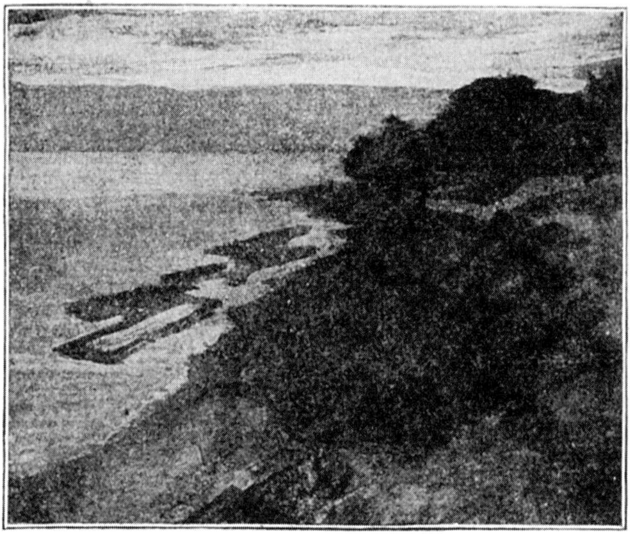

The River Bank. *D. Burleigh Parkhurst.*

Half-hour sunset sketch.

same, and use no more effort than will suffice to express that which is most important. The rest will come another time.

Try to keep things simple. Keep the impression of unity; have the sketch one thing only.

Express things as they look. As they look to *you* and at *this time*. How they seem to some one else, or seemed at some other time, is not to the point. What you know they are or may be will not help you, but only hinder you in a sketch. The more facts the worse, in sketching. Remember always what a sketch is for. Don't be beguiled into trying to make a picture of it, nor a study of it. Above all, don't try to make a clever thing of it. Make something sincere and purposeful of it, and have it as concise, as terse, as direct, and as expressive of one thing as you can.

Keep Looking. — Always keep your eyes open and your mind receptive; do not be always looking for reasons. Accept the charm as it presents itself; note it, if you have anything handy to express it with; if not, study it, and get something into your mind and memory from it. The simplest way of expressing it, and the simplest elements which cause it, you can study without the materials to preserve it, and you so keep your receptivity and quicken your power of observation.

Your sketch will be more quickly done, directly and more forcefully, if you map out the thing rather deliberately first with a few very exact lines and masses in some way: then you have a free mind to concentrate on the effect. A few values and masses well placed are the things you most want; you can almost always spare time to ensure their exactness by a few measurements and two or three rubs of color first. Of course if the sketch is of a passing gleam you can do nothing but get a few smudges of color. But get them true in value and in color relation; get the glow of it, or you will get nothing.

Canvases of a Size. — In sketching from nature, have the habit of using always the same sized canvases or panels. They pack better, and you learn to know your spaces, and so you do quicker and better work. Make them big enough to do free work on, yet small enough to cover easily, so that you lose no time in mere covering of surface. Ten inches by fourteen is plenty small enough, and fifteen by twenty large enough, for most persons. Suit yourself as to the size, but settle on a size, and stick to it. Nothing is more awkward and inconvenient than to have stacks of canvases of all sizes and shapes.

Always have plenty of sketching materials on hand. You will lose many a good effect which will pass while you are getting your kit ready.

In sketching, avoid details. When you want them, make a study of them. In a sketch they only interfere with frankness of expression. One or two details for the sake of accent only, may be admitted.

Make a frame with your hand, or, better, cut a square hole in a card, and look through it.

Decide what is the essence of it, what is vital to the effect, and do that; concentrate on that. Put in what you need for the conveying of that, and leave out everything else.

Work Solidly. — Work in body color, and lay on your paint fully and freely. In getting an effect of light, don't be afraid of contrast either of value or of color. Paint loosely; get the vibration which results from half-mixed color. Don't flatten out the tone. Load the color if you want to. In twenty years you will wonder to see how smooth it has become.

Freedom and breadth give life to a sketch. Don't work close to your work. Don't bend over it. Use plenty of color, large brushes, and strike from the shoulder.

CHAPTER XXVII

THE STUDY

THE qualities which make a good study are the reverse of those which make a good sketch. In the sketch all is sacrificed to the effect, or to the one thing which is its purpose. The study is what its name implies, and its purpose is not one thing, but many. In a study you put in everything which may be valuable. You store it with facts. You leave out nothing which you wish to put in. It is all material. You can take and leave in using it afterwards, as you could from nature. Of course every study has some main intention, but you must take the trouble to give everything that goes to the making of that.

A study is less of a picture than a sketch is. For unity of effect is vital to both a sketch and a picture. But this quality is of no essential value in a study — unless it be a study of unity. For you can make a *study* of anything, from a foreground weed to a detailed interior, from a bit of pebble to a cavalry charge.

But in a study of one thing you concentrate on that thing, you deliberately and carefully study everything in it, while in a sketch you work only for general effect. The study is the storehouse of facts to the painter. By it he assures himself of the literal truths he needs, collecting them as material in color or black and white, and as mental material by his mental understanding of them, only to be gained in this way.

In making a study you may work as long as you please, timing yourself by the difficulty and size of the thing you are studying. A study of an interior or a landscape may occupy a week or two; one of a simple object for some detail in a picture may be a matter of only a few hours. But in any work of this kind you should be deliberate, and remember that what you are doing is neither a sketch nor a picture, but the gathering of material which is to be useful, but which can be useful only so far as it is accurate.

In making studies, don't try for surface finish; get the facts, and leave all other qualities for the picture. Don't glaze and scumble, but work as directly as you can. Study the structure and texture of whatever you are doing. Understand it thoroughly as you go on, and search out whatever is not clear to you. This is no place for effects; nor for slighting or shirking. If you do not do work of this kind thoroughly, you might as well not do it at all — better; for you are at least not training yourself to be careless.

There are places where you may be careless, but the making of a study is not that place.

Take plenty of trouble with preliminaries. Get all your foundation work true. Have a good drawing, get the groundwork well laid in, and then build your superstructure of careful study.

Don't be afraid of over-exactness, nor of hardness and edginess here. All that is only an excess of precision, and it is just as well to have it. You can leave it out if you want to in your picture, but a groundwork of exactness is not to be despised.

Be exact also with your values. If your study is not sure of its values, it will weaken the results you should get from it later.

Make your studies in the same light as that which the picture will represent. You can paint a picture under any light you please if your studies give you the facts as to light and shade that the truth to nature requires; but studies made in one light for a picture representing another are useless to that picture.

No good painting was ever made without preliminary studies. When you are to make a picture, therefore, take plenty of time to prepare yourself with all the material in the form of facts that you may require. Don't trust to building up a picture from a sketch or two and your "general knowledge." That sort of thing is something which a painter of experience may do after stor-

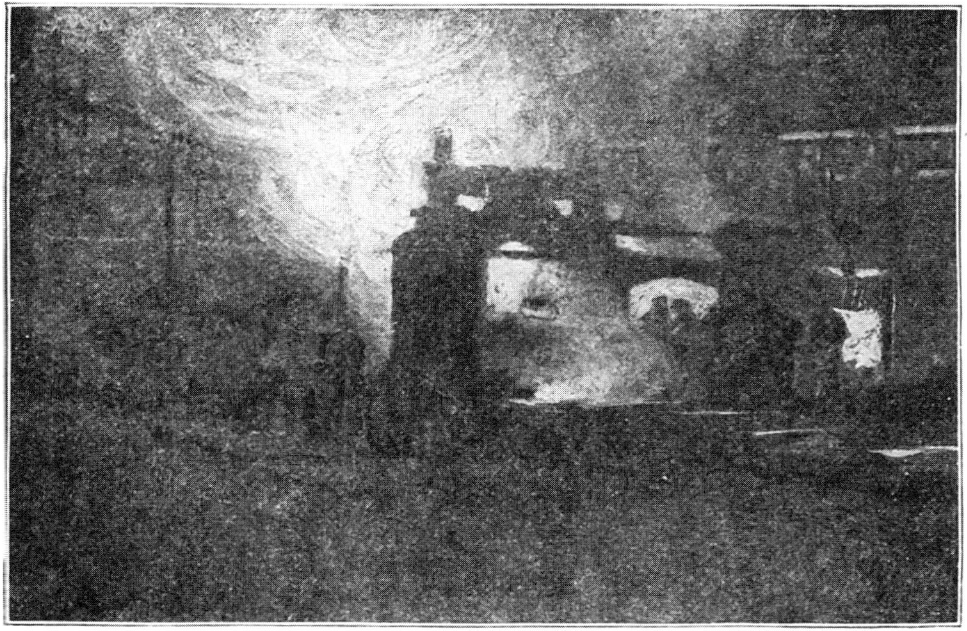

Study of a Blooming-Mill. *D. Burleigh Parkhurst.*

ing his mind for years with all sorts of knowledge; but it will not do for most people—least of all for a student. And it is a dangerous way for any one to work. Even the experienced painter is apt to do the worse work for it, and if he does so constantly, his reputation may suffer for it. Take time to be right.

Don't be afraid of taking measurements. Every one who did anything worth looking at took measurements. Leonardo laid down a complete system of proportions. You can't get your proportions right without measurements, and if your proportions are not right, nothing will be right. Use a plumb-line: use it frequently, and measure horizontals and verticals. If you are in doubt about anything, stop a minute and measure. It takes less time than correcting.

Whatever you do, get the character first, then the details. Character is not a conglomeration of details. The detail is the incident of character. See what the vital things are first, then search farther.

Use your intelligence as well as your eye and hand. Think as you work. Don't for a moment let your hand get ahead of your brain. Don't work absent-mindedly, nor without purpose. If your mind is tired, if your eye won't see, stop and rest a while. Tired work runs your picture down hill.

CHAPTER XXVIII

STILL LIFE

THE name of still life is used in English for all sorts of pictures which represent groupings of inanimate objects except flowers. The French word for it is better than ours. They call it "*nature morte*," or dead nature.

There is no kind of painting which is more universally useful — to the student as well as to the painter. It furnishes the means for constant, regular, and convenient study and practice. You need never lack for something interesting to paint, nor for a model who will sit quietly and steadily without pay, if you have some pieces of drapery, and a few articles, of whatever shape or form, which you can group in a convenient light.

You can make the group as simple or as difficult as you wish, and make it include any phase of study. The advantage of its possible variety, scope, and particularly, its convenience and cheapness and manageableness, make it the fundamental work for the beginner.

Materials. — Practically anything and everything is available for still life. You should be constantly on the lookout for interesting objects of all kinds. Try to get a collection which has as much variety in form, size, and surface as you can. Old things are generally good, but it is a mistake to suppose old and broken things the best. An object is not intrinsically better because of its being more or less damaged, although it sometimes has interesting qualities, as of color or history, because of its age.

What you should avoid is bad proportion, line, and color in the things you get. The cost is not of any importance at all. You can pick up things for a few cents which will be most useful. Have all sorts of things, tall slim vases, and short fat jugs. Have metals and glass, and books and plaques. They all come in, and they add to the variety and interest of your compositions.

Draperies. — The study of drapery particularly is facilitated by still-life study. You can arrange your draperies so that they are an essential part of your study, and will stay as long as you care to paint from them, and need not be moved at all. This fact of "staying power" in still life is one of importance in its use, as it reduces to the minimum the movement and change which add to the difficulties in any other kinds of work. The value of the antique in drawing lies in its unvarying sameness of qualities from day to day. In still life you have the same, with color added. You can give all your attention and time unhurriedly, with the assurance that you can work day after day if you want to, and find it just the same to-morrow morning as you left it to-day. This as it applies to drapery is only the more useful. You can hardly have a lay figure of full size, because of its cost. To study drapery on a model carefully and long, is out of the question, because it is disarranged every time the model moves, and cannot be gotten into exactly the same lines again.

Still life steps in and gives you the power to make the drapery into any form of study, and to have it by itself or as a part of a picture.

In draperies you should try to have a considerable variety just as you have of the more massive objects, — variety of surface, of color, and of texture. Do not have all velvet and silk. These are very useful and beautiful, but you will not always paint a model in velvet and silk. Satins and laces are also worn by women, and cloth of all kinds by men, and so you should study them. Sometimes you want the drapery as a background, to give color or line; and yet to have also marked surface qualities (texture), would take from the effect of those qualities in the other objects of the group.

As to color, in the same way you should have all sorts of colors; but see to it that the colors are good, — in themselves "good color," not harsh nor crude. It does you no good as a student to learn how to express bad color. Neither is it good training for you, in studying how to represent what you see, to have to change bad color in your group into good color in your picture.

Good useful drapery does not mean either large pieces, or pieces with much variety of color in one piece; on the contrary, you should avoid spotty or prominent design in it. Still, the more kinds you have, the more you can vary your work.

If your drapery is a little strong in color, you can always make it more quiet by washing or fading it to any extent. There is very little material which is absolutely fast color. But when it is so, and the color is too strong, don't use it.

Don't scorn old and faded cloth, especially silk and velvet, or plush. The fact that it would look out of place on furniture or as a dress does not imply that it may not be beautiful as a background or as a foreground color. These old and faded materials furnish some of the most useful things you can have; a fact the reverse of what is true in general of other still-life things.

The Use of Still Life. — There is no way in which you can better study the principles of composition than by the use of still life. The fact that you can bring together a large number of objects of any color and form, and can arrange and rearrange them, study the effect and result before painting, and be working with actual objects and not by merely drawing them, gives a positiveness and actuality to composition that is of the greatest service to you. You can use (and should at times) the whole side or corner of a room, and so practise composition on the large scale, or you can make a small group on a table. That you are using furniture and drapery or vases, flowers, and books, instead of men and women, does not affect the seriousness and usefulness of the problem; for the principles of composition and color do not have to do with the materials which you use to bring about the effect, but the effect itself.

It is practically impossible for the student and the amateur to make very advanced study of composition in line and mass with more than one or two living models; but with still life he may and should get all the practical knowledge possible.

Practical Composition. — Suppose you were going to work with still life, how would you begin? In the first place, get a good composition. Never work from a bad one. You must learn composition some time, so you might as well study it every time you have occasion to start a still-life study. Take any number of things and put them on a table, get a simple background to group them against. Consider your things, and eliminate those which are not necessary, or will not tell in the composition. It is a law that whatever does not help your picture (or composition) tells against it; so get rid of anything which will not help the composition.

For instance, here are a lot of things indiscriminately grouped on a table. You might paint

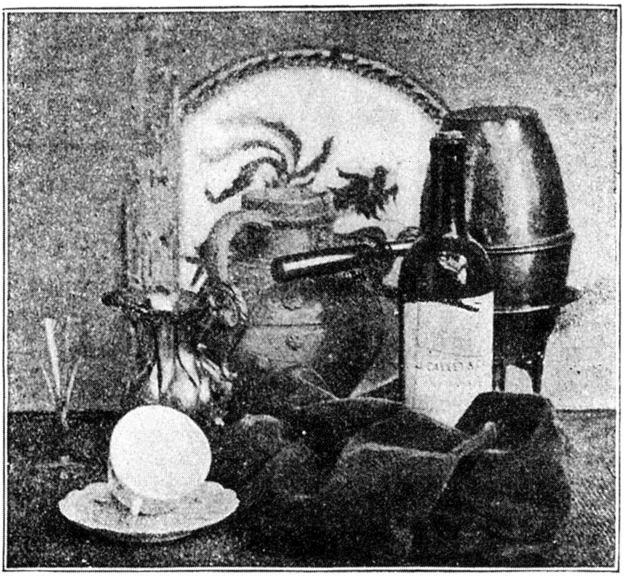

Still Life, No. 1.

them, but they are not arranged. There is no composition. They would lack one commanding characteristic of a good picture if you were to paint them so. What do they lack as they are? They have no logical connection with each other, either in arrangement or in the placing, to begin with. They do not help each other either in line or mass. They are crowded, huddled together. You could do with less of them; or, if you want

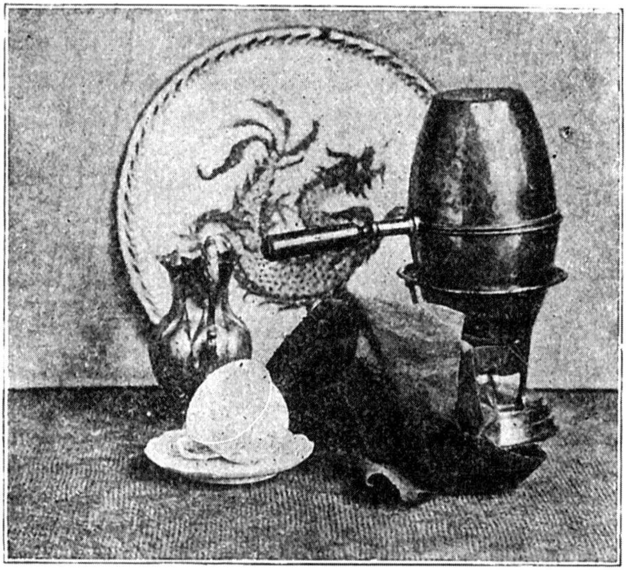

Still Life, No. 2.

them all, you can place them better. But suppose we take some of them away for simplicity, and re-arrange the rest.

Here are some of the things, with others taken away. The combination is simpler, but still it is not satisfactory. There is some logical connection among the objects, but none in the grouping. They are still huddled; there is no line; it is too square; no attempt at balance; they are simply things. If you change them about a little, having

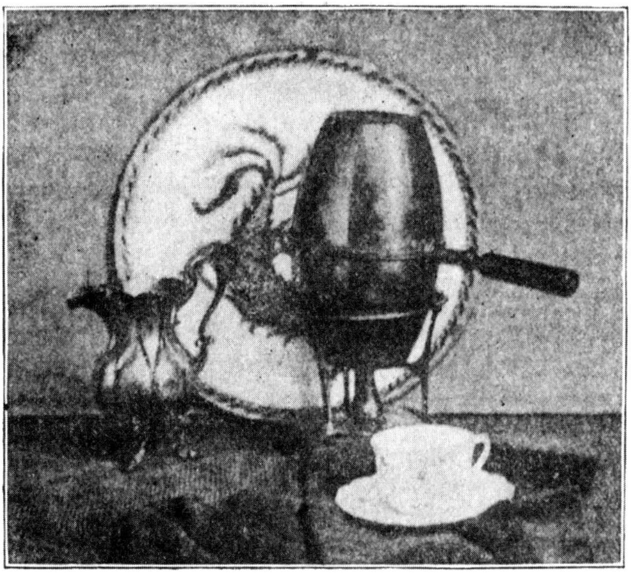

Still Life. No. 3.

regard to size, proportion, balance, and line, you can get something better out of these same objects.

Here the coffee-pot is moved toward the centre, to give height and mass, and to break up the round of the plaque; the handle turned around to give more looseness and freedom; the pitcher is placed where it will break the line of the plaque, yet not too obviously or awkwardly; the handle is placed at a good angle with that of the coffee-pot, and the relation of distance with the coffee-pot in balancing the whole is considered. The drapery is spread out so as to have some probability. It does not help much in line, but it does in mass and in color (in the original). It could be bettered, but it will do for the present. The cup also has a reasonable position, and helps to balance and to give weight to the main mass, which is the coffee-pot. There is not much light and shade in this composition, nor much distinction. But it does balance, and would make a good study, and is a very respectable piece of composition, — simple, modest, and dignified.

Now if you wanted to add some of those things which were eliminated, and make a more complicated composition, you would look for the same things in it when completed. We have simply the same group, with the bottle and glass added. The stout jug in the first group is left out because it is not needed, and it will not mass with the rest easily. The tall glass vase is left out because it is too transparent to count either as line, mass, or color, and does not in any way help, and therefore counts against, because it does not count for, our composition. The things we have here are enough, but they are not right as they are now. They injure rather than help the last arrangement. The bottle and glass are in the composition, but not of

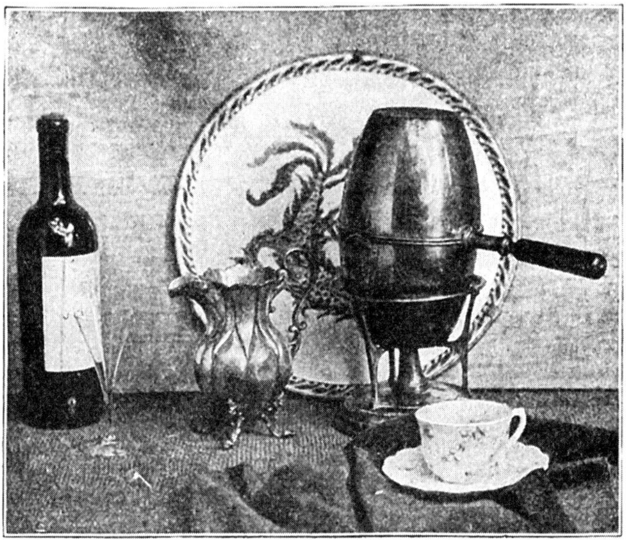

Still Life No. 4.

it; a composition must be *one thing*, no matter how many objects go to the making of it. This is two things. Draw a line down between the bottle and glass and the other things, and you get two compositions, both good, instead of one, which we must have for good arrangement.

Let's change them again. This is worse, if anything. We have now got two groups and a thing. The coffee-pot and cup and saucer alone, the bottle and glass alone, and the pitcher; the drapery tries to pull them together, but can't. The plaque has

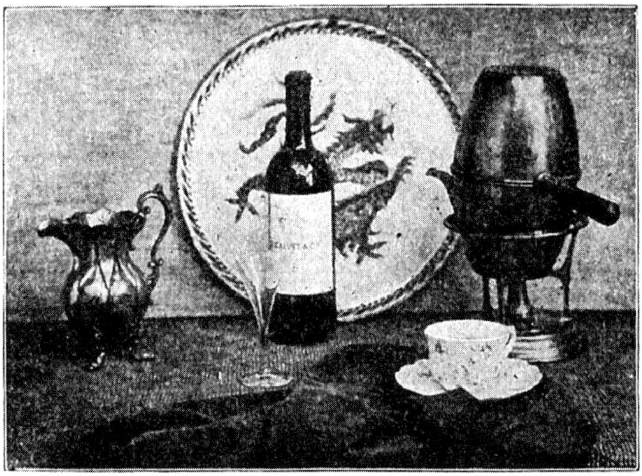

Still Life, No. 5.

no connection with anything. They are all pulled apart. In the last group at least there was some chief mass, the first complete composition. Now every one is for himself; three up and down lines and a circle — that's about what it amounts to.

Let's group them, — push them together. Place the bottle near the coffee-pot. Because they are about the same height, one cannot dominate the other in height; then make them pull together as a mass.

Place the cup about as before, and the mass pretty well towards the centre of the plaque.

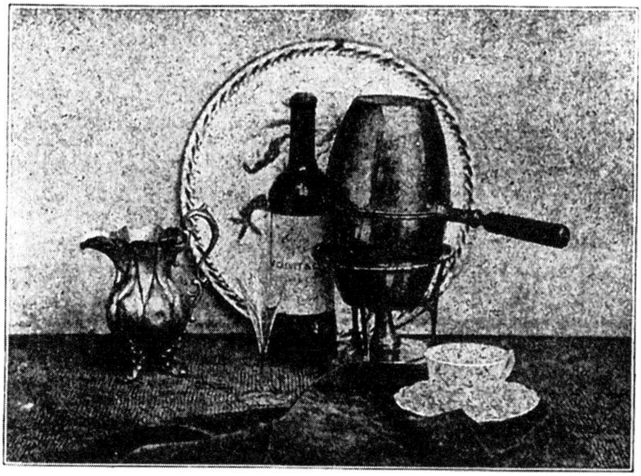

Still Life, No. 6.

Put the pitcher where it will balance, and the glass where it will count unobtrusively, and help break the line of the bottoms of the objects. The drapery now helps in line also, and gives more unity, as well as mass and weight and color, to the whole. This group is about as well placed as these objects will come. There is balance, mass, proportion, dignity, unity.

Of course you may make a paintable and interesting composition with only two things. But you must give them some relation both as to fact and as to position. The same elements of unity and balance and line come in, no matter how many or how few are the objects which enter as elements in your group.

In this way study composition with still life. Move things about and see how they look; use your eye and judgment. Get to see things together, and apply the principles spoken of in the chapter on "Composition" to all sorts of things in nature.

Scope of Study. — Drawing is always drawing, whatever the objects to which it is applied, and you can study all the problems of drawing and values with still life. The drawing is not so severe as that of the antique, nor so difficult as study from the life, but you can learn to draw and then apply it to other things, and advance as far as you please; and as I said at first, you need never lack an amiable model.

All sorts of effects of lighting you can study easily with still life; and of color and texture also. The study of surface and texture is most important to you. If you were to undertake to paint a sheep or a cow the first time; if you were to paint without previous experience a background which contained metal and glass, or a model with a velvet or satin dress, you would not succeed. These all involve problems of skill and facility of representation. When you paint a portrait or figure picture, or a landscape with animals, you should not have to deal with, as new, problems of this sort. You should have arrived at some understanding of this sort of thing in studies which are not complicated by other problems of greater difficulty. This is where still life comes in again to make the study of painting easier.

Interest. — But the use of this sort of painting is not only its practical *use*. You need not feel that it is all drudgery — which is something that most students do not love! You may make pictures with a much clearer conscience along this line; for the better the picture, and the more interesting and charming it is, the more successful is your work as study. You can be as interested in the beauty and the picture of it as you please, and it will only make you work the better. To see the picture in a group of bottles and books is to be the more able to see the picture in a tree and sky. An artist's eye is sensitive to beauty of color and line and form wherever he sees it. The student's should be also. No artist but has found delight in painting still life. No student should think it beneath his serious study.

Procedure. — Study painting first in still-life compositions. When you set up your canvas first, and set your palette, let it be in front of a few simple objects grouped interestingly; or, better, set up a single jar or a book, with a simply arranged background for color contrast. All the problems of manipulation are there for you to study. No processes of handling, no manner of color effect, which you cannot use in this study.

Learn here what you will need in other lines of work.

Beginning. — The best way to make a study from still life is to begin with a careful charcoal drawing on the canvas. You may shade it more or less as you please, but be most careful about proportions and forms. The shading means the modelling and the values in black and white; and you can do this either in charcoal as you draw, or it can be put in with monochrome when you begin with paint. But you must have the drawing sure and true first; for drawing is position, locality. You must know *where* a value is to go before you can justly place it. The value is the *how much*. You must have the *where* before the *how much* can mean anything in drawing. It would be well to lay in some of the planes of light and shade, because you feel proportion more naturally and truly so than with mere outline. The outline encloses the form, but with nothing but outline you are less apt to feel the reality of the form. The planes of values fill in the outline and give substance to it. They map it out so that it takes thickness and proportion; it is more real. And any fault of outline is more quickly seen, because you cannot get your masses of shade of the right form and proportion if the outline enclosing them is not right.

The Frottée. — Make, then, a careful light-and-shade drawing with charcoal directly on the canvas, working in the background where it tells against the group, but without carrying it out to the edges of the canvas.

Be accurate with your modelling and values, and keep the planes simple and well defined. Draw all characteristic details, but only the most important, nearly as if it were not to be painted, but were to remain a drawing.

Fix this drawing with fixative and an atomizer.

In beginning with paint go over the drawing with a thin *frottée* which shall re-enforce the drawing with color. You may do this with one color, making a monochrome painting very thin, leaving the canvas bare for the lights. Many of the best painters lay in all pictures this way. What color is to be used is a matter for consideration. It should be one so sympathetic to the coloring of the whole picture that if it is left without any other paint over it in places it will still look all right. Raw umber is a good color, or raw umber modified with burnt sienna and black. You can make a mixture that seems right. This establishes your larger values, and gives you something better than a bare canvas, and something with which you can have a more just idea of the effect of each touch of color you put on.

If there is much variety of color in the various objects of your composition, it is better to make your *frottée* suggest the different colors. Instead of making a monochrome *frottée*, rub in each object with a thin mixture, approximating the color and value, but not solid, nor as strong as it will become when painted, of course. Nevertheless, you can get in this first rubbing in, a strong effect, which at a distance has a very solid look, though the relations are not so carefully studied. When you come to put on solid color with this sort of an under-painting, it is easy to judge pretty closely of color as well as light-and-shade relations, and you can work more frankly into it.

Into this painting, when it is dry, you may begin to paint with body color, beginning with the true color and value of the lights, and working down through the half darks into the darks. Paint the background pretty carefully as to color and value, but loosely as to handling. Paint slowly, deliberately, and thoughtfully. There is no need to pile up masses of wrong color. You should try to be sure of the color before you lay it on. Study the color in the group, mix on the palette, and compare them. Think at least two minutes for every one minute of actually laying on paint. You save time in the end by being deliberate and by working thoughtfully. Put on color firmly and with a full brush, but there is no need to load color for the sake of the body of it.

Loaded Lights. — It was a principle with the older painters to paint the shadows thinly and with transparent color, and to load the lights. It gave a richness to the shadows and a solidity to the lights which was much valued. But don't think about this; don't let it influence the frankness of your painting. The theory is in itself largely obsolete now, and in fact has been disregarded by almost every able painter who ever lived, in practice, no matter what he said about it. I only speak of it because almost all books on painting have laid it down as a rule, and you had better know its true relation to painting. Like all other traditional methods of painting it has been used by the greatest of painters, and has also been disregarded by the greatest of painters; and as far as you are concerned, you may use it or not as suits your purpose. The main thing is to get the right color and value in the right place, in the most dircct and natural, in the least affected, manner possible.

You may work into your *frottée*, then, more or less solidly as you feel will give you the best representation of the color you see.

Solid Painting. — Don't paint always in the same way. It is a mistake to get too accustomed to one manner of procedure. Different things require different handling. Let the thing suggest how you shall paint it. If you want to paint directly, paint solidly from first to last instead of rubbing in thinly first. But always have an accurate drawing underneath.

In working solidly without previous laying in, begin where each brush-stroke will have the greatest effect toward establishing the appearance of reality. If the canvas is light, begin by putting in the main darks, and if the canvas is dark, do the reverse. You get the most immediate effect of reality by the *relief;* the relief you get most directly by putting in first those values which contrast with what is already there. Establish your most telling values first, then work from them towards less immediately effective things.

Color and Values. — Study the color at the same time you do the value. Put on no touch of paint as a value or a color alone. If you do, you will have to paint that spot twice, — once for the value, and again for the color. You might as well paint for the two qualities in one stroke. It takes more thought, but it gives you more command of your work. It doesn't load your canvas with useless paint, and it saves time in the long run.

Relations and Directness. — Study to give the true relations of things. Try to get the just color quality. Give it at once. Don't get it half way and trust to luck and a subsequent painting to correct it. You will never learn to paint that way. Paint intensely while you paint. Use all the energy you have. Paint with your whole strength for a half or a whole hour, and then rest. You will accomplish more so than by painting all day in a languid, half-hearted way.

Directness. — Directness comes from making up your mind just what tint of color and value is needed, and just where it is to go, first, then putting it there with no coaxing. Get the right color on your brush and plenty of it; then put the brush deliberately and firmly down in the right place, and take it directly away, and look at the result without touching it again till you have made up your mind that it needs something else, and what it is that it needs. Then do that and stop.

Directness and justness of relation are the most important things in painting. They tell for most, result in most, both to the picture and to the student. Whatever you do, work for that. Try to have no vagueness in your mind as to what you will do or why you do it, and the effect of it will show on your canvas.

CHAPTER XXIX

FLOWERS

FLOWER painting is the refinement of still life. You have the same control of combination, but you have not the same control of time. Flowers will change, and change more rapidly than any other models you can have; and at the same time they are so subtle that the most exquisite truth and justness are necessary to paint them well.

People seem to think that any one can paint flowers. On the contrary, almost no one can paint them well. There are not a dozen painters in the world who can really paint flowers as they ought to be painted. Why? Because while they are so exquisite in drawing and color, and so infinitely delicate in value, they are also even more infinitely subtle in substance and sentiment.

When you have got the drawing and the color and the value, you have not got the *quality*.

What is the petal of a flower? It is not paper, and it is not wax, neither is it flesh and blood, of the most exquisite kind. All these are gross as substance compared to the tender firmness of the flower petal; and the whole bunch of flowers is made up of petals.

Yet you cannot paint the *petals* either, else you lose the *flower*. You must paint the *quality* of the petal, and the *character* of the flower.

All these things make the mere perception of facts most difficult, and it must be done with full knowledge that in an hour it will be something else, and you can never get it back to its original form again. Yet you cannot paint a bunch of flowers in an hour. What will you do?

Mass and Value. — There is something besides the flower and the petal; there is the *mass*. The mass is *one thing*, and it is surrounded with air, and air goes through the interstices of it. You must make this visible. The difference in value in flowers is something "infinitely little," as a great flower painter said to me once. Yet the difference is there. The bunch has its nearer and its farther sides, and the way the light falls on it is the most obvious expression of it.

When you begin a group of flowers, get the *whole* first. Make up your mind that you cannot complete your work from the flower you have in front of you, and that you must constantly change your models. Do not paint the little things, the personal things first then. Paint what is common to all the flowers in the group first. Paint the mass and the rotundity of it, and express most vaguely the *forms* of the accents, and of the darks which fall between the flowers, but get their values. For you will have to change these, and you should have nothing there which will influence you to shirk. In this way only can you get the larger things without hampering your future work by what may be wrong.

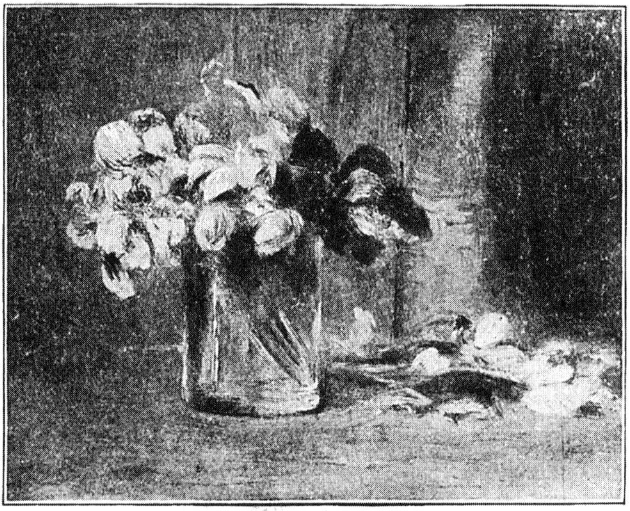

Sweet Peas.

Get the large values, and as little as possible of the expression of the individual flowers; then as the flowers fade and change, substitute one or two fresh ones at a time, in this or that part of the partially wilted group, using the same kind of flower as that which was in that place before;

then work more closely from these new flowers, letting the whole bunch preserve for you the mass and general relation. As you work, the bunch will be gradually changing and constantly renewed from part to part, and you can work slowly from general to particular. Finally, from new flowers, put in those more individual touches which give the personal flowers.

This is the only way you can work a long time, and it is not easy. But it should not discourage you. Nothing takes the place of the flower picture, and the only way to learn to paint flowers is to paint flowers.

General Principles Hold Always. — Still, the principles of all painting hold here as elsewhere, and what is said of painting in general will have its application to flowers.

Paint flowers because you love them; and if you love them, love them enough to study patiently to express the qualities most worth painting, even if there be difficulties.

Details Again. — Don't make too much of unimportant things. The whole is more than the part; the flower than the petal. Of course you can't paint a flower without painting the petals, but you need not paint the petals so that you can't see anything else. If the character of the flower as a whole is to be seen at a glance without the emphasis of any special petal, suggest the petals only. If the petal is important to the expression of character, then paint it; and if you do, paint it well. Use your judgment; make the less expressive of the greater, or do not paint it at all.

Colors. — Colors and tints in flowers are always more rather than less subtle than you think them. If you have a doubt, make it more delicate — give delicacy the benefit of the doubt. Still, flowers are never weak in color. Subtle as they are, it is the very subtlety of strength. Black will be the most useless color of your palette. Make your grays by mixing your richer colors. A gray in a flower is shadow on rich color, and it must not be painted by negation of color, but by refinement of color.

Sketches. — Make sketches of flowers constantly. Try to carry the painting of a single flower or of a group as far as you can in an hour. Practise getting as much of the effect of detail as possible with as little actual painting of it, and then apply this to your picture.

Get to know your work in studies and sketches, and you will work better in more difficult combinations.

When you have, as you generally will have, still-life accessories to your flowers, rub in quickly the color and values of the vase or what not first, but leave the painting of it till the flowers are done. It will be a more patient sitter than they.

Apply the ways of painting spoken of with reference to still life to the sketching of flowers. Either rub in quickly a *frottée* and then paint solidly into that, or work frankly and solidly but deliberately to render the characteristic qualities. When you sketch flowers don't take too many at a time; calculate to work not more than an hour and a half or two hours, and have no more flowers in your sketch than you can complete in that time.

When you sketch, quite as much as when you work at more ambitious canvases, get the mass first, especially if the group is large. Then put in the accents which do most to give the character or type of the flower. Make studies of single flowers and sketches of groups. In the study search detail and modelling; in the sketch search relations and relief, effect and large accent.

CHAPTER XXX

PORTRAITS

DON'T look upon portraits as something any one can do. A portrait is more than a likeness, and the painting of it gives scope for all of the great qualities possible in art. Only a great painter can paint a great portrait. Some great painters rest their fame on work in this field, and others have added by this to the fame derived from other kinds of work.

You must not think it easy to paint a portrait, or rest satisfied with having got a likeness. Likeness is a very commonplace thing, which almost any one can get. If there were no other qualities to be tried for, it would hardly be worth while to paint a portrait. Back of the likeness, which a few superficial lines may give, is the character, which needs not only skill and power to express but great perception to see, and judgment to make use of to the best advantage.

Character. — The first requisite in a good portrait is character, — more than likeness, more than color or grace, before everything else, it needs this; nothing can take the place of it and make a portrait in any real sense of the word. Everything else may be added to this, and the picture be only so much the greater; but this is the fundamental beauty of the portrait. Some of the greatest painters made pictures which were very beautiful, yet the greatest beauty lay in the perception and expression of character. Holbein's wonderful work is the apotheosis of the direct, simple, sincere expression of character in the most frank and unaffected rectitude of drawing. There are masterpieces of Albrecht Dürer which rest on the same qualities, as you can see in the Portrait of Himself by Dürer. Likeness is incidental to character; get that, and the likeness will be there in spite of you.

Hubert Herkomer said once that he did not try for likeness; if only he got the right values in the right places, the likeness had to be there. The same can hardly be said of character, for this depends on the selection from the phases of expression which are constantly passing on the face, those which speak most of the personality of the man; and the emphasis of these to the sacrifice of others. The painting of character is interpretation of individuality through the painting of the features, and, like all interpretation, depends more on insight and selection than on representation. Try for this always. Search for it in the manner, in the pose and occupation, of your sitter. Get likeness if you will, of course; but remember that there is a petty likeness, which may be accident or not, which you can always get by a little care in drawing; and that there is a larger character which includes this, and does not depend on exaggeration of feature or emphasis of accidental lines, but on the large expressiveness of the individual. You may find it elsewhere than in the face. The character affects the whole movement of the man. The set of the head and the great lines of the face, the head and shoulders alone would give it to you even if the features were left out. Study to see this, and to express it first, and then put in as much detail as you see fit, only taking care never to lose the main thing in getting those details.

Qualities. — There are other great qualities also which you can get in a portrait. All the qualities of color and tone, of course. But the simplicity of a single figure does not preclude the qualities of line and mass. The great things to be done with composition may as well be done in portrait as elsewhere. If you would see what may be done with a single figure, study the Portrait of his Mother, by Whistler. You could not have a better example. It is one of the greatest portraits of the world. Notice the character which is shown in every line and plane in the figure. The very pose speaks of the individuality. Notice the grace and repose of line, and the relations of mass to mass and space —

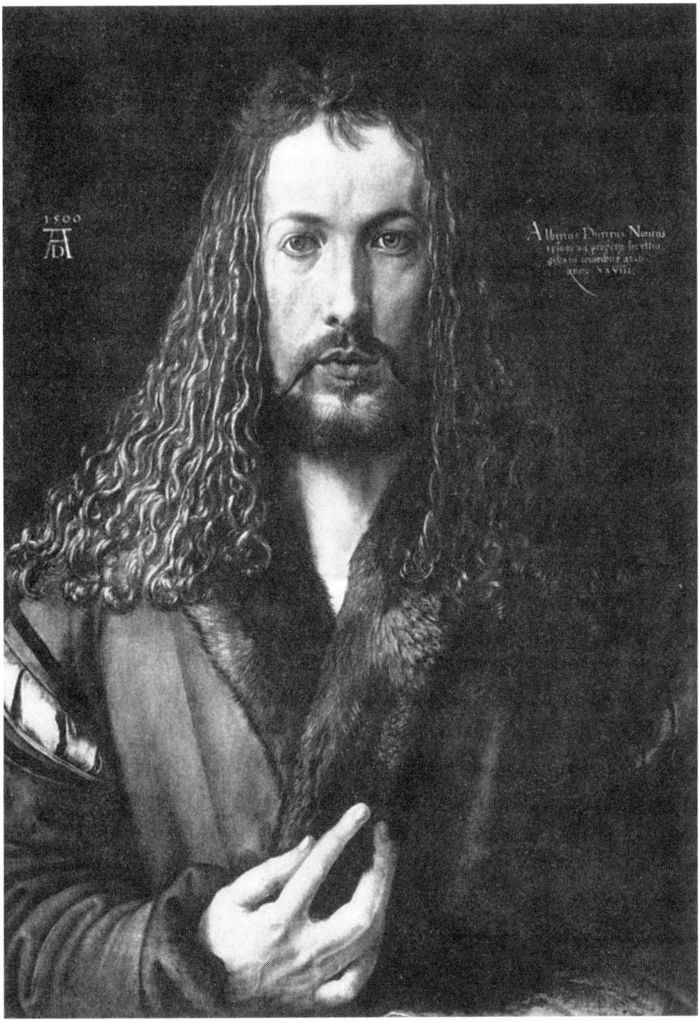

Dürer, *by Himself.*

To be studied as an example of directness and näiveté of painting.

the proportion. See how quiet it is and simple, yet how just and true. Of the color you cannot judge in a black and white, but you can see the relations of tones, the values and the drawing. It

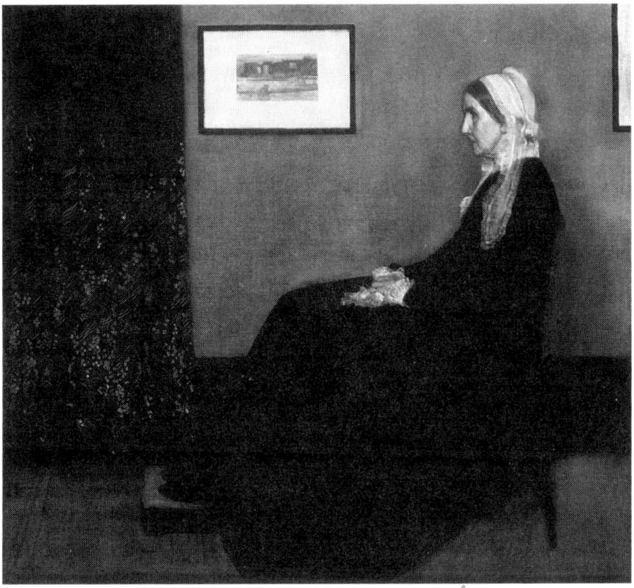

Portrait of his Mother. *Whistler.*

is these things which make a picture; not only a portrait, but a great work of art as well.

Drawing. — Good work in portraiture depends on good drawing, just as other work does. Don't think that because it is only a head you can make it more easily than anything else. As in other kinds of work, the drawing you should try for is the drawing of the proportions and characteristic lines. Get the masses and the more important planes, and don't try for details. You can get these afterwards, or leave them out altogether, and they will not be missed if your work has been well done.

Don't undertake too much in your work. Make up your mind how much you can do well, and don't be too ambitious; the best painters who ever lived have been content to work on a head and shoulders, and have made masterpieces of such paintings. You may be content also. See how little Velasquez could make a picture of! and notice also the placing of the head, and the simplicity of mass, and of light and shade.

Painting. — Of course you can help your color with glazing and scumbling, but work for simplicity first. It is not necessary to use all sorts of processes; you can get fine results and admirable training from portrait studies, and the more directly you do it, the better the training will be.

Study the Portrait of Himself, by Albrecht Dürer. You will find no affectation here; the most simple and direct brush-work only. You will not be able to do this sort of thing, but that is no reason why you should not try for it. It will depend on the brush-stroke. It implies a precision

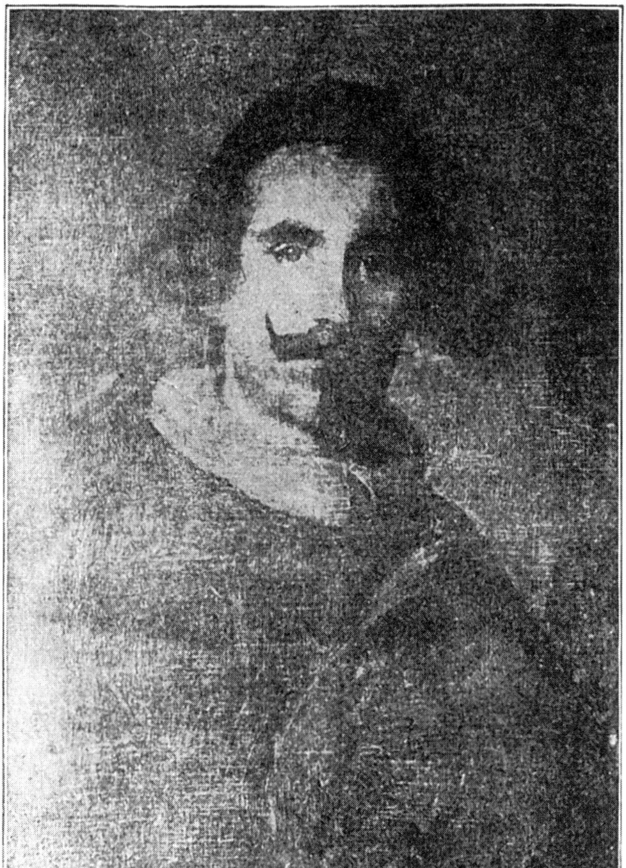

Portrait of Himself. *Velasquez.*

of eye as well as of hand. It means drawing quite as much as painting, — drawing in the painting. You will not get this great precision; nevertheless, try for it, and get as near it as you can. Don't try for too much cleverness; be content with good sincere study, and the most direct expression of planes that you can give.

Let your brush follow lines of structure. Don't lay on paint across a cheek, for instance. Notice the direction of the muscle fibre. It is the line of contraction of the muscle which gives the anatomical structure to a face. If your brush follows those, you will find that it takes the most natural course of direction.

Do the same with the planes of the body and of the clothing. Note the lines of action, and the brush-stroke will naturally follow them.

See that the whole form, and particularly the head, "constructs." The head is round, more or less; it is not flat. The planes of it cross the plane of the canvas, recede from it, cross behind, and return. This in all directions. You must make your painting express this. It is not enough that there be features, the features must be part of a whole which is surrounded, behind as well as in front, by the atmosphere. The hair is not just hair, it is the outer covering of the skull, and of necessity follows the curves of the skull; and there is a back part to the skull which you cannot see, but which you can feel—can know the presence of, because of the way it is connected with the front part by the sides. All this you must make evident in your painting, as well as the facts which are on the side of the skull turned toward you. How make it evident? By values and directness of brush-stroke.

Background. — Never treat the background as something different from the head. The whole thing must go together. The slightest change in the background is equivalent to that much change of the head itself. For the change means necessarily a different contrast, either of color or light and shade, and it will have its effect on the color or relief of the head.

Paint the two together, then. Make the head and all that goes with it or around it as equally parts of the picture, which all tend to affect each other. Your background is not something which can be laid in after the head is finished. True you can paint the background immediately around the head first, and then, after painting the head, extend the background to the edge of the canvas; but the color, tone, and character of the background must be decided upon at the time the head is painted, and carried on in the same feeling.

It is never good work to paint the head and then paint a background behind it. Particularly

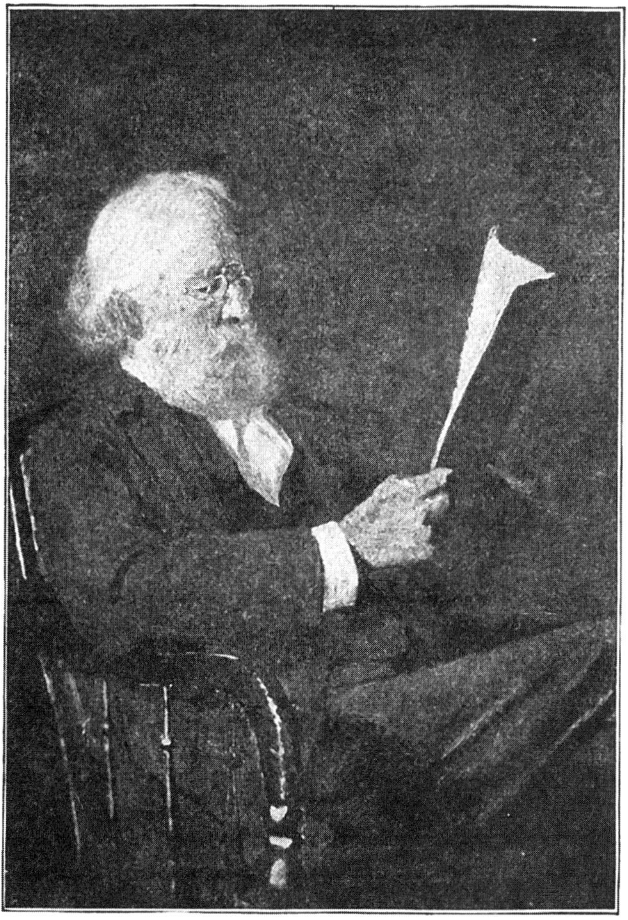

Portrait. *D. Burleigh Parkhurst.*

is this true when there are windows or any objects whatever in the background. It is most important that the whole thing shall be seen in the same kind of light, and in the same relation of light. This is hardly to be done when the head is one painting and the background another.

This is not rigidly true, however, in cases when the whole thing is planned beforehand, and studies made for each part, as in elaborate portraits and compositions which include several figures or special surroundings. But the principle holds good here also. The relation must be kept of the head to the surroundings, and the effect of the one upon the other always kept in mind.

Complex Portraits. — It is often possible to pose your model so as to bring out some characteristic occupation. This is often done in portraits of distinguished men. Such a treatment gives opportunity for composition both of the figure and of the various objects which may make up the background.

In such pictures you should study arrangement of line and mass, to make the thing æsthetically interesting as well as interesting as a portrait. Composition in mass, — the consideration of the head and shoulders in relation to the space of the canvas, — is necessary in the simplest head; but as soon as the canvas takes in a representation of action on the part of the figure, line and movement must be considered, as was done so beautifully in Whistler's portrait. In this the study of composition is your problem. You may study it all the time and in every picture you do, but it should be worked out before you begin to paint.

Plan your canvas carefully always. Know just where everything is coming. When you leave things to chance, you are pretty sure to have trouble later.

Portraits Good Training. — I would not have you undertake to paint a portrait rashly. You should know what you are to expect. If you are not pretty sure of your drawing, and of the first principles of seeing color in nature, and of representing it on canvas, you are likely to get discouraged. Particularly if a friend poses for you, you may expect disappointment on both sides. Drawing a head from the life is a very different thing from drawing an inanimate object which will stay in one position as long as you can pay the rent. So in the painting of it, too, the color itself is alive. Flesh is something very elusive to see the color of. And when you find that just as you begin to get things well under way, or are in a particularly tight place, just at that moment your model must rest, you must stop while the position is changed and gotten back to again; then you will begin to realize that "*la nature ne s'arrête pas.*"

I would have you know all this, I say, before

you begin on your first portrait ; but, nevertheless, if you can get a start at it you will find it extremely good practice. The very difficulties bring more definitely to you the real problems of painting. The fact that it is really the representation of something which has life has an interest quite of its own. The constant change of position on the part of the model will make you more observant, and less regardful of details ; or if you do regard the details, and forget the other things, it will show you how inadequate those details are to real expression, unless there is something larger to place them on.

Don't undertake the painting of a head without considering well that you are likely to have trouble, and that the trouble you will have is most likely to be of a kind that you don't expect. But, having begun, keep your head and your grit, and do the best you can. Remember that you learn by mistakes, and failures are a part of every man's work, and of every painter's experience, and not only of your own.

You will save your self-esteem from considerable bruising if you make it a point never to let your sitter see your work till you are pretty well over the worst of it. The knowledge that it is to be seen will make you work less unconsciously, and you will find yourself trying for likeness, and all that sort of thing, when that is not what you should be thinking about; and if, after all, the thing is a failure, it is a great consolation to know that no one but yourself has seen it!

Beginning a Portrait. — The ways of beginning portraits are innumerable. There is no one right way. Some are right for one painter or subject, and some for others; but there are some methods which are more advisable for the beginner.

You can begin and carry through your painting entirely with body color, or you can begin it with *frottées*, and paint solidly into that. Take these two methods as types, and work in one or the other, according to what are the special qualities you want your work to have.

If you have never painted a head, and have some knowledge of the use of paint and of drawing, I would suggest that you make a few studies of the head and shoulders, life size, in solid color, and on a not too large canvas, say sixteen by twenty inches. This will leave you no extra space, and you can devote your whole attention to the study of the head, with only a few inches of background around it. You will probably make the head too large. A head looks larger than it really is, especially when you are putting it on canvas. If you measure them you will find that few heads will be longer than nine inches from the top of the hair to the bottom of the chin. Take this as the regular size in drawing it on your canvas, and make the other proportions according to that.

Make a drawing of the outlines in straight lines, which shall give only the main proportions of the head, neck, and shoulders. Within this, block out the features largely. Don't draw the eyes, but only the shape of the orbit; nor the nostril, but only the mass of light and shade of the nose.

Construction. — In these studies avoid trying to get anything more than what will be suggested by this simple drawing. Use body color. Don't think of anything but what you have to represent. Never mind how the paint goes on, nor what colors you use, except that it is right in value, and as near the color as you can get. Put it on with the full brush, and try to get first the large masses and planes. Get it light where it is light, and dark where it is dark, and have contrast enough to give some relief. Don't try for any problems. Set your model in a simple, strong light and go ahead.

No details, no eyes, only the great structural masses. Try to feel the skull under these planes of light and dark. Have the edges of them pronounced and firm.

Do a lot of these studies; learn structure first. You will never be able to put an eye in its place in the orbit till you can make the plane of dark which expresses the bony structure of the orbit. You will feel the edge of the brow, of the cheekbone, and where the light falls on the temple and on the side of the nose. Inside of this is the dark of the cavity, broken for your purpose only by the light on the upper lid. Lay these in. Do the same with the other planes, and put your brush down firmly where you want the color, with no consideration but the simplest and most direct expression of value and color.

Now, when you can lay in a head in this way, so that you can express the likeness with nothing but these dozen or so of simple planes, you have got some idea of what are the main things which give character to a head. You will begin to understand how it should "construct." Into this you can put all the detail you want, and if the detail is in value with this beginning it will keep its proper relation to the whole.

Always when painting a head solidly, work this way. Get the action and character of the head as a whole. Block in the planes of the face and the features; and then go ahead to give the details which express the lesser characteristics. But always get the character, even the first look of resemblance, with this blocking in. Details and features will not give you the likeness, to say nothing of the character, if you have not gotten the character first by the representation of those proportions which mean the structure which underlies all the accidental positions of the detail of feature.

The Frottée. — If you want to be more exact with your drawing before you begin to paint, lay in your canvas with a light-and-shade drawing in charcoal. Then make a *frottée* in one color, and paint into and over that, as was described in the Chapter on "Still Life."

By careful and studious use of these two methods of work you can learn the main principles of painting portraits, and modify the handling as you have need; for all the various methods of manipulation are modifications of one or the other, or combinations of both of these fundamentally different ways of working.

If you paint more than one sitting, get as good a drawing as you can the first day. Put in your *frottée* the next, or make your blocking in; then after that do your painting into the *frottée*, or the working out of such details as you decide to put in.

Titian painted solidly, probably with no details; then worked these in and glazed, then touched rich colors into the glaze.

But you had better not bother with all these ways of painting. When you can work well in the simplest way, you will find yourself making all sorts of experiments without any suggestions from me. Work first for facts of utmost importance, and technical methods are not such facts. Perception and representation by any most convenient means are the first things to be thought of, and nothing else is of importance until a certain amount of advance is made along this line.

Learn to see and paint the wholeness of the thing at once, not the details, but the *fact* of it. Try to lay in things so that you have a solid ground to work onto and into later.

Look for the vital things. Don't try for "finish." Finish is not worked for nor painted into a picture; finish *occurs* when you have represented all you have to express. When you have got character and values and true representation of color, you will find that the "finish" is there without your having bothered about it.

The masses you are to look for and emphasize are the great spaces where the light strikes and the shadows fall. Close your eyes. The lines disappear. You only see large planes of values; express these at once and simply.

Don't be afraid of rudeness, either of handling or of color, at first. Don't try for finesse. All these delicacies will come later. But you must get the important things first. Learn to be strong *first*, or you never will be. Delicacy comes after strength, not before.

So, too, freedom comes after knowledge — is the result of knowledge. So paint to learn. If it is rigid at first and hard, never mind. Get the understanding and the representation as well as you can, and try for other things later.

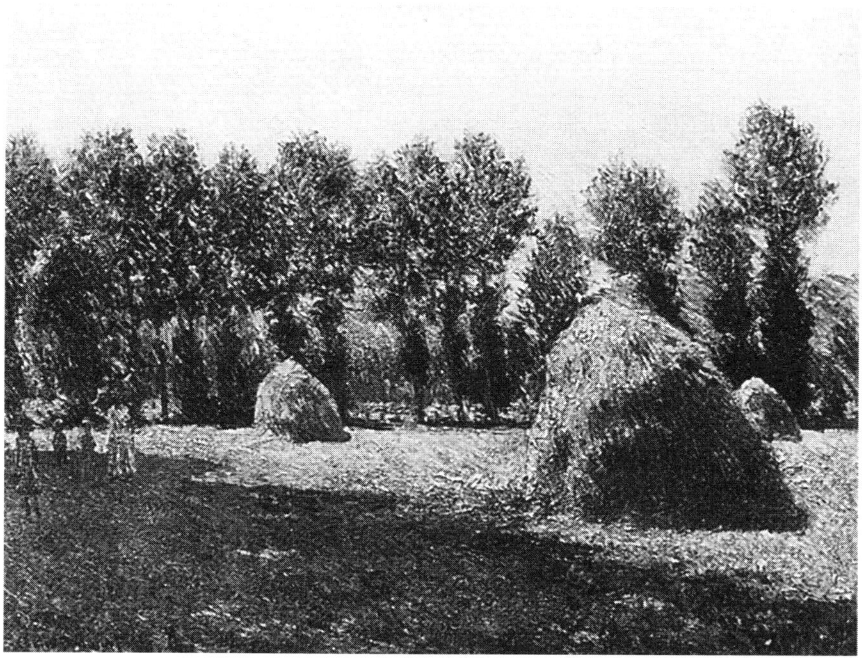

Haystacks in Sunshine. *Monet.*

To show certain characteristics of handling in "Impressionist" work.

A Procedure. — Walter Thor of Munich had a way of painting a head which arrived at a very masterly result, working with single square brush strokes, each discriminated carefully as to value, color and size, somewhat like what used to be called in Paris, *"premier coup"*; and he saved a great deal of time by going about it in a way which he strongly recommended to me. You may find it a good way, as I have. First lay in your head with three or four strokes of a large brush, establishing the hair, the forehead, the light and dark sides of the face, and a swipe across for the eyes. Do it in ten minutes. On this paint, lay your three main lights and your three main darks simply but justly. The background contiguous to the head should be a part of this lay-in. Now paint the eyes as one feature, with their immediate surroundings. Go from these to the nose and paint that; and then the mouth and then the chin. Do these separate features one after the other and almost finish each before going on to the next one, leaving the rest of the face and head as they were first laid in. You will find that in painting them, with what you have to do around them and as they join each other towards their common center, you will have pretty much finished the face and will have only to paint the ears, sides of the head, the hair, and with comparatively few touches you are ready to finish the whole of this part of your picture.

Hands. — Consider hands as at least as important

and difficult as the face. Not only have they much character, but they have so much more flexibility than the head and face that they are more liable to involuntary movement and so much the harder to draw and paint.

The bony structure of the face is permanent, and even the musculature of it changes comparatively little, and the main masses change only all together as the whole position of it changes. But the hand, with its five fingers each with three joints, and connected with the arm by another set of joints, all in constant unconscious motion, is a model whose slightest change may make an entirely different construction.

Many men can paint a head well, but comparatively few can paint a hand equally well. Study the anatomy and consequent action of the hand. Get a jointed skeleton hand if you can, and place it in all sorts of positions and lights. Notice particularly its great planes, where it changes most easily and inevitably, where it changes least; and try to understand the logic of it. I won't ask you to try to paint a wrist well. There are not many who can. Even sculptors who have only form and construction to consider, fail most commonly here and in the ankle. Nevertheless, study it and try to understand it. But know that when you can paint a wrist and hand as they ought to be painted you will have nothing to learn from me!

CHAPTER XXXI

LANDSCAPE

From the usual rating of figures as the most important branch of painting, it would be natural to speak of that kind of work first. But work from the head must come before you attempt the figure, and there are a good many things that you can learn from landscape which will help you in figure-work. The manner of painting figures has been much modified, too, of late years, owing to certain qualities and points of view which are due to the study of landscape and the important position that it has come to occupy.

In the old days landscape was only a secondary thing, not only as a branch of art in itself, but particularly as it was used by figure painters. In this century it has so broadened in its scope that it is now recognized to be as important a field of work as any. But further than this, it has become the most influential study in the whole range of painting. From the development of the study of outdoor nature, and particularly outdoor light, it has come about that certain facts of nature have been recognized which were before neglected, ignored, or unsuspected, and these facts bear quite as much on the painting of the figure as on the painting of landscape. So that it is no more possible to paint the figure, in some respects, as it was painted as a matter of course a hundred years ago, while other ways of painting the figure, which were undreamed of at that time, are the matters of course now.

The whole problem of light has taken a new phase, and the treatment of color in that relation is modified in the painting of figures as well as in the other branches of work.

Pitch. — In no direction is this more marked than in the matter of *pitch*, or *key*. With the study of landscape, the range of gradation from light to dark has broadened. A picture may now be painted in a "high key;" the picture may be, from the highest to the lowest note in it, far lighter than would have been thought possible even thirty years ago.

This question of "bright pictures" is one which demands consideration. One has only to go into any exhibition of pictures to-day to be struck with the fact that the key of almost every picture in it, of whatever kind, has changed from what it would have been in the last generation. This is not merely the result of the spread of the "Impressionist" idea. That influence has only been strongly felt in this country within the last ten years. It is not that which I am speaking of now I mean the fact that even the grayer pictures — those which do not in any ordinary sense of the word belong to Impressionist work — are light in color, where they would once have been dark, or at least darker. The impressionists have had a definite influence, it is true; but the work of the earlier "*plein air*" men — the men who posed their models out-of-doors as a matter of principle, who studied landscape out-of-doors — was the first and most powerful influence, and that of the impressionists, coming along after it, has simply emphasized and carried it farther.

Bright Pictures. — Whatever may be thought of the work of those painters who are called "impressionists," it must be recognized that they have taught us how some things may be possible. And the present quality of brightness will necessarily be to a certain extent a permanent one in art. For like it or not as we may, it is true — true to a certain great, fundamental characteristic of nature. For outdoor light *is bright*, even on a gray day. The luminosity of color is too great to be represented with dark paint or lifeless color. And once this fact is recognized, it is a fact which will inevitably influence all kinds of work. What is possible and right at a certain stage of knowledge or recognition may be impossible when other points of view have once been accepted. We see only what we look for, and we look for only what we expect to see or are interested to see. You cannot go out-of-doors now and paint as you would have painted a hundred years ago. Then you would have painted what you saw then; but you would not have seen nor looked for things which you cannot help seeing now. For our eyes have been opened to new qualities and new facts, and once the eyes have been opened to them they can never be closed to them again.

Average Observation. — I say we see only what we look for, what we expect to find; anything out of the ordinary is hard to believe at first. In looking at nature the average observer does not even see the obvious. Certain general facts he accepts in the general, but as a rule there is no real recognition of what is there; no perception of the relations of things; no analysis; no real *seeing*, only a conventional acceptance of a thing as a *thing*. Men look at nature with one idea, and at a picture of nature with an entirely different idea. Nature in the picture is to most people just what they have been accustomed to see in other pictures. They get their idea of how nature looks from those pictures, and if you show them a picture differently conceived they have difficulty in taking it in.

For this reason the "bright picture" does not "look right." I remember being asked by a man in a modern exhibition what I thought of "these bright pictures." When I asked which pictures he had reference to, I found that he meant the work of a man whose whole aim in painting landscape was, as he once said to me, to get "the just note" in color and value. One would think that the fact that the whole force of an extremely able and sincere mind was directed to that purpose, would produce a picture with at least truth of observation. Yet this was not what my passing acquaintance wanted to see. The picture he liked, which "had some nature in it," as he pointed out to me, was an extremely commonplace landscape with a black tree against a garish sky, reflected in a pool of water. The "bright picture" seemed to me exquisitely gray and quiet, though high in key, and the one with "nature in it," harsh and crude, but conventional; and that was just the point. The average observer wants to see, and does see, in nature what he is accustomed to accept in a picture as nature.

But a painter cannot go on such a basis. He may paint a dark picture, but he must find a subject which is dark to do so. He may not paint daylight with false pitch and false relations, and say he sees it so. With every liberty for personal seeing, there are still certain facts so established and obvious that personality must take them and deal with them, must use them and not ignore them, in its self-expression.

The pitch of daylight is one of these facts. Light and luminosity may not be qualities which appeal to your temperament. You may therefore not make them the main theme of your painting

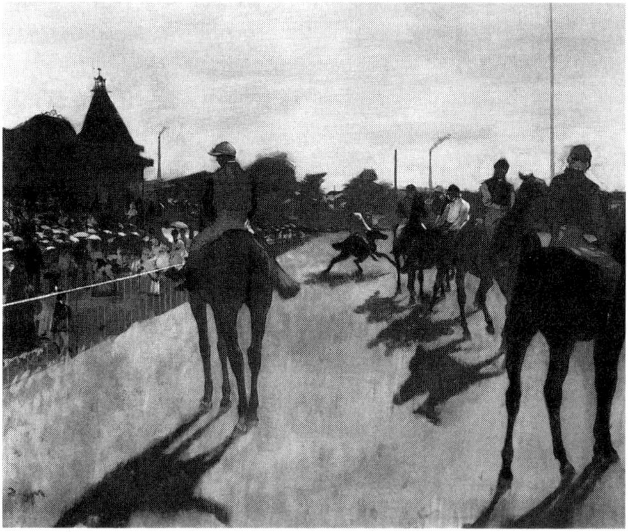

On the Race Track. *Degas.*

To show relations ot pitch and contrast out-doors.

of landscape; but you cannot paint a daylight picture without in some way making it obvious that luminosity is a fundamental characteristic of day light. There is no other quality so universally present and pervasive. In sunlight it is the most vital quality. You might as well paint water without recognizing the fact that water is wet, as to paint daylight without recognizing the fact that diffused sunlight is brilliant.

A Help. — You will find it very useful as a help in seeing pitch as well as color to have a card with a square hole cut in it to look through at your landscape. Have one side covered with black velvet and the other left white. Compare darks with the black, and the lights with the white, and make the picture compose in the opening as in a frame.

Key and Harmony. — But you should remember that the high key for out-of-door work does not mean crude nor unsympathetic color, neither does it mean that there is nothing but sunshine and shadow. Your picture may be as high as you please in pitch, and yet be harmonious and pleasing. I have seen impressionist pictures of most pronounced type hung in the same room with old pictures and in perfect harmony with them. It means that good color is always good color, and will always be harmonious with other good color, whatever the pitch of either. One picture is simply a different note from the other, that is all. The color in nature is not crude in not being dark. The relations of spots of color are just; you have only to be as just in observing them, and your picture will be harmonious.

Make your notes just *all over* your canvas. Have some of them just and the rest false, and of course it will be wrong. Or if you try to make crudity take the place of brilliancy, you will not get harmony. The harmony which comes from the presence in just relation of all the colors is none the less beautiful because more alive. You need not try for the most contrasting and most sparkling qualities of out-of-door color, but you should feel for the out-of-doorness of it.

The space, the breadth, lack of confines, the largeness and movement, vibration and life,—these are the things which the modern painter has discovered in landscape and has emphasized; and this is what has made modern landscape a vital force in modern art. Whatever you do or do not see, feel, and express in your painting, these you must see, feel, and express; for once these qualities are recognized and accepted they are as universal as the law of gravity, and can be as little ignored.

Landscape Drawing.—Landscape is more difficult to draw than is generally thought; not only is the character affected by the *scale* of the main masses, but there is great probability of overdrawing. The curves that mark the modelling of the ground are very difficult to give justly. The altitude and slope of mountains are almost invariably exaggerated. The twists and windings of roadways and fences are seldom carefully drawn; yet the most exquisite movement of line is to be gained by just representation of them. To give the character of a tree, too, without making out too much of the

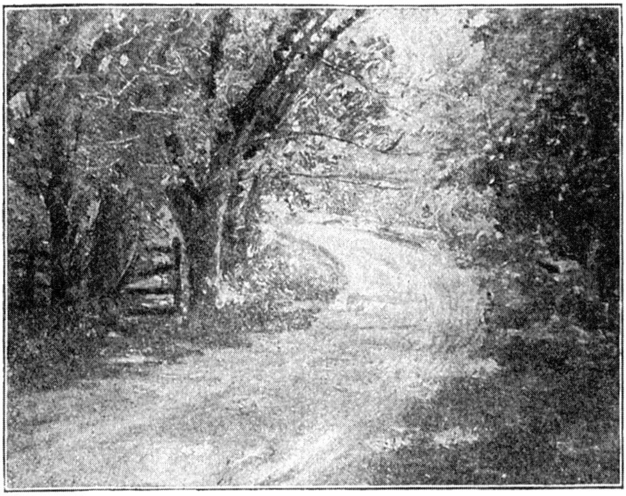

Willow Road. *D. Burleigh Parkhurst.*

detail of it, needs more precise observation than it generally gets.

Get the character; get the sentiment of it. Search for the important things here first, and be more particular about the placing of each line than about the number of lines.

Don't draw too many lines in a landscape;

don't draw too many objects. Carefully study the scene before you till you have decided what parts are most essential in giving the character that you want to express, and then draw most carefully those parts. See which are the *most expressive lines* in it. Get the swing and movement of those lines in the large; then study the more subtle movement of them. Get these things on the canvas first, and put everything else in as subsidiary to them. Have all this well placed before you begin to paint, and allow for little things being painted on to this.

Don't get too many things into one landscape. The spirit of the time and place is what will make the beauty of it, not the details nor the mere facts. This spirit you will find in a few things, not in many. Having found which lines and forms, which masses and relations of color and value, express this, the more carefully you avoid putting in other things the more entirely you emphasize the quality which is the real reason of existence of your picture.

In studying landscape, work for one thing at a time. What has been said of sketching and studies applies here. Landscape is the most bewildering of subjects in its multiplicity of facts and objects and colors and contrasts. If you cannot find a way to simplify it you will neither know where to begin nor where to leave off. I cannot tell you just what to do or not to do, because no two landscapes are alike. Recipes will do nothing in helping you to paint. But there is the general principle which you may follow, and I try to keep it before you even at the risk of over-repetition. In no kind of picture can you drag in unimportant things simply because they exist in nature. In landscape more than elsewhere, because you cannot arrange it, but must select in the actual presence of everything, you must learn to concentrate on the things which mean most, and to refuse to recognize those which will not lend themselves to the central idea.

Selection.—When you select your subject, or "*motif*," as the French call it, select it for something definite. There is always something which makes you think this particular view will make a good picture. State to yourself what it is that you see in it, not in detail, but in the general. Is it the general color effect of the whole, or a contrast? Is it a sense of largeness and space, or a beautiful combination of line in the track of a road, or row of trees, or a river? Perhaps it is the mass and majesty of a mountain or a group of trees. Something definite or definable catches you—else you had better not do it at all; and what that something is you must know quite precisely, or you will not have a well-understood picture.

When you have distinctly in your mind what

you want to paint it for, then see that the composition is so placed on your canvas that that characteristic is the main thing in evidence. With this done it is a very easy thing to concentrate on that characteristic, and to leave out whatever tends to break it up or distract from it. This is the only way you can simplify your subject. First by a distinct conception of *what* you paint it for, then by so much analysis of the whole field of vision as will show you what does and what does not help in the expression of it.

Detail.—Much detail in landscape is never good painting. Whether big or little, your canvas must express something larger and more important than detail. Give detail when it is needed to express character or to avoid slovenliness. Give as much detail *where the emphasis lies* as will insure the completeness of representation—not a touch more.

Structure.—Have your foreground details well understood in drawing and value. This does not require the drawing of leaf and twig, but it does require *structure*. Everything requires structure. *Structure is fundamental to character.* If you will not take the trouble to study the character of any least thing you put in, don't put it in at all. Nothing is important enough to put in, if it is not important enough to have its character and its purpose in the picture understood.

I spoke of structure in speaking of the head.

If I said nothing but "structure, structure, structure" to the end of the section, you would get the impression of what is the most important thing in drawing. If you will look for and find the line and proportion expressing the anatomy which makes the thing fulfil its particular function in the world, you will understand its character, and that is what is important everywhere.

Work in Season. — Make your picture in the season which it represents. I don't say that a good summer picture may not be made in winter; but I do say that you are more likely to express the summer quality while the summer is around you. There is too much half painting of pictures, and then leaving them to be "finished up" afterwards.

Of course you can make all your studies and sketches, and then begin and finish the picture from them. If you are careful to have plenty of material, to accumulate all your facts with the intention of working from those facts, all right; but it would be better if you were to work your picture in the season of it, as long as you are a student at least. For until you have had a great deal of experience, you will find when you come to paint your picture that some very much needed material you have neglected to collect, and you cannot safely supply it from memory. If this occurs in the time of year represented in the picture, you can just go out and study it.

Out-of-door Landscapes.—The most important movement in modern art, the most important in its effects on all kinds of work, is what I have mentioned as the *plein air* movement. It was thought by some clear-headed men that the best way to paint an out-door picture was to take their canvases out-of-doors to paint it. Instead of working from a few color sketches and many pencil studies, they painted the whole picture from first to last in the open air. Working in this way, certain qualities got into the pictures unavoidably. Necessarily the color was fresher and truer. Necessarily there was more breadth and frankness, and less conventionality and mere picture-making. The spirit of the open got onto the canvas, and the whole type of picture was changed. For the first time out-of-door values were studied as things in themselves interesting and important. The result on landscape pictures was that pictures painted in the studio seemed unreal and insincere, and that men looked and studied less for the making of pictures, and more for what nature had to reveal.

It would be a good thing for you as a student if you would do as these men did whenever you want to do any work at landscape, whether for itself or for background. If you wish to pose any kind of figure with landscape background, pose and paint your figure out-of-doors. Make sketches as much as you please, make studies as much as you please; but make them for the suggestions and knowledge they will give you, and not for material to be used in painting a picture at home. For your picture, start, and go on with, and finish it out-doors; you will get a feeling of freshness and truth in your work which you cannot get any other way. You will also acquire a power of concentration and of selection and rejection in the presence of nature which is of the utmost importance to you.

Impressionism. — It is not possible to speak of landscape and *plein air* without mention of the "Impressionists." You should understand what "impressionism" really is, and what it is not, and what the impressionist stands for. Whether we like it or not, this work is not to be ignored. It has tried for certain things, and has shown that they can be much more justly represented than had before been believed to be possible, and fad or no fad, that result stands.

In the first place, impressionism does not mean "purple and yellow." Any one who says "purple and yellow" and throws the whole thing aside, is a very superficial critic. The purple and yellow are incidental to the impressionist, not essential. It is only one of the ways of handling color by means of which it was found possible to express certain qualities of light.

Before everything else the real impressionist

stands for the representation of the personal conception and method as against the traditional. He believes that if a man has anything of his own to say, he must say it in his own way; and that if he cannot find that nature has anything to say to him personally, if nature cannot give him a personal message, if he can only paint by giving another man's ideas and another man's method, then he had better not paint at all; so that whatever he may see to paint, and however he finds a way to express it, the value of it and the truth of it lie in the fact that it is *his*, his way of seeing, and his way of expressing, — that it is "personal."

Luminosity. — The impressionist is imbued with the fact that all the light by means of which things are at all visible is luminous — that it vibrates. He does not think that living light can be represented by dead color. He strives to make his color live also. This is the secret of the purple and yellow. By the contrast of these two colors, by the combination and contrast and juxtaposition of the complementary colors and the use of pure pigments, he can make his colors more vibrant, and so give more of the pitch of real sunlight. He actually applies on his canvas the laws which are known to hold with light and color scientifically. He applies practically in his work those laws which the scientist furnishes him with theoretically. The result in some hands is garish, crude. But the best men have shown that it is possible to use the means so as make a subtle harmony and a luminous brilliancy that have never before been attained. The crudity is the result of the man, not of the method.

The Application. — The application of all this to your own work is that when you want pitch and sunlight you can get it through the observance of the laws of color contrast, and such a laying on of pigment as will bring this about. Try to study the actual contrasts of color, not as they seem, but as they are in nature. Study the facts which have been observed as to colors in their effects on each other, and then try to see these in nature and to paint the results.

The Luminists. — This is the principle of all "loose painting" carried out scientifically. It is the cause of the peculiar technique of those impressionists who paint in streaks and spots of pigment. The manner of putting on paint does interfere with the continuity of outline in the drawing necessarily, but there is a marked gain in the quality of light; and as these men are "luminists," and light is what they want primarily, the sacrifice is justifiable, or at any rate explicable.

Now if you understand the scientific principle, and the practical application and its result on canvas, you have in your hands one of the main instrumentalities in the rendering of one great quality of out-of-doors. How far you adopt it is a matter for you to decide for yourself. If the complete adoption of it implies too much of a sacrifice of other things of equal or greater value to you, then modify it, or take advantage of it as much as will give you the balance of qualities you most want. There is one way to get light and brilliancy and life into your color: adapt it to your purpose if you need it.

This is the application of color juxtaposition to mixing. The placing of complementaries so as to increase contrast is another way of adding to the brilliancy of light. You will find this most useful when you want to give the greatest possible emphasis to the effect of sunlight and shadow. If you keep your shadows cool, your lights will be the richer and more sparkling because of that contrast. If you want more strength in a note of color, get its complement as near it as you can. Look for their iridescence of edges of shadow, and of the contours of objects. You will get greater relief of light and shade by contrast of warm and cool than contrast of light and dark.

Do not misunderstand me. I am not advising you to be an impressionist. I wish only that you shall see what there is in this way of looking at nature and of representation of certain effects of nature, which will be of use to you in the painting of landscape. I would have you know what means are at your command, what is possible to accomplish in certain directions, and how it is possible to accomplish it; then I would have you make use of whatever will most directly and completely serve your purpose.

Do not use any color or colors, any method or point of view, because of any advocacy whatsoever. Know first what you want to paint and why. Let nature speak to you. Go out and look at landscape. Study and observe; see the effect which makes you want to paint it, and then use the means and method which seem most entirely adapted to it. Don't ask yourself, nor let any one else ask you, Is this So-and-So's method? or, Does this belong to this or that school? Don't bother about schools or methods at all. Look frankly to see, accept frankly, and then work to render and convey as frankly as you have seen. Be sincere — sincere with yourself and with your painting: then you will surely work at whatever you do from conviction, and not from fad; and whether it makes you paint as an impressionist or not is a very minor matter, because sincerity of purpose is the most important thing in painting, and method of representation one of the least.

Atmosphere. — A universal characteristic of nature will be a fundamental one in landscape. A landscape which you cannot breathe in is not a perfect one. We live and breathe in atmosphere, and the expression of atmosphere will go far to make your landscape true. But atmosphere is not haziness. Neither is it vagueness nor negativeness of color. Truth of color-quality, and justness of relation will do most in getting it. You had better not try for atmosphere as a thing, but as a result. Anything so universal and so indefinite can be expressed by no one thing. If you try to get it by any one means you will miss it. Study, then, the subtlety of color relation and justness of value. Try to be sensitive to the slightest variety of tone, and be satisfied with no least falsity of rendering, and you will find that your picture will not lack atmosphere.

Color of Contour. — An important thing for you to look for and to study is the color of contours. You will not find it easy; not easy even to know what it is that you are looking for. But consider it as a combination of contiguous values and color vibrations, and things will reveal themselves to you.

No form is composed of unvarying color. No combination of color surrounding it lacks variety. All along the edge of forms and objects, of whatever kind, the value and color relation constantly change. The outline is not constant. Here and there it becomes lost from identity of value and color with what surrounds it, and again defines itself. The edge is not sharp. The color rays vibrate across each other. The inevitable variety of tint and value, of definiteness and vagueness, gives a never-ending play of contrasts and blendings. These are qualities which go to the harmonizing of color, to the expression of light, and particularly to the feeling of atmosphere. This constant variety of contrasting edges is the constant movement and play of the visual rays, and the study of it gives life and vibration to the picture, and all the objects represented in it.

Outdoors, particularly when the play of diffused light and the movement of all the objects is continually felt, either through their own elasticity or because of the heat and light waves, this study is most necessary, if you would get the feeling of freedom, space, and air.

Skies. — In the painting of the sky there are several points to be kept in mind. The sky, even on the quietest day, is full of movement. Cloud masses change continually. If there are no clouds there is constant vibration in the blue; constant variety in the plane of color, — a throb of color sensation which is not to be expressed by a dead, flat tint.

Paint the sky loosely. Lay on the color as you will, with a broad, flat brush, or with a loose, smudgy handling; put it on with horizontal strokes, or with criss-cross touches, but never make it a lifeless tone. Have variety in it; keep a pulsation between the warm and cool color. You can work in the separate touches of half-mixed color, warm and cool, all through the sky, so that the whole tone will be flat and even, but not dense and dead. So far as the sky is concerned, the atmosphere is essential, and is to be represented not by dense color, but by free, loose, vibrating color.

Clouds. — If you have clouds to paint, do not draw them rigidly. Get the effect of the mass and movement, and the lightness of them. As they constantly change in form, any one form they may assume cannot be characteristic. The type form is what you must get, and the suggestion of the motion and lightness. You can suggest, too, the direction of the wind by the way they mass and sway and flow. The direction of the sun's rays, too, counts in the color of them. The outline of a cloud mass is never hard, never rigid. The pitch and luminosity and subtlety are what give you most of the effect of it.

Study the type of cloud, of course. It is a *cumulus*, *cirrus*, *stratus*, or what not. This character is important; but the character lies in the whole body of the cloud form, not in the accidental outlines or the special position of it for the moment.

Sky Composition. — The massing of cloud forms is a very useful factor in the composition of the landscape. The cloud bank or cloud line is capable of giving accent or balance to the picture.

As it is not constant in position any more than in form, you can place it with truth to nature pretty nearly always where it will do the most good as an element in the composition. Make use of them, then, and study the forms and the possible phases of them so as to make the best use of them.

Diffused Light. — Much of the characteristic quality of out-door light is the result of the diffusion of light due to both the refraction and the reflection of the sky. The light which bathes the landscape comes in all directions from the sky. Necessarily, then, the sky will be in most cases far higher in value than anything under it. Even the blue of the sky, which looks darker than some bit of light in the landscape, you will find, if you can manage to get them to tell against each other, will be the more luminous of the two, and will look lighter. There are times when the sun glares on a white building or a piece of white sand, when the white tells light against the blue. But these are exceptions, and if we could get a blue paint which would give the intensity of color, and also the brilliancy of the light, even these cases would be most truly represented with the sky as the higher value. It is a case of whether to sacrifice value to color, or the reverse, as we cannot have both.

Sometimes, however, in a storm, the dense dark

of the storm sky is really lower in value than some white object against it, especially if there be a bit of sun breaking through on it.

But in general, nevertheless, you should consider the sky as always lighter and more luminous than anything under it.

Three Planes. — It will help you in understanding the way the light falls on landscape to consider everything as in one of three planes, and these planes taking greater or less proportions of light according to the position of the sun with reference to them.

The position of the sun changes from a point immediately over, to a point practically at right angles to all objects in nature. Everything that can exist under the sun will come in one of these planes, and at some time in the day in each. The vertical, the horizontal, or some sort of an oblique between these two. If the sun is overhead exactly, the flat ground, the tops of trees and houses, will get the full amount of sunlight. The vertical planes, sides of houses, depths of foliage, etc., will get the least, some of them being lighted only by diffused and reflected light. The planes lying between these two extremes will get more or less, according as they are more or less at right angles to the direct rays of the sun. And as the sun declines from the zenith, the vertical planes get more and more and the horizontal planes less and less of the light, till in the late afternoon the banks of trees and sides of buildings and cloud-masses are gilded with light, and the broad horizontal plains of land and water are in shadow.

However obscured the sun may be, this principle holds more or less; and it makes clear and helps you to observe and notice many facts in landscape light and shade which it is necessary to know.

Millet said that all the beauty of color and value, and the whole art of painting, rested on the comprehension and observance of these facts.

He said that as the planes of any form turned towards or away from the light and so got more or less of it, and as one form stood more or less far back of another and the atmosphere came between, the color and value changed; and in the observance of this, and its representation as applied to any and every object or group of objects, lay the whole of painting. All the possible beauties of the art rested on it. He showed a painting of a single pear in which these things were most subtly observed, and said that that painting was as complete and perfect as any painting he could do simply because in the observance of these relations was implied the observance of everything which was vital to painting.

Short Sittings. — This characteristic, and the steady change of position of the sun and its effects on all the objects which are directly lighted by it, make it necessary, whenever you are painting from nature out-of-doors, that you should not paint at one thing very long at a time. The light changes pretty rapidly; at high noon it only takes a few moments to exactly reverse the light. It is seldom that you can do any just study for more than an hour or an hour and a half at a sitting. Some men do work two or three hours, but they are not studying justly all that time; for that which was light is dark three hours later, and any true study of value and color is impossible under these conditions. Of course on gray days this is less marked, but you must suit your sittings to the time and facts.

It would be better if you had more canvases, and worked a short time on each, and many days on all. You would have the truest work.

Monet works never more than a half-hour on one canvas; but when he starts out he takes a half-dozen or more different canvases, and paints on each till the light has changed. Theodore Robinson seldom worked more than three-quarters of an hour, or at most an hour, on one canvas; but, he worked for twenty or thirty days on each canvas, and sometimes had a single canvas under way for successive seasons.

Any man who would truly study for the just value and note of color must work more or less in this way when he works out-of-doors.

CHAPTER XXXII

MARINES

ALL that has been said on landscape painting applies to marines. You have the same open-air feeling and vibration of light and color. There is no need to say the same things over again. It is only necessary to take all these things for granted, and emphasize certain other things which are peculiar to the sea.

Sea and Sky. — To begin with, the relation of the sky to what is under it is markedly different in color from any other relations in painting. The sea is always more or less of a perfect reflecting surface, and always strongly influenced in color, value, and key by the reflections of the sky on its surface. The sky color is always modifying the water — when and how depends on the condition of the weather, and the degree of quiet or movement of the water. Sometimes the water is a perfect mirror; sometimes the mirror quality is almost lost, but the influence is there.

This relation is the most important thing, because the sea and the sky is always the main part of your picture; and no matter what else is there, or how well painted it may be, if these things are not recognized, if they are not justly observed, your picture is bad.

I cannot tell you all about these things. The variety of effects and relations is infinite. You must study them, paint them in the presence of nature, and use your eyes; only remember the general principles of air and atmosphere and light and color that I have spoken of elsewhere — all have most vital importance on marine painting. You must study these, and think of them, and in the presence of sea or sky observe their bearings, and apply them as well as you can.

Movement. — If "*la nature ne s'arrête pas*" ordinarily, the fact is even more marked in marines; for the water is the very type of ceaseless motion. Somehow, you must not only study in spite of the continual motion, but you must manage to make that motion itself felt. This you will find is in the larger modelling of the whole surface — the "heave" of it as distinguished from the waves themselves. The waves are a part of that motion of course; but give the wave-drawing only, without their relation to the great swing of the whole body of water, and you get rigidity rather than movement. The wave movement is in and because of this larger motion. See that first, and make it most evident, then let the waves themselves cut it up and help to express it.

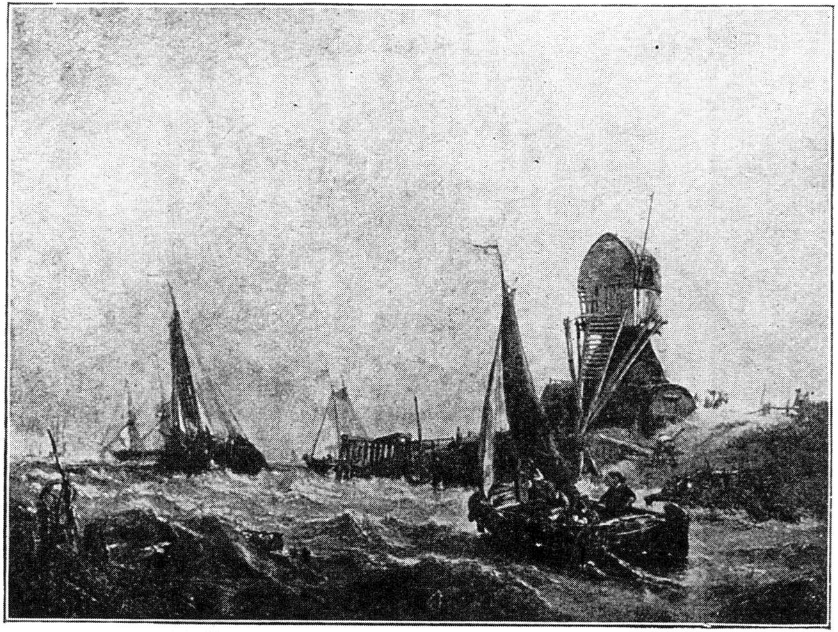

Entrance to Zuyder Zee. *Clarkson Stanfield.*

Wave Drawing. — How shall you "draw" so changeable a thing as a wave? Every wave has a type of form, has a characteristic movement and shape; and as it changes it comes into a new position and shape in logical and practically identical sequence of movement. You can only study this by constant watching. You look at the wave, and then turn your eyes away to fix it on your canvas; as you look back, the wave is not there. Well, you can only not try to make a portrait of each wave; it isn't possible. Don't expect to. Study the movement and type forms; think of it; fix it in your mind; decide on the mass and suggestive relation of it to other masses, and put that down.

There is never a recurrence of the same thing either in exact form or color, but fix your eyes on one place, and over and over again you will see a succession of waves of similar kind. Or look at a wave and follow it as it drives on; changes come and go, but the wave form in the main keeps itself for some time.

Look over a large field of the water without too sharply focussing the eyes, you will see the great lines and planes of modelled surface over and over again taking the same or similar shapes, positions, and relations. And as you look your eye will follow the movement in spite of yourself. Your gaze will gradually come nearer and nearer;

but meanwhile, in following the wave, it will have felt that the wave was the same in shape, but only varied in position.

In this way you will come to know the wave forms. Jot them down, either in color or with charcoal; but do not look for outline too much. Try to study the forms and relations, mainly by the broad touch, with a characteristic direction and movement. No amount of explanation will tell you anything. You must sit and look, think, analyze, and suggest, then generalize as well as you can.

Open Sea and Coast. — The open sea is all movement. Even a ship, the most rigid thing on it, moves with it. But you do not have to study these things from the standpoint of invariable movement. You can start from a stable base. Study coast things first. You have then the relation of the movement of the water to the rock or land, and you can simplify the thing somewhat. What has been said of motion holds good still; but you can get something definite in a rock mass, and study the changes near it, and then extend your study as you feel strong enough.

The study of coast scenery is quite as full of changing beauty as the open sea, and it has certain types that belong to it alone. Breakers and surf, and the contrast of land and sea colors and forms, give great variety of subject and problem.

In the drawing of rocks the study of character is quite as important, but not so evasive, as the study of wave forms. You must try to give the feeling of weight to them. The mass and immovability add to the charm and character of the water about them.

Subject. — Don't undertake too much expanse on one canvas. Of course there are times when expanse is itself the main theme; but aside from that, too much expanse will make too little of other things which you should study. Whether your canvas be big or little, to get expanse everything in the way of detail and form must be relatively small, otherwise there is no room on the canvas for the expanse. So if you would paint some surf, or a rock and breakers, or a ship, place the main thing in proper proportion to the canvas, and let the expanse take care of itself, making the main thing large enough to study it adequately. If it is too small on the canvas, you cannot do this.

Ships. — The painting of the sea necessarily involves more or less the painting of vessels of different kinds. You may put the ship in so insignificant a relation to the picture that a very vague representation of it will do, but you must have a thorough knowledge of all the details of structure and type if you give any prominence to the ship in your picture.

Detail. — You do not need to put in every rope

in a vessel. You do not need to follow out every line in the standing rigging even, in order to paint a ship properly. To do this would miss the spirit of it, and make the thing rigid and lifeless. But ignorance will not take the place of pedantry for all that. Every kind of vessel has its own peculiar structure, its own peculiar proportions, and its own peculiar arrangement of spar and rigging. Whether you are complete or not in the detailing of the masts and rigging, you must know and represent the true character of the craft you are painting. You must take the trouble to know how, why, and when sails are set, and what are the kinds, number, and proportion of them, and their arrangement on any kind of vessel or boat you may paint. There is again only one way to know this. If you are not especially a painter of marines, you may find that the study of some particular vessel in its present condition and relation to surrounding things will serve your turn; but if you go in for the painting of marine pictures generally, you can only get to know vessels by being on and about them at all seasons and places. Your regular marine painter fills dozens and hundreds of sketch-books with pencilled notes of details and positions and accidents and incidents of all sorts and conditions of ships. Ships under full sail and under reefed canvas; ships in a squall and ships in dead calm — he can never have too many of these facts to refer to.

The true marine painter is nine parts a sailor. If he does not take, or has not taken a voyage at sea, at least has passed and does pass a large part of his time among vessels and sailors. He knows them both; his details are facts that he understands. And what he puts in or leaves out of a painting is done with the full knowledge of its relative importance to his picture and to the significance of the ship.

All this sounds like a good deal to undertake; but to the man who loves the water and what sails upon it, it is only following his liking, and any one who does not love all this should content himself with only the most incidental sea painting; for sea pictures are not to be painted from recipes any more than any other thing, and ships particularly cannot be represented without an understanding of them. And after all, you do not have to do all this study at once. If you will only study well each thing that you do, and never paint one vessel or boat without understanding that one; if you will study the one you are doing now, and will do the same every time, — eventually you will have piled up a vast deal of knowledge without having realized how much you were doing.

Color of Water. — You must study the color of water in the large when you paint it. Remember that its color depends on other things than what it is itself. The character of the bottom, whether it be rocky or sandy, and the depth of the water, will affect its color; and to one accustomed to see these things, the picture betrays its truth or falsity at a glance, especially as the character of the wave and the great movement of the whole surface are influenced by the same things.

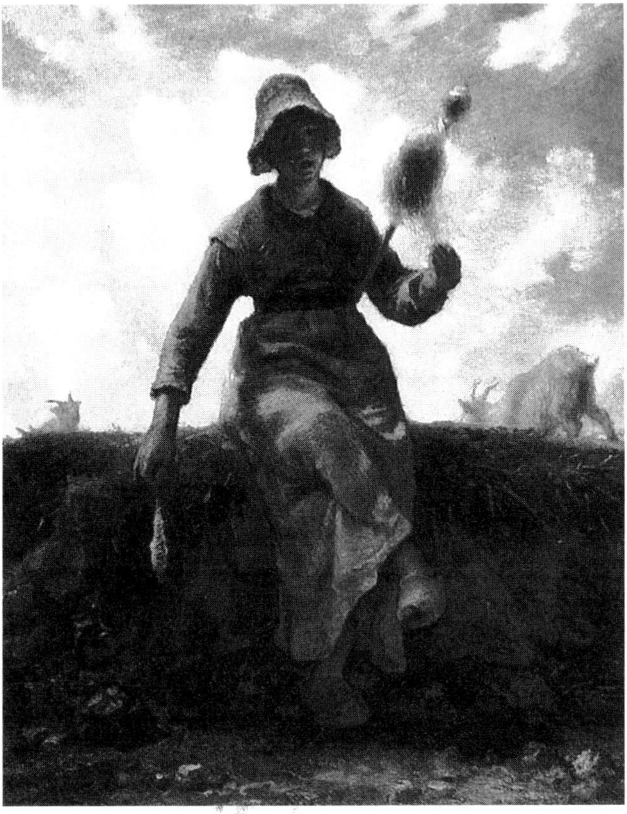

Girl Spinning. *Millet.*

Example of "*contre jour*" and out-of-door contrast of light and shade.

CHAPTER XXXIII

FIGURES

THE broadest classification of figure pictures is to consider them as of two kinds, — those painted in an out-door or diffused light, and those painted in an in-door or concentrated light. The painting of figures out-of-doors you will find more difficult if you have had no experience in painting them in the studio. The problems of light and shade and color are more complex in the diffused light, and the knowledge of structure and modelling, as well as of special values gained by studio study, will be most helpful to you when you paint out-of-doors. I should say, then, don't attempt any serious painting of the human figure in the open air till you have had some experience with its special problems in the house.

The Nude. — No good figure-work has ever been done which was not founded on a knowledge of the nude. Whether the figure is draped or not, the nude is the basis of form. The best painters have always made their studies of pose and action in the nude, and then drawn the draperies over that. This insures the truth of action and structure, which is almost sure to be lost when the drawing of the form is made through drapery or clothing. The underlying structure is as essential here as in portrait. It is the more imperative that the body be felt within the clothes from the fact that it cannot be seen. There must be no ambiguity, no doubt as to the anatomy underneath; for without this there can be no sense of actuality.

I do not say paint the nude. On the contrary, if you want to go so far as that in the study of the figure, you must not attempt to do it with the aid of a book. Go to a good life class. But I wish to emphasize the principle that when you undertake to paint anything involving the figure, you must know something of the structure of what is more or less hidden, and must make allowance for the disguising of form which the draping of it will inevitably cause.

And when you draw your figure, you should lay in your main lines, at any rate, from the nude figure if you can. If you cannot command a professional model for this purpose, you can only be more careful about your study of the underlying lines and forms as they are suggested by the saliencies of the draperies.

If this is the case, be most accurate in those measurements which place the proportions of the parts which show through the covering, and try to trace out by the modelling where the lines would run. By mapping out these proportions, and drawing the lines over the drapery masses wherever you can make them out, you can judge to a certain extent of the truth of action in your drawing.

The use of a lay figure will help you somewhat if you can get one which is true in proportion. It will not help you much in the finer modelling, but it will at least insure your structural lines being in the right place, and that is as much as you can hope for without the special study of the nude.

A lay figure is expensive, costing about three hundred dollars in this country. You will hardly be apt to aspire to a full-sized one, as only professional painters can afford to pay so much for accessories. But small wooden ones are within the means of most people, and will be found useful for the purpose I have mentioned, and one should be obtained.

When you have assured yourself, as far as you can by its use with and without special draperies, of the right action of your drawing, you must do your painting from the draped model.

The Model. —Never paint without nature before you. If you paint the figure, never paint without the model. For the sake of the study of it, it goes without saying that you can learn to paint the figure only by studying from the figure. But beyond that, for the sake of your picture, you can have no hope of doing good work without working from the actual object represented. The greatest masters have never done pictures "out of their heads." The compositions and æsthetic qualities came from their heads it is true, but they never worked these things out on canvas without the aid of nature. And the greater the master, the more humble was he in his dependence on nature for the truth of his facts.

Much more, then, the student needs to keep himself rigidly to the guidance of nature; and this he can only do by the constant use of the model.

One Figure or Many. — Whether you have one or more figures, the problem may be kept the same. The canvas must balance in mass and line and in color. When you decide to make a picture with several figures, study the composition first as if they were not *figures*, but groups of masses and line. Get the whole to balance and compose, then decide your color composition. Simplify rather than make complex. The more you have of number, the more you should consider them as parts of a whole. Keep the idea of grouping; combine the figures, rather than divide them. Have every figure in some logical relation to its group, and then the group in relation to the other parts. Don't string them out or spot them about. Study the spaces between as well as the spaces they occupy. And don't fill up these spaces with background objects. That will not bind the group together, but will separate it. Fill the spaces with air and with values — even more important!

All this arranged, paint each group and each figure as if it were one thing instead of many. As you treat the head, the body, the dress, and the chair as all parts of a whole in a single sitting figure, so treat the various heads, bodies, dresses, etc., in a group as parts of a whole, by studying always the relations of each to each. And then study to keep the different groups as parts of whole canvas in the same way.

Simplicity of Subject. — But do not be too ambitious in your attempts. Keep your subjects simple. Don't be in a hurry to paint many figures. Paint one figure well before you try several.

You will find plenty of scope for your knowledge and skill in single figures. Practise with sketches and compositions, if you will, in grouping several figures, and try to manage them so that the whole shall be simple in mass and effect; but do not attempt, as a student, without experience and skill in the painting of one figure, to paint pictures containing several. By the time you can really paint a single figure well, you can dispense with a manual of painting, and branch out as ambitiously as you please. In the meantime, everything that you have knowledge enough to express well, you can express with the single figure.

With the model, the background, the pose and occupation, the clothing and draperies, and whatever accessories may be natural to the thing as elements, it is possible to work out all the problems of line and mass and color. If a really fine thing cannot be made with one figure, more figures will only make it worse.

Look again at Whistler's portrait of his mother. Consider it now, not as a portrait, but as a single figure. What are the qualities of it which would be helped if there were more in it? The very simplicity of it makes the handling of it more masterly.

Look also at the one simple figure of Millet's "Sower;" all the great qualities of painting that are likely to get themselves onto one canvas you will find in this.

See what movement and dignity there are in it. How statuesque it is! It is monumental. It has scale; it imposes its own standard of measurement. There are air and envelopment and light and breadth. Are these not qualities enough for one canvas?

Nature the Suggester. — Take your suggestions, your ideas, for pictures from nature. Keep your eyes open. Observe all poses which may hint of possible schemes of light and shade, of composition, or of color. It is marvellous how constantly groupings and poses and effects of all kinds occur in every-day life. Humanity is kaleidoscopic in its succession of changes; one after another giving a phase new and different, but equally suggestive of a picture if you will take the hint. The picture which originates in a natural occurrence is always true if it is sincerely and frankly painted. Truth is more various than fiction. It is easier to see than to invent. And in the arrangement of the material which nature freely and constantly furnishes to him there is scope for all the invention of man.

Action and Character. — The picture comes from the action — resides in it. The action comes from the act, and is natural to it, expressive of it. Any gesture or position which is the natural and unaffected result of an essential action will be true and vital, suggestive of nature, and beautiful because it will inevitably have character — be characteristic. The beauty of the picture is not something external to the costumes, occupations, and life which surround you, but is to be found, contained in it, and brought out, manifested, made visible, by the mere logical working out of the need, the custom, or the occasion.

Emphasis is only the salience of the most natural movement.

Daily life swarms with pictures. You do not need to go to other places and other times for subjects. If you are awake to what is going on around you, if you see the essential line of the occupation, or the mass and color which is incidental to every least activity, you will have more suggested to you than you have time to do justice to. And it is your business to see the beautiful in the commonplace. Everything is commonplace till you see the charm in it. The artistic possibility does not lie in the unusual in any subject, but in the fact that the thing cannot get done without action and grouping and color and contrast; and these are the artist's opportunities. Keep your eyes open for them; learn to recognize them when you see them; look for these rather than for the details of the accidental fact which brings them out. See the movement of it, and the relation of it to what surrounds it, and you will hardly avoid seeing the picture in it.

Here is a composition which is an almost literal rendering of the movement and light and shade effect of a position quite accidentally seen.

The whole effect of lighting and of line, the grouping and the pose, resulted purely from the musician's desire to get a good light on his music. There was no need to add to it. It was simply necessary to recognize the charm of it, and to represent that charm through it as frankly as it could be done.

Posing the Model. — Let the character of the model suggest the pose. If you have a scheme for a pic-

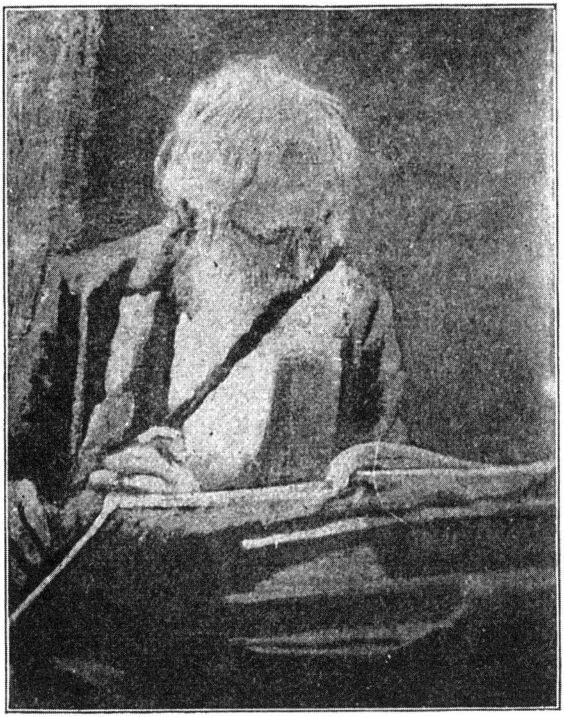

Sketch of a Flute Player. *D. Burleigh Parkhurst.*

ture, choose a model whose personality will lend itself naturally to the occupation or action natural to that scheme. Then follow the suggestion which you find in the model. Some rearrangement will always be necessary if you do not use as a model the same person who originally gave you the idea for the picture. Every human being has a different manner. You cannot hope for exactly the same expression in one person that you found in another. But put the model as nearly as you can in the same situation and pose, and then when the model eases from the unnatural muscular balance into the one natural to him, you will find the idea taken from your first observation translated into the characteristics of your present model.

Never try to place a model in a pose which he can only hold by an unnatural strain. You will not get a satisfactory result from it. Study your model; see what poses he most naturally falls into, and then take advantage of one of these, and arrange your picture with reference to it.

Never attempt to represent a character in your picture by using a model of a different class or type from it; you will not be successful either in painting a lady from a model who is a peasant, nor in painting a peasant from a model who is a lady. The life and occupation and thought common to your model will get into your painting of her; and if that is not in accordance to the idea in the picture, your picture will be false. The dress, no less than the pose and occupation, must be such as is natural to your model. The accessories of your picture must befit the character you wish to paint; otherwise your model becomes no more than a lay figure.

Take note of the characteristics which are peculiar to your model, and use them; do not change them nor idealize them. Rather paint them as they are, and make them a vital part of your study of the subject. This is the best you can do with these characteristics. They may be the most expressive thing in your picture. If they are of such a nature that you cannot use them in this way, then do not use this model at all; you cannot get rid of these things. In trying to obscure or idealize them, you only lose character, or paint a character into your model which is unnatural to him; the result will not be satisfactory.

Quiet Sitters. — An inexperienced painter should not use a model with too much vivacity of body or of expression. The quiet, reposeful, thoughtful model, who will change little in position or manner, will simplify the problem. A model too wide awake or too sleepy will either of them give you trouble.

Avoid very young children as models, and particularly babies. They are never quiet, and the problems you will have even with the best of models will be made enormously more difficult by their restlessness.

For your first work choose models with well-marked faces, and pose them in a direct light which will give you the simplest and strongest effect of light and shade.

See that your sitter is in as comfortable a position as you can get him into, so that the pose can be held easily. Don't attempt difficult and unusual attitudes. Such things require much skill and knowledge to take advantage of, and to use successfully. Make your effect more in the study of composition and color than in fanciful poses. Later, when you have gained experience, you may do this sort of thing.

If you are painting a face, see that the eyes are in at a restful angle with the head, and that they are not facing a too strong light, nor are obliged to look at a blank space. Give them room to have a restful focus, and perhaps something pleasant or interesting to look at.

Length of Pose. — No sitter can hold a pose in perfect motionlessness. Do not expect it. You must learn to make allowance for certain slight changes which are always occurring. You must give your model plenty of rest, too, especially if he be not a professional model. A half-hour pose to ten minutes' rest is as much as a regular model expects to do as a rule. If you have a friend posing for you, particularly if it be a woman, twenty minutes' pose and ten minutes' rest, for a couple of hours, is all you should expect; and if the pose is a standing one, this will probably be more than she can hold — make the rests longer.

An inexperienced model — and sometimes even a trained one — is likely to faint while posing, particularly if the room be close. Look out for this; watch your sitter, and see that she is not looking tired. The minute that you see the least sign of fatigue, if she shows pallor — rest. Do not get so absorbed in your canvas that you do not notice your model's condition. If you are observing and studying your model as closely as you should, you can hardly fail to notice any change that may occur, and you should at once give her relief.

Distance. — Don't work too near your model, nor too near your canvas. As regards the first, be far enough away to see the whole of the figure you are painting, or of that part which you are doing, entirely at one focus of the eye, and yet near enough to see the detail clearly. If you are too near, you see parts at a time, and do not see it as a whole. If you are too far, you see too generally for good study. You might make it a rule to be away from your subject a distance of about three or four times the extreme measurement of it. If it is a full length, say fifteen to twenty feet, if you can get so large a room. If it is a head and shoulders, about six or eight feet. Never get closer than six feet.

As to your canvas, work at arm's length. Don't bend over — again you see parts, and you must treat your canvas as a whole. Never rest your hand or arm on the canvas. Train your arm to be steady. Sit up straight, hold your brush well out at the end of the handle, and your arm extended; now and then, if you need closer work, lean forward, and if necessary use a rest-stick; but as a rule your work will be stronger and hang together better if you work as I have suggested. Of course you will often get up, and walk away from your work. Set your easel alongside the model, and go away to a distance, and compare them. Too intense application to the canvas forgets that relations, effect, and wholeness of impression are of the greatest importance, and are only to be judged of when seen at some distance.

Background. — Under the general title of background you may place everything which will come in as accessory to the figure, and against or alongside of which it stands. The picture must "hang together;" must have envelopment; must be a whole, not an aggregation of parts. Everything that goes to the making up of this whole must have a natural and logical connection with it. From the first conception of the picture you must consider the background as an essential part of it, and as something which will have a vital effect upon the figure. The color of the background must be thought of as a part of, because affecting, the figure itself. The simplicity or variety in the background, the number of objects in it, must be considered as to the effect on the figure also. You cannot make the background a patchwork of objects and colors without interfering with the effect of the main thing in the picture.

If your figure is simple and quiet, keep the background the same. Make it a principle to treat the background simply always. If the character of the case demands some detail, and a variety of objects, then treat them so that their effect is as simple as possible; and the figure must be made stronger, in order that the variety in the background shall not overpower it. Control it by the way the light or the color masses, or simplify the painting of them. Keep the background in value as regards prominence and relief of objects as well as in the matter of color.

Composition of Backgrounds. — You can make the background help the figure, not merely by the painting of objects which help to explain, — that is of course, — but in the placing and arranging of them you may emphasize the composition. Whether the background be a curtain with its folds, or an interior with its furniture, you can and must make every object, every fold of the drapery, every mass of wall or object, distinctly help out in the composition as line and mass. Your composition must balance; the line and movement of the figure must have its true relation. The way you use whatever goes into the picture, the objects which make up the background, the way they group, and the spaces between them, must have a helpful reference to that movement, and to the balance of the whole.

Simplicity. — Lean always towards simplicity in composition as against complexity. In backgrounds particularly, avoid detail and over-variety. Don't have the whole surface of the canvas spotted with *things*. If it is necessary, put it in; if it is not necessary, leave it out; and if there is the slightest doubt which it is, leave it out.

The most common and the most fatal mistake is to make the picture too "interesting." The interest in a picture does not lie in the quantity of things expressed, but in the character of them, and in the quality of their representation. If you cannot treat a simple composition well, if you cannot make a picture balance well, and make it interesting with a quiet background, be sure a multitude of objects will not help it. The more you put into it the worse it will be. Learn to be master of the less before you try to be master of the more.

Lighting. — I have spoken of lighting in general in other chapters. You must apply the principles to your use of figures. Study the different effects

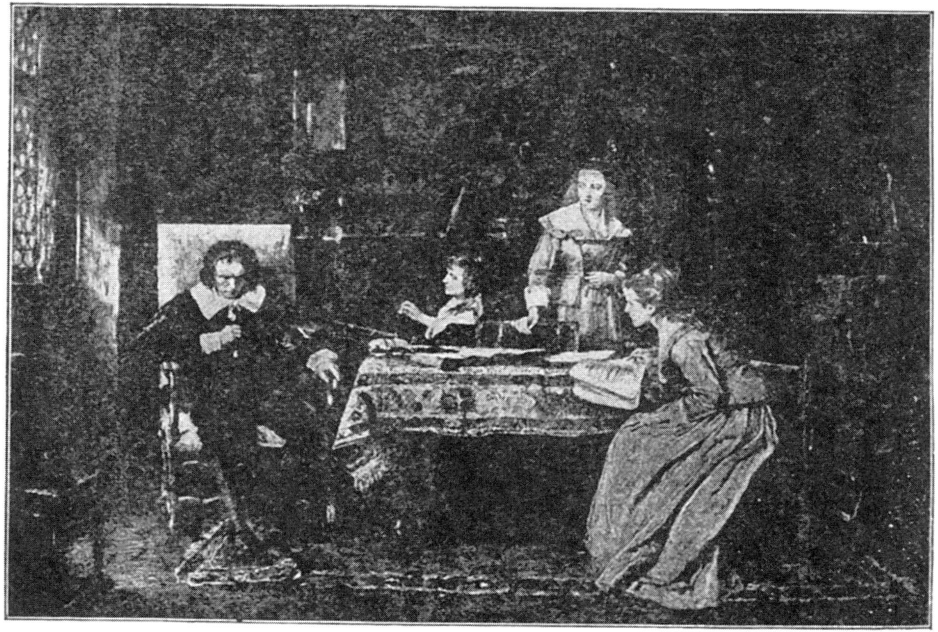

Milton Dictating "Paradise Lost." *Munkacsy.*

To show use of background. Notice also the composition.

which you can get on the model by the different ways of placing in reference to the window. Whatever lighting will be difficult in one kind of painting will be no less so in another. Avoid cross-lights, and do not be ambitious to try unusual and exceptional effects. If one should occur to you as charming, of course do it, if it is not too difficult, but don't go around hunting for the strange and weird. There is beauty enough for all occasions in such effects as are constantly coming under your observation. What was said about simplicity of subject will apply here as well, for the light and color effect is naturally a part of the subject. The most practical lights are those which fall from one side, so as to give simple masses of light and dark; they should come from above the level of the head, so as to throw the shadow somewhat downwards.

"Contre Jour." — One kind of posing with reference to lighting, gives very beautiful effect, but calls for close study of values, and is very difficult. It is called in French, *contre jour;* that is, literally, "against the day," or, against the light. It is a placing of the model so that the light comes from behind, and the figure is dark against the light. From its difficulty it should not be taken as a study by a beginner, for modelling and color are difficult enough at best. When they are to be gotten in the low key that the light behind necessitates, and with the close values which this implies, the difficulty is enormously increased. But before you attempt the human figure in the open air, you will find it very good study to work in the house *contre jour.* The effect of a figure out-doors has many of the qualities of *contre jour.* The diffusion of light and the many reflections make the problem more complex; but the contrast, the close values, and the subtle modelling which you must study in *contre jour* will be good previous training before going out-doors with a model.

Look at Millet's "Shepherdess Spinning," at the head of this chapter, as an example of *contre jour.*

Figures Out-of-doors. — In painting, an object is always a part of its environment. So a figure must partake of the characteristics of its surroundings. Out-of-doors it is part of the landscape, characterized by the qualities which are peculiar to landscape. The diffusion of light, the vibration and the movement of it, the brilliancy and pitch, the cross-reflections and the envelopment, — all these give to the figure a quality quite different from that which it has in the house. There is no such definiteness either of drawing, or of light and shade, or of color. The problem is a different one. You must treat your figure no more as something which you can control the effect of, but as something which, place it in what position, in what surroundings, you will, it will still be affected by conditions over which you have no control.

Textures and surface qualities, local or personal colors, lose their significance to the figure out-of-doors. They become lost in other things. The pose, the action, the mass, the note of color or value, — these are what are of importance. The more you search for the qualities which would be a matter of course in the house, the more you will lose the essential quality, — the quality of the fact of out-doors.

When in the house, you can have things as definite as you wish; out-doors you will find a continual play of varying color and light. The shadows do not fall where you expect them to. The values are less marked. The stillness of the pose is interfered with by the constant movement of nature. The color is influenced by the diffused color of the atmosphere and the reflected color of the grass, the trees, and the sky. The light does not fall *on* the face so much as it falls *around* it. The modelling is less, the planes are not precise. The expression is as much due to the influence of what is around it as to the face itself.

All this means that you must study and paint the figure from a new point of view. You do not make so much of what the model is as how the model looks in these surroundings. You must not look for so much decision, and you must study values closely. Look more for the modelling of the mass than for the modelling of surface. Look more for the vibration of light and air on the flesh and drapery colors than for these colors in themselves. Look for color of contours in the model.

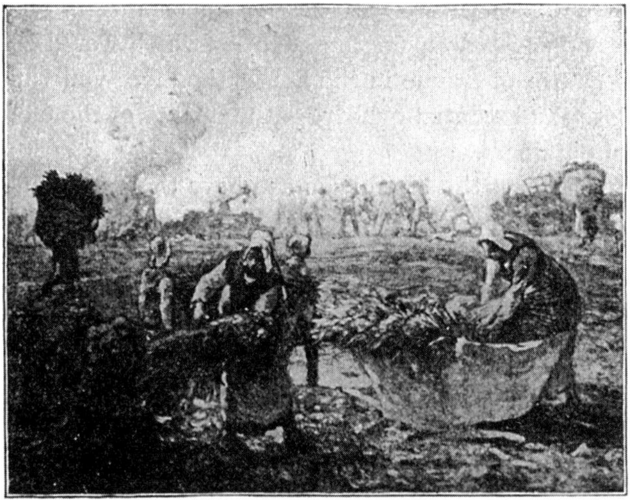

Buckwheat Harvest. *Millet.*

Study the subtleties of values of contours, and make your figure relieve by the contrast of value in mass rather than by the modelling within the outline. See how the figure "tells" as a whole against what is behind it first, and keep all within that first relation.

It is possible to look for and to find many of the qualities which distinguish the figure in the studio light; sometimes you may want to do so. The telling of a story, the literary side of the picture, if you want that side, sometimes needs help that way. But in this you lose larger characteristics, and the picture as a whole will not have the spirit of open air in it.

What has been said of the painting of landscape applies to the painting of figures in landscapes. Pose your figure out-of-doors if you would represent it out-of-doors. Then paint it as if it were any other out-door object. If the figure is more important to the composition than anything else in the landscape, as it often will be, then study that mainly, and treat the rest as background, but as background which has an influence which must be constantly recognized.

Never finish a figure begun out-doors by painting afterwards from a model posed in the house. Leave the figure as you bring it in. If it is not finished, at least it will be in keeping with itself; and this will surely be lost if you try to work it from a model in different conditions.

Animals. — Animals should be considered as "figures out-of-doors." There is no essential difference in the handling one sort of a figure or another. The anatomy is different, and the light falls on different textures, but the principle is not changed. You must consider them as forms influenced by diffused light and diffused color, and paint them so. You will find that often, especially in full sunlight, the color peculiar to the thing itself is not to be seen at all. The character of the light which falls on it gives the note, and controls. In the shade the effect is less marked, but the constant flicker makes the same sort of variation, though not to the same extent.

There is no secret of painting animals either in the house or out-of-doors which is not the same as the secret of painting the human figure. If you would paint an animal, get one for a model and study it. Work in some sort of a house-light first, in a barn or shed, or, if it be a small animal, in your studio. Study as you would any other thing, from a chair to a man. The principles of drawing do not change with the character of anatomy. The animal may be less amiable a poser, but you must make allowance for that.

When you have got a knowledge of the form, and the character of color and surface, take the animal out-doors, get some one to help hold him, and apply the same principles that would govern your study of a rock or a tree in the open air.

As for fur, and all that sort of thing, treat it as you would any other texture-problem in still life.

CHAPTER XXXIV

PROCEDURE IN A PICTURE

SOME pictures, particularly those begun and finished in the open air, may be frankly commenced immediately on the canvas from nature as she is before the painter, and without any special processes or methods of procedure carried on to completion. But many pictures are of a sort which renders this manner of work unwise or impossible. There may be too many figures involved. The composition, the drawing, or other arrangement may be too complicated for it, and then the painter has to have some methodical and systematic way of bringing his picture into existence. He must take preliminary measures to ensure his work coming out as he intends, and must proceed in an orderly and regular manner in accordance with the planning of the work. It is in this sort of thing that he finds sketches and studies essential to the painting of the picture as distinguished from their more common use as training for him, or accumulation of general facts.

Preliminaries. — There must be made numbers of sketches, first of the slightest and merely suggestive, and then of a more complete, kind, to develop the general idea of composition from the first and perhaps crude conception of the picture. All the great painters have left examples of work in these various stages. It is a part of the training of every student in art schools to make these composition sketches, and to develop them more or less fully in larger work. In the French schools there are monthly *concours*, when men compete for prizes with work, and their success is influenced by a previous *concour* of these composition sketches.

This preliminary sketch in its completed stage gives the number and position and movement of the figures and accessories, with the arrangement of light and shade and color. There is no attempt to give anything more than the most general kind of drawing, such details as the features, fingers, etc., being neglected. The light and shade on the single figures also is not expressed, but the light and shade effect of the whole picture is carefully shown, and the same with the color-scheme. It is this first sketch that establishes the character of the future picture in everything but the details. Sometimes this work is done on a quite large canvas, but usually is not more than a foot or two long, and of corresponding width.

Studies. — After this there must be studies made for the drawing of the single figures, and for more

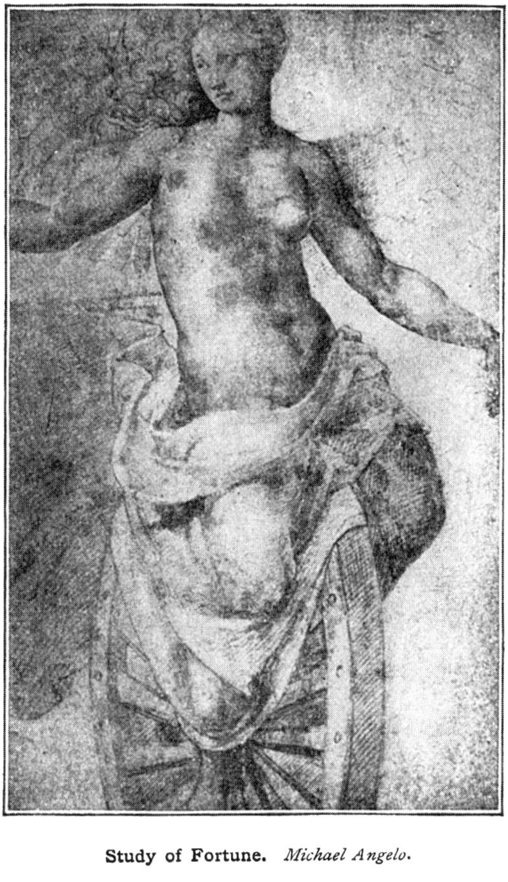

Study of Fortune. *Michael Angelo.*

exactness of line and action in the bringing of all together into the whole. This work is usually done in charcoal, from the life, and sometimes on a piece of drawing-paper stretched over the same canvas that the picture will be painted on, or otherwise arranged, but of the same size. Often, however, this work, too, is done on a smaller scale than that of the picture, especially when the picture is to be very large. This is based on the preliminary sketch as composition, and is intended to carry that idea out more in full, and perfect the drawing of the different figures, and to harmonize the composition. The composition and relation of figures both as to size and position on the final canvas depend on this study.

Corrections. — In making these studies and in transferring them to the canvas, corrections are of course often necessary. The correction may or may not be satisfactory. To avoid too great confusion from the number of corrections in the same place, they are not made always directly on the study or canvas, but on a curtain of tissue paper dropped over it. The figure may be completely drawn, and is to be modified in whole or in part. The tissue paper receives the new drawing, and the old drawing shows through it, and the effect of the correction can be compared with that of the first idea. The study itself need not then be changed until the alteration which is satisfactory is found, as the process may be repeated as many times as necessary on the tissue paper, and the alterations finally embodied in the completed study.

Figure Studies. — The studies for the various single figures are now made in the nude from the model, generally a quarter or half life size — a careful, accurate light and shade drawing of every figure in the picture, the model being posed in the position determined on in the study just spoken of. Sometimes further single studies are made with the same models draped, and generally special studies of drapery are made as well; these studies are afterwards used to place the figures in position on the canvas before the painting begins.

Transferring. — The composition study must now be transferred to the canvas, to give the general arrangement and relative position, size, and action of the figures, etc. If the drawing is the same size as the canvas it is done by tracing, if not, then it is "squared up." In this stage of the process mechanical exactness of proportion is the thing required, as well as the saving of time; all things having been planned beforehand, and freedom of execution coming in later. This establishes the proportions, the sizes, and positions of the several figures on the final canvas. The drawing is not at this stage complete. The more general relations only are the purpose of this.

Onto this preparation the studies drawn from

the nude model are "squared up," and the drawing corrected again from the nude model. This drawing is now covered with its drapery, which is drawn from the life in charcoal, or a *frottée* of some sort. At this stage the canvas should represent, in monochrome, very justly, what the finished picture will be in composition, drawing, and light and shade. If the *frottée* of various colors (as suggested in the chapter on "Still Life") has been used, the general color scheme will show also. This completes the preliminary process of the picture, and when the painting is begun with a *frottée*, this stage includes also the *first painting*.

"The Ébouch." — An *ébouch* is a painting which, mainly with body color, blocks in broadly and simply the main masses of a composition. Sometimes an *ébouch* is used as one of the preliminary color studies for a picture, especially if there is some problem of drapery massing to be determined, or other motive purely of color and mass. Or if there is some piece of landscape detail such as a building or what not to come in, *ébouches* for it will be made to be used in completing the picture. But more commonly the *ébouch* is the first blocking-in painting of the picture, by means of which the greater masses of color and value are laid onto the canvas, somewhat rudely, but strongly, so as to give a strong, firm impression of the picture, and a solid under-painting on which future work may be done. Whether this *ébouch* is rough or smooth, just how much of it will be body or solid color and how much transparent, just what degree of finish this painting will have, — these depend on the man who does it. No two men work precisely the same way.

Some men make what is practically a large and very complete sketch. Some paint quite smoothly or frankly, with more or less of an effect of being finished as they go, working from one side of the picture gradually across the whole canvas. Others work a bit here and a bit there, and fill in between as they feel inclined. Another way is to patch in little spots of rather pure color, so that the *ébouch* looks like a sort of mosaic of paint.

In the matter of color, too, there is great difference of method. Some men lay in the picture with stronger color than they intend the finished picture to have, and gray it and bring it together with after-painting. Others go to the other extreme, and paint grayer and lighter, depending on glazings and full touches of color later on to richen and deepen the color. All the way between these two are modifications of method. The main difference between these extremes is that when stronger color is used in the first painting, the process is to paint with solid color all through; while if glazings are to be much used, the *ébouch* must be lighter and quieter in color, to allow for

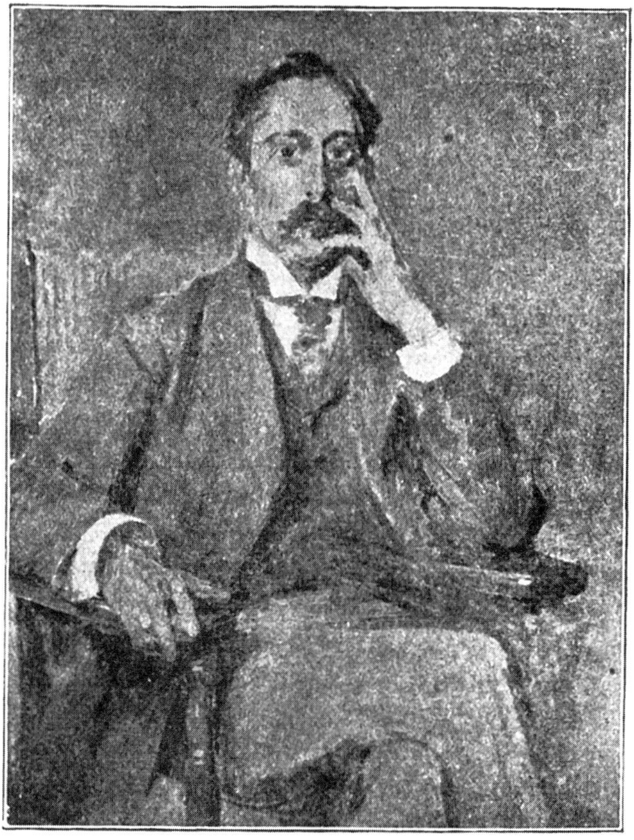

Ébouch of Portrait. *Th. Robinson.*

One sitting of one hour and a half.

the results of after-painting. For you cannot glaze *up*. You always glaze *down*. The glaze being a transparent color, used without white, will naturally make the color under it more brilliant in color, but darker in value, just as it would if you laid a piece of colored glass over it. And this result must be calculated on beforehand.

Which of all these methods is best to use depends altogether on which best suits the man and his purpose in the picture or his temperament. A rough *ébouch* will not make a smooth picture. A mosaic gives a pure, clear basis of color to gray down and work over, and may be scraped for a good surface. It is a deliberate method, and will be successful only with a thoughtful, deliberate painter. If a man is a timid colorist, a strong, even crude, under-painting will help to strengthen his color. A good colorist will get color any way. For a student, the more directly he puts down what he sees, the less he calculates on the effect of future after-painting, the better.

But whichever way a man works as to these various beginnings, the chief thing is, that he understand beforehand what are the peculiar advantages and qualities of each, and that he consider before he begins what he expects to do, and how he purposes to do it.

Further Painting. — The first painting may be put in from nature with the help of the several models in succession. More probably it will be put in from the color sketch which furnishes the general scheme, and from a number of studies and *ébouches* which will give the principal material for each part of the canvas. With the next painting comes the more exact study from models and accessories themselves. The under-painting is in, the color relations and the contrasts of masses, but all is more or less crude and undeveloped. Every one thing in the picture must be gradually brought to a further stage of completion. The background is not as yet to be carried farther as a whole. If the canvas is all covered, so that the background effect is there, it is all that is needed as yet. The most important figures are to be painted, beginning with the heads and hands, and at the same time painting the parts next to them, the background and drapery close around them, so that the immediate values shall all be true as far as it has gone.

No small details are painted yet. The whole canvas is carried forward by painting all over it, no one thing being entirely finished ; for the same degree of progress should be kept up for the whole picture. To finish any one part long before the rest is done, would be to run the risk of over-painting that part.

After the heads and other flesh parts, the draperies should be brought up, and the background and all objects in it painted, to bring the whole picture to the same degree of completion. This finishes the second painting. It is all done from nature direct, and is painted solidly as a rule. Even if the first painting has been a *frottée* this one will have been solidly painted into that *frottée*, although the transparent rubbing may have been left showing, whenever it was true in effect; most probably in the shadows and broader dark masses of the backgrounds. In this second painting no glazings or scumblings come in. The canvas is brought forward as far as possible with direct frank brush-work with body color before these other processes can be used. Glazes and such manipulations require a solid under-painting, and a comparative completion of the picture for safe work. These processes are for the modifying of color mainly; you do not draw nor represent the more important and fundamental facts of the picture with them. All these things are painted first, in the most frank and direct way, and then you can do anything you want to on a sure basis of well-understood representation. There will be structure underneath your future processes.

The Third Painting. — The third painting simply goes over the picture in the same manner as the second, but marking out more carefully the important details and enforcing the accuracy of features, or strengthening the accents of dark and bringing up those of the lights. The procedure will, of course, be different, according as the picture was begun with an *ébouch* of body color or a *frottée* of transparent color. The third painting will, in either case, carry the picture as a whole further toward being finished.

Rough and Smooth. — If body color has been used pretty freely in the two first paintings, the surface of paint will be pretty rough in places by the time it is ready for the third painting. Whether that roughness is a thing to be got rid of or not is something for the painter to decide for himself. Among the greatest of painters there have always been men who painted smoothly and men who painted roughly. I have considered elsewhere the subject of detail, but the question of detail bears on that of the roughness of the painting; for minute detail is not possible with much roughness of surface; the fineness of the stroke which secures the detail is lost in the corrugations of the heavier brush-strokes. The effect of color, and especially luminosity, has much to do with the way the paint is put on also, and all these things are to be considered. As a rule, it might be well to look upon either extreme as something not of importance in itself. The mere quality of smoothness on the canvas is of no consequence or value, any more than the mere quality of roughness is. If these things are necessary to or consequent upon the getting of certain other qualities which are justly to be considered worth striving for, then these qualities will be seen on the canvas, and will be all right. The painter will do well to look on them as something incidental merely to the picture. If he will simply work quite frankly, intent on the expression of what is true and vital to his picture, the question of the surface quality of his canvas will not bother him beyond the effect that it has upon his attaining of that expression.

Scraping. — The second painting will be well dry before the third begins, especially if the paint be more rough and uneven than is for any reason desirable. Almost every painter scrapes his pictures more or less. There is pretty sure to be some part of it in which there is roughness just where he doesn't want it. For the third painting, that is to say, after the main things in the picture are practically entirely finished, there remains to be done the strengthening and richening and modifying of the colors, values, and accents, and the bringing of the whole picture together by a general overworking. Before this begins, the picture may need scraping more or less all over. If it does need it, you may use a regular tool made for that purpose; or the blade of a razor may be used, it being held firmly in such a position that there is no danger of its cutting the canvas.

It is not necessary to scrape the paint smooth,

but only to take off such projections and unevenness of paint as would interfere with the proper over-painting.

The third painting represents any and all processes that may be used to complete the picture. There is no rule as to the number of processes or "paintings." You may have a dozen paintings if you want them, and after the first two they are all modifications and subdivisions of the third painting; for they all add to furthering the completion of the picture. They are all done more or less from nature, as the second painting was. There should be very little done to any picture without constant reference to nature.

If you glaze your picture, glaze one part at a time. Don't "tone" it with a general wash of some color. That is not the way pictures are "brought into tone," nor is that the purpose of the glaze. The glaze, like any other application of paint, is put on just where it is needed to modify the color of that place where the color goes. The use of a scumble is the same; and both the glaze and the scumble will be painted into and over with solid color, and that again modified as much as is called for. The thing which is to be carefully avoided is not the use of any special process, but the ceasing from the use of some process or other before the thing is as it should be, — don't stop before the picture represents the best, the completest expression of the idea of the picture.

This completeness of expression may even go to the elimination of what is ordinarily looked upon as "finish." Finish is not surface, but expression; and completeness of expression may demand roughness and avoidance of detail and surface at one time quite as positively as it demands more detail and consequent smoothness at another.

And this final completeness comes from the last paintings which I group together as the "third." Scumble and glaze and paint into them, and glaze and scumble again. Use any process which will help your picture to have those qualities which are always essential to any picture being a good one. The qualities of line and mass, composition that is, you get from the first, or you never can get it at all. Those qualities of character, and truth of representation, and exactness of meaning, you get in the first paintings, together with the more general qualities of color and tone. Emphasis and force of accent, such detail as you want, and the final and more delicate perceptions of color and tone, you get in the third or last painting, which may be divided into several paintings.

Between Paintings. — When a painting is dry and you begin to work on it again, you will probably find parts of its surface covered with a kind of bluish haze, which quite changes its color or obscures the work altogether. It is "dried in." In drying, some of the oil of the last painting is absorbed by what is beneath it, and the dead haze is the result. You cannot paint on it without in some way bringing it back to its original color. You cannot varnish it out at this stage, for this will not have a good effect on your picture.

"Oiling Out." — You can oil it all over, and then rub all the oil off that you can. This will bring it out. But the oil will tend to darken the picture; too much oil should be avoided. Turpentine with a little oil in it will bring it out also, but it will not stay out so long, but perhaps long enough for you to work on it. If you put a little siccative de Harlem in it, or use any picture varnish thinned with turpentine, it will serve well enough. There is a retouching varnish, *vernis à retoucher*, which is made for this purpose, and is perfectly safe and good.

The picture must be well dried before it is finally varnished.

CHAPTER XXXV

DIFFICULTIES OF BEGINNERS

ALL painters have difficulty with their pictures, but the trouble with the beginner is that he has not experience enough to know how to meet it. The solving of all difficulties is a matter of application of fundamental principles to them; but it is necessary to know these principles, and to have applied them to simple problems, before one can know how to apply them to less simple ones.

I have tried to deal fully with these principles rather than to tell how to do any one thing, and to point out the application whenever it could be done.

There are, however, some things that almost always bother the beginner, and it may be helpful to speak of them particularly.

Selection of Subject. — One of the chief objections to copying as a method of beginning study is that while it teaches a good deal about surface-work, it gives no practical training just when it is most needed. The student who has only copied has no idea how to look for a composition, how to place it on his canvas, or how to translate into line and color the actual forms which he sees in nature. These things are all done for him in the picture he is copying, yet these are the very first things he should have practised in. The making of a picture begins before the drawing and painting begins. You see something out-doors, or you see a group of people or a single person in an interesting position. It is one thing to see it; how are you practically to grasp it so as to get it on canvas? That is quite a different thing. How much shall you take in? How much leave out? What proportion of the canvas shall the main object or figure take up? All these are questions which need some experience to answer.

In dealing with figures experience comes somewhat naturally, because you will of course not undertake more than a head and shoulders, with a plain background, for your first work. The selecting of subject in this is chiefly the choice of lighting and position of head, which have been spoken of elsewhere; and the placing of them on the canvas should be reduced to the making of the head as large as it will come conveniently. The old rule was that the point of the nose should be about the middle of the canvas, and in most cases on the ordinary canvas this brings the head in the right place. As you paint more you will put in more and more of the figure, and so progress comes very naturally.

But in landscape you are more than likely to

be almost helpless at first. There is so much all around you, and so little saliency, that it is hard to say where to begin and where to leave off. Practice in still life will help you somewhat, but still things in nature are seldom arranged with that centralization which makes a subject easy to see. Even the simplicity which is sometimes obvious is, when you come to paint it, only the more difficult to handle because of its simplicity. The simplicity which you should look for to make your selection of a subject easy is not the lack of something to draw, but the definiteness of some marked object or effect. What is good as a "view" is apt to be the reverse of suitable for a picture. You want something tangible, and you do not want too much or too little of it. A long line of hill with a broad field beneath it, for instance, is simple enough, but what is there for you to take hold of? In an ordinary light it is only a few broad planes of value and color without an accent object to emphasize or centre on. It can be painted, of course, and can be made a beautiful picture, but it is a subject for a master, not for a student. But suppose there were a tree or a group of trees in the field; suppose a mass of cloud obscured the sky, and a ray of sunlight fell on and around the tree through a rift in the clouds. Or suppose the opposite of this. Suppose all was in broad light, and the tree was strongly lighted on one side, on the other shadowed, and that it threw a mass of shadow below and to one side of it. Immediately there is something which you can take hold of and make your picture around. The field and hill alone will make a study of distance and middle distance and foreground, but it would not make an effective sketch. The two effects I have supposed give the possibility for a sketch at once, and what suggests a sketch suggests a picture.

This central object or effect which I have supposed also clears up the matter of the placing of your subject on the canvas. With merely the hill and plain you might cut it off anywhere, a mile or two one side or the other would make little or no difference to your picture. But the tree and the effect of light decide the thing for you. The tree and the lighting are the central idea of the picture. Very well, then, make them large enough on your canvas to be of that importance. Then what is around them is only so much more as the canvas will hold, and you will place the tree where, having the proper proportionate size, it will also "compose well" and make the canvas balance, being neither in the middle exactly nor too much to one side.

Here are two photographs taken in the same field and of the same view, with the camera pointed in the same direction in both. One shows the lack of saliency, although the tree is there. In the other the camera was simply carried forward a hundred yards or so, until the tree became large enough to be of importance in the composition. The placing is simply a better position with reference to the tree in this case.

Centralize. — Now, as you go about looking for things to sketch, look always for some central object or effect. If you find that what seems very beautiful will not give you anything definite and graspable, — some contrast of form, or light and shade, or color, — don't attempt it. The thing is beautiful, and has doubtless a picture in it, but not for you. You are learning how to look for and to find a subject, and you must begin with what is readily sketched, without too much subtlety either of form or color or value.

Placing. — Having found your subject with something definite in it, you must place it on your canvas so that it "tells." It will not do to put it in haphazard, letting any part of it come anywhere as it happens. You will not be satisfied with the effect of this. The object of a picture is to make visible something which you wish to call attention to; to show something that seems to you worth looking at. Then you must arrange it so that that particular something is sure to be seen whether anything else is seen or not. This is the first thing to be thought of in placing your subject.

Where is it to come on the canvas? How much room is it to take up? If it is too large, there is not enough surrounding it to make an interesting whole. If it is to be emphasized, it must have

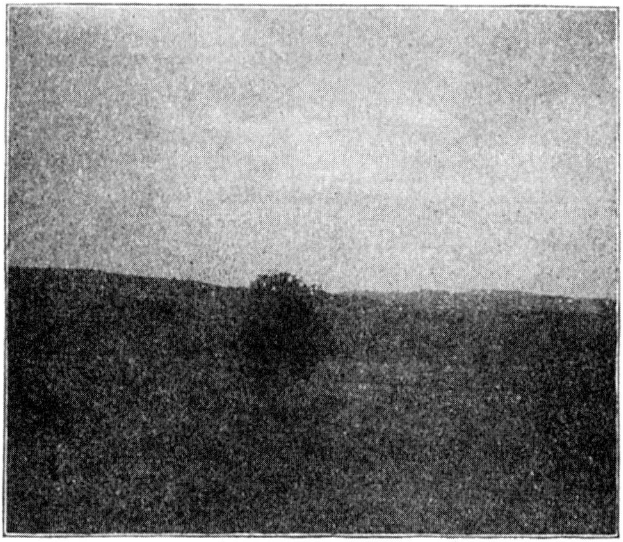

Landscape Photo. No. 1.

something to be emphasized with reference to. On the other hand, if it is too small, its very size makes it insignificant.

If it is a landscape, decide first the proportions of land and sky, — where your horizon line will come. Then, having drawn that line, make three or four lines which will give the mass of the main effect or object — a barn, a tree, a slope of hill, or whatever it be, get merely its simplest suggestion of outline. These two things will show you, on

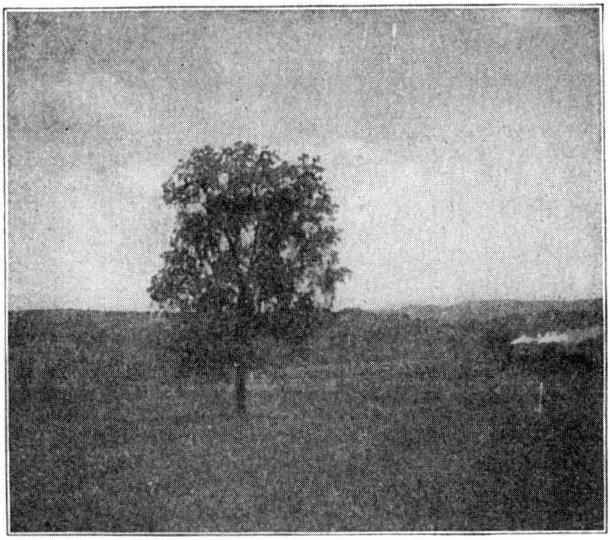

Landscape Photo. No. 2.

considering their relation to each other and to the rest of the canvas, about what its emphasis will be. If it isn't right, rub it out and do it again, a little larger or smaller, a little more to one side or the other, higher or lower, as you find needed. When you have done this to your satisfaction, you have done the first important thing.

Still Life, etc. — If your subject be still life, flowers, or an animal or other figure, go about it in the same way. Look at it well. Try to get an idea of its general shape, and block that out with a few lines. You will almost always find a horizontal line which by cutting across the mass will help you to decide where the mass will best come. First, the mass must be about the right size, and then it must balance well on the canvas. Any of the things suggested as helping about drawing and values will of course help you here. The reducing-glass will help you to get the size and position of things. The card with a square hole in it will do the same. Even a sort of little frame made with the fingers and thumbs of your two hands will cut off the surrounding objects, and help you see your group as a whole with other things out of the way.

Walk About. — A change of position of a very few feet sometimes makes a great difference in the looks of a subject. The first view of it is not always the best. Walk around a little; look at it from one point and from another. Take your time. Better begin a little later than stop because you don't like it and feel discouraged. Time taken to consider well beforehand is never lost. "Well begun is half done."

Relief. — In beginning a thing you want to have the first few minutes' work to do the most possible towards giving you something to judge by. You want from the very first to get something recognizable. Then every subsequent touch, having reference to that, will be so much the more sure and effective. Look, then, first for what will count most.

What to look for. — Whether you lay your work out first with black-and-white or with paint, look to see where the greatest contrast is. Where is there a strong light against dark and a strong dark against light? Not the little accents, but that which marks the contact of two great planes. Find this first, and represent it as soon as you have got the main values, in this way the whole thing will tell as an actuality. It will not yet carry much expression, but it will look like a *fact*, and it will have established certain relations from which you can work forward.

Colors. — It ought to go without saying that the colors as they come from the tube are not right for any color you see in nature however you think they look. But beginners are very apt to think that if they cannot get the color they want, they can get it in another kind of tube. This is a mistake. The tubes of color that are actually necessary for almost every possible tint or combination in nature are very few. But they must be used to advantage. Now and then one finds his palette lacking, and must add to it; but after one has experimented a while he settles down to some eight or ten colors which will do almost everything, and two or three more that will do what remains. When you work out-of-doors you may find that more variety will help you and gain time for you; that several blues and some secondaries it is well to have in tubes besides the regular outfit. Still even then, when you have got beyond the first frantic gropings, you will be surprised to see yourself constantly using certain colors and neglecting others. These others, then, you do not need, and you may leave them out of your box.

Too Many Tubes. — If you have too many colors, they are a trouble rather than a help to you. You must carry them all in your mind, and you do not so soon get to thinking of the color in nature and taking up the paint from different parts of your palette instinctively — which means that you are gaining command of it. Never put a new color on your palette unless you feel the actual need of it, or have a special reason for it. Better get well acquainted with the regular colors you have, and have only as many as you can handle well.

Mixing. — Use some system in mixing your paint. Have your palette set the same way always, so that your brush can find the color without having to hunt for it. Have a reasonable way too of taking up your color before you mix it. Don't always begin with the same one. Is the tint light or dark? strong or delicate? What is the prevailing color in it? Let these things affect the sequence of bringing the colors together for mixing. Let these things have to do also with the proportionate quantity of each. Suppose you have a heavy dark green to mix, what will you take first? Make a dash at the white, put it in the middle of the palette, and then tone it down to the green? How much paint would you have to take before you got your color? Yet I've seen this very thing done, and others equally senseless. What is the green? Dark. Bluish or warm? Will reddish or yellowish blue do it best? How much space do you want that brushful to cover? Take enough blue, add to it a yellow of the sort that will make approximately the color. Don't stir them up; drag one into the other a little — very little. The color is crude? Another color or two will bring it into tone. Don't mix it much. Don't smear it all over your palette. Make a smallish dab of it, keeping it well piled up. If you get any one color too great in quantity, then you will have to take more of the others again to keep it in balance. Be careful to take as nearly the right proportions of each at the first picking up, so as to mix but few times; for every time you add and mix you flatten out the tone more, and lose its vibration and life.

Now, if the color is too dark, what will you

lighten it with? White? Wait a minute. Think. Will white take away the richness of it? White always grays and flattens the color. Don't put it into a warm, rich color unless it belongs there. Then only as much as is needed.

Treat all your tints this way. Is it a high value on a forehead in full light? White first, then a little modifying color, yellow first, then red; perhaps no red: the kind of yellow may do it. When you have a rich color to mix, get it as strong as you can first. Then gray it as much as you need to, never the reverse. But when you want a delicate color, make it delicate first, and then strengthen it cautiously.

These seem but common-sense. Hardly necessary to take the trouble to write it down? But common-sense is not always attributed to artists, and the beginner does not seem able always to apply his common-sense to his painting at first. To say it to him opens his eyes. Best be on the safe side.

Crude Color. — The beginner is sure to get crude color, either from lack of perception of color qualities, or inability to mix the tints he knows he wants. In the latter case crude color either comes from too few colors in the mixture, or from inharmonious colors brought together, which is only another form of the same, for an added complementary would make it right. For instance, Prussian blue and chrome yellow mixed will make a powerful green which you could hardly put anywhere — a strong, crude green. Well, what is the complementary? Red? And what does a complementary do to a color? Neutralizes, grays. Then add a very little red, enough to gray the green, not enough to kill its quality.

Or if you don't want the color that makes, take a little reddish yellow, ochre say, and possibly a little reddish blue, new blue or ultramarine; add these, and see how it grays it and still keeps the same kind of green. This is the principle in extreme. Still, the best way would be not to try to make a green of Prussian blue and chrome yellow. It is better to know the qualities of each tube color on your palette. Know which two colors mix to make a crude color, and which will be gray, more or less, without a third.

Muddy Color. — Dirty or muddy color comes from lack of this last. You do not know how your colors are going to affect each other. You mix, and the color looks right on the palette, but on the canvas it is not right. You mix again and put it on the canvas; it mixes with the first tint and you get — mud. Why? Both wrong. Scrape the whole thing off. With a clean spot of canvas mix a fresh color. Put it on frankly and freshly and let it alone — don't dabble it. The chances are it will be at least fresh, clean color.

Over-mixing makes color muddy sometimes, especially when more than three colors are used. When you don't get the right tint with three colors, the chances are that you have got the wrong three. If that is not so, and you must add a fourth, do so with some thoughtfulness, or you will have to mix the tint again.

Dirty Brushes and Palette. — Using dirty brushes causes muddy color. Don't be too economical about the number of brushes you use. Keep a good big rag at your hand, and wipe the paint out of your brush often. If the color is getting muddy, clean your palette and take a clean brush. Your palette is sure to get covered with paint of all colors when you have painted a little while. You can't mix colors with any degree of certainty if the palette is smeared with all sorts of tints. Use your palette-knife — that's what it's for. Scrape the palette clean every once in a while as it gets crowded. Wipe it off. Take some fresh brushes. Then, if your color is dirty, it is your fault, not the fault of your tools.

Out-door and In-door Colors. — There is one source of discouragement and difficulty that every one has to contend against; that is, the difference in the apparent key of paint when, having been put on out-of-doors, it is seen in the house. Out-of-doors the color looked bright and light, and when you get it in-doors it looks dark and gray, and perhaps muddy and dead. This is something you must expect, and must learn how to control.

As everything that the out-door light falls upon looks the brighter for it, so will your paint look brighter than it really is because of the brilliancy of the light which you see it in. You must learn to make allowance for that. You must learn by experience how much the color will go down when you take it into the house.

Of course an umbrella is a most useful and necessary thing in working out-of-doors, and if it is lined with black so much the better for you; for there is sure to be a good deal of light coming through the cloth, and while it shades your canvas, it does to some extent give a false glow to your canvas, which a black lining counterbalances.

Mere experience will give you that knowledge more or less; but there are ways in which you can help yourself.

When you first begin to work out-doors try to find a good solid shade in which to place your easel, and then try to paint up to the full key, even at the risk of a little crudeness of color. Use colors that seem rather pure than otherwise. You may be sure that the color will "come down" a little anyhow, so keep the pitch well up. Then, if the shade has been pretty even, and your canvas has had a fair light, you will get a fairly good color-key.

Predetermined Pitch. — Another way is to determine the pitch of the painting in some way before you take the canvas out-of-doors. There are various ways of doing this. The most practical is, perhaps, to know the relative value, in the house and out-doors, of the priming of your canvas. Have a definite knowledge of how near to the highest light you will want that priming is. Then, when you put on the light paint, if you keep it light with reference to the known pitch of the priming, you will keep the whole painting light.

Discouragement. — We all get discouraged sometimes, but it is something to know that the case is not hopeless because we are. That what we are trying to do does not get done easily is no reason that it may not get done eventually. Often the discouragement is not even a sign that what we are doing is not going well. The discouragement may be one way that fatigue shows itself, and we may feel discouraged after a particularly successful day's work — in consequence of it very probably. Make it a rule not to judge of a day's work at the end of that day. Wait till next morning, when fresh and rested, and you will have a much more just notion of what you have done.

When you begin to get blue about your work is the time to stop and rest. If the blues are the result of tire, working longer will only make your picture worse. A tired brain and eye never improved a piece of painting. And in the same spirit rest often while you are painting. If your model rests, it is as well that you rest also. Turn away from your work, and when you get to work again you will look at it with a fresh eye.

Change Your Work Often. — Too continued and concentrated work on the same picture also will lead to discouragement. Change your work, keep several things going at the same time, and when you are tired of one you may work with fresh perceptions and interest on another.

Stop often to walk away from your work. Lay down your palette and brushes, and put the canvas at the other end of the room. Straighten your back and look at the picture at a distance. You get an impression of the thing as a whole. What you have been doing will be judged of less by itself and more in relation to the rest of the picture, and so more justly.

When things are going wrong, stop work for the day. Take a rest. Then, before you begin again on it to-morrow, take plenty of time to look the picture over — consider it, compare it with nature, and make up your mind just what it lacks, just what it needs, just what you will do first to make it as it should be. It is marvellous how it drives off the blues to know just what you are going to do next.

INDEX

INDEX

A CATALOG OF SELECTED

DOVER BOOKS

IN ALL FIELDS OF INTEREST

A CATALOG OF SELECTED DOVER BOOKS IN ALL FIELDS OF INTEREST

CONCERNING THE SPIRITUAL IN ART, Wassily Kandinsky. Pioneering work by father of abstract art. Thoughts on color theory, nature of art. Analysis of earlier masters. 12 illustrations. 80pp. of text. 5⅜ x 8½. 0-486-23411-8

CELTIC ART: The Methods of Construction, George Bain. Simple geometric techniques for making Celtic interlacements, spirals, Kells-type initials, animals, humans, etc. Over 500 illustrations. 160pp. 9 x 12. (Available in U.S. only.) 0-486-22923-8

AN ATLAS OF ANATOMY FOR ARTISTS, Fritz Schider. Most thorough reference work on art anatomy in the world. Hundreds of illustrations, including selections from works by Vesalius, Leonardo, Goya, Ingres, Michelangelo, others. 593 illustrations. 192pp. 7⅛ x 10¼. 0-486-20241-0

CELTIC HAND STROKE-BY-STROKE (Irish Half-Uncial from "The Book of Kells"): An Arthur Baker Calligraphy Manual, Arthur Baker. Complete guide to creating each letter of the alphabet in distinctive Celtic manner. Covers hand position, strokes, pens, inks, paper, more. Illustrated. 48pp. 8¼ x 11. 0-486-24336-2

EASY ORIGAMI, John Montroll. Charming collection of 32 projects (hat, cup, pelican, piano, swan, many more) specially designed for the novice origami hobbyist. Clearly illustrated easy-to-follow instructions insure that even beginning papercrafters will achieve successful results. 48pp. 8¼ x 11. 0-486-27298-2

BLOOMINGDALE'S ILLUSTRATED 1886 CATALOG: Fashions, Dry Goods and Housewares, Bloomingdale Brothers. Famed merchants' extremely rare catalog depicting about 1,700 products: clothing, housewares, firearms, dry goods, jewelry, more. Invaluable for dating, identifying vintage items. Also, copyright-free graphics for artists, designers. Co-published with Henry Ford Museum & Greenfield Village. 160pp. 8¼ x 11. 0-486-25780-0

THE ART OF WORLDLY WISDOM, Baltasar Gracian. "Think with the few and speak with the many," "Friends are a second existence," and "Be able to forget" are among this 1637 volume's 300 pithy maxims. A perfect source of mental and spiritual refreshment, it can be opened at random and appreciated either in brief or at length. 128pp. 5⅜ x 8½. 0-486-44034-6

JOHNSON'S DICTIONARY: A Modern Selection, Samuel Johnson (E. L. McAdam and George Milne, eds.). This modern version reduces the original 1755 edition's 2,300 pages of definitions and literary examples to a more manageable length, retaining the verbal pleasure and historical curiosity of the original. 480pp. 5$\frac{3}{16}$ x 8¼. 0-486-44089-3

ADVENTURES OF HUCKLEBERRY FINN, Mark Twain, Illustrated by E. W. Kemble. A work of eternal richness and complexity, a source of ongoing critical debate, and a literary landmark, Twain's 1885 masterpiece about a barefoot boy's journey of self-discovery has enthralled readers around the world. This handsome clothbound reproduction of the first edition features all 174 of the original black-and-white illustrations. 368pp. 5⅜ x 8½. 0-486-44322-1

STICKLEY CRAFTSMAN FURNITURE CATALOGS, Gustav Stickley and L. & J. G. Stickley. Beautiful, functional furniture in two authentic catalogs from 1910. 594 illustrations, including 277 photos, show settles, rockers, armchairs, reclining chairs, bookcases, desks, tables. 183pp. 6½ x 9¼. 0-486-23838-5

AMERICAN LOCOMOTIVES IN HISTORIC PHOTOGRAPHS: 1858 to 1949, Ron Ziel (ed.). A rare collection of 126 meticulously detailed official photographs, called "builder portraits," of American locomotives that majestically chronicle the rise of steam locomotive power in America. Introduction. Detailed captions. xi+ 129pp. 9 x 12. 0-486-27393-8

AMERICA'S LIGHTHOUSES: An Illustrated History, Francis Ross Holland, Jr. Delightfully written, profusely illustrated fact-filled survey of over 200 American lighthouses since 1716. History, anecdotes, technological advances, more. 240pp. 8 x 10¾. 0-486-25576-X

TOWARDS A NEW ARCHITECTURE, Le Corbusier. Pioneering manifesto by founder of "International School." Technical and aesthetic theories, views of industry, economics, relation of form to function, "mass-production split" and much more. Profusely illustrated. 320pp. 6⅛ x 9¼. (Available in U.S. only.) 0-486-25023-7

HOW THE OTHER HALF LIVES, Jacob Riis. Famous journalistic record, exposing poverty and degradation of New York slums around 1900, by major social reformer. 100 striking and influential photographs. 233pp. 10 x 7⅞. 0-486-22012-5

FRUIT KEY AND TWIG KEY TO TREES AND SHRUBS, William M. Harlow. One of the handiest and most widely used identification aids. Fruit key covers 120 deciduous and evergreen species; twig key 160 deciduous species. Easily used. Over 300 photographs. 126pp. 5⅜ x 8½. 0-486-20511-8

COMMON BIRD SONGS, Dr. Donald J. Borror. Songs of 60 most common U.S. birds: robins, sparrows, cardinals, bluejays, finches, more–arranged in order of increasing complexity. Up to 9 variations of songs of each species.
Cassette and manual 0-486-99911-4

ORCHIDS AS HOUSE PLANTS, Rebecca Tyson Northen. Grow cattleyas and many other kinds of orchids–in a window, in a case, or under artificial light. 63 illustrations. 148pp. 5⅜ x 8½. 0-486-23261-1

MONSTER MAZES, Dave Phillips. Masterful mazes at four levels of difficulty. Avoid deadly perils and evil creatures to find magical treasures. Solutions for all 32 exciting illustrated puzzles. 48pp. 8¼ x 11. 0-486-26005-4

MOZART'S DON GIOVANNI (DOVER OPERA LIBRETTO SERIES), Wolfgang Amadeus Mozart. Introduced and translated by Ellen H. Bleiler. Standard Italian libretto, with complete English translation. Convenient and thoroughly portable–an ideal companion for reading along with a recording or the performance itself. Introduction. List of characters. Plot summary. 121pp. 5¼ x 8½. 0-486-24944-1

FRANK LLOYD WRIGHT'S DANA HOUSE, Donald Hoffmann. Pictorial essay of residential masterpiece with over 160 interior and exterior photos, plans, elevations, sketches and studies. 128pp. 9¼ x 10¾. 0-486-29120-0

THE CLARINET AND CLARINET PLAYING, David Pino. Lively, comprehensive work features suggestions about technique, musicianship, and musical interpretation, as well as guidelines for teaching, making your own reeds, and preparing for public performance. Includes an intriguing look at clarinet history. "A godsend," *The Clarinet*, Journal of the International Clarinet Society. Appendixes. 7 illus. 320pp. 5⅜ x 8½. 0-486-40270-3

HOLLYWOOD GLAMOR PORTRAITS, John Kobal (ed.). 145 photos from 1926-49. Harlow, Gable, Bogart, Bacall; 94 stars in all. Full background on photographers, technical aspects. 160pp. 8⅜ x 11¼. 0-486-23352-9

THE RAVEN AND OTHER FAVORITE POEMS, Edgar Allan Poe. Over 40 of the author's most memorable poems: "The Bells," "Ulalume," "Israfel," "To Helen," "The Conqueror Worm," "Eldorado," "Annabel Lee," many more. Alphabetic lists of titles and first lines. 64pp. 5$\frac{3}{16}$ x 8¼. 0-486-26685-0

PERSONAL MEMOIRS OF U. S. GRANT, Ulysses Simpson Grant. Intelligent, deeply moving firsthand account of Civil War campaigns, considered by many the finest military memoirs ever written. Includes letters, historic photographs, maps and more. 528pp. 6⅛ x 9¼. 0-486-28587-1

ANCIENT EGYPTIAN MATERIALS AND INDUSTRIES, A. Lucas and J. Harris. Fascinating, comprehensive, thoroughly documented text describes this ancient civilization's vast resources and the processes that incorporated them in daily life, including the use of animal products, building materials, cosmetics, perfumes and incense, fibers, glazed ware, glass and its manufacture, materials used in the mummification process, and much more. 544pp. 6⅛ x 9¼. (Available in U.S. only.) 0-486-40446-3

RUSSIAN STORIES/RUSSKIE RASSKAZY: A Dual-Language Book, edited by Gleb Struve. Twelve tales by such masters as Chekhov, Tolstoy, Dostoevsky, Pushkin, others. Excellent word-for-word English translations on facing pages, plus teaching and study aids, Russian/English vocabulary, biographical/critical introductions, more. 416pp. 5⅜ x 8½. 0-486-26244-8

PHILADELPHIA THEN AND NOW: 60 Sites Photographed in the Past and Present, Kenneth Finkel and Susan Oyama. Rare photographs of City Hall, Logan Square, Independence Hall, Betsy Ross House, other landmarks juxtaposed with contemporary views. Captures changing face of historic city. Introduction. Captions. 128pp. 8¼ x 11. 0-486-25790-8

NORTH AMERICAN INDIAN LIFE: Customs and Traditions of 23 Tribes, Elsie Clews Parsons (ed.). 27 fictionalized essays by noted anthropologists examine religion, customs, government, additional facets of life among the Winnebago, Crow, Zuni, Eskimo, other tribes. 480pp. 6⅛ x 9¼. 0-486-27377-6

TECHNICAL MANUAL AND DICTIONARY OF CLASSICAL BALLET, Gail Grant. Defines, explains, comments on steps, movements, poses and concepts. 15-page pictorial section. Basic book for student, viewer. 127pp. 5⅜ x 8½. 0-486-21843-0

THE MALE AND FEMALE FIGURE IN MOTION: 60 Classic Photographic Sequences, Eadweard Muybridge. 60 true-action photographs of men and women walking, running, climbing, bending, turning, etc., reproduced from rare 19th-century masterpiece. vi + 121pp. 9 x 12. 0-486-24745-7

ANIMALS: 1,419 Copyright-Free Illustrations of Mammals, Birds, Fish, Insects, etc., Jim Harter (ed.). Clear wood engravings present, in extremely lifelike poses, over 1,000 species of animals. One of the most extensive pictorial sourcebooks of its kind. Captions. Index. 284pp. 9 x 12. 0-486-23766-4

1001 QUESTIONS ANSWERED ABOUT THE SEASHORE, N. J. Berrill and Jacquelyn Berrill. Queries answered about dolphins, sea snails, sponges, starfish, fishes, shore birds, many others. Covers appearance, breeding, growth, feeding, much more. 305pp. 5¼ x 8¼. 0-486-23366-9

ATTRACTING BIRDS TO YOUR YARD, William J. Weber. Easy-to-follow guide offers advice on how to attract the greatest diversity of birds: birdhouses, feeders, water and waterers, much more. 96pp. 5³⁄₁₆ x 8¼. 0-486-28927-3

MEDICINAL AND OTHER USES OF NORTH AMERICAN PLANTS: A Historical Survey with Special Reference to the Eastern Indian Tribes, Charlotte Erichsen-Brown. Chronological historical citations document 500 years of usage of plants, trees, shrubs native to eastern Canada, northeastern U.S. Also complete identifying information. 343 illustrations. 544pp. 6½ x 9¼. 0-486-25951-X

STORYBOOK MAZES, Dave Phillips. 23 stories and mazes on two-page spreads: Wizard of Oz, Treasure Island, Robin Hood, etc. Solutions. 64pp. 8¼ x 11. 0-486-23628-5

AMERICAN NEGRO SONGS: 230 Folk Songs and Spirituals, Religious and Secular, John W. Work. This authoritative study traces the African influences of songs sung and played by black Americans at work, in church, and as entertainment. The author discusses the lyric significance of such songs as "Swing Low, Sweet Chariot," "John Henry," and others and offers the words and music for 230 songs. Bibliography. Index of Song Titles. 272pp. 6½ x 9¼. 0-486-40271-1

MOVIE-STAR PORTRAITS OF THE FORTIES, John Kobal (ed.). 163 glamor, studio photos of 106 stars of the 1940s: Rita Hayworth, Ava Gardner, Marlon Brando, Clark Gable, many more. 176pp. 8⅜ x 11¼. 0-486-23546-7

YEKL and THE IMPORTED BRIDEGROOM AND OTHER STORIES OF YIDDISH NEW YORK, Abraham Cahan. Film Hester Street based on *Yekl* (1896). Novel, other stories among first about Jewish immigrants on N.Y.'s East Side. 240pp. 5⅜ x 8½. 0-486-22427-9

SELECTED POEMS, Walt Whitman. Generous sampling from *Leaves of Grass*. Twenty-four poems include "I Hear America Singing," "Song of the Open Road," "I Sing the Body Electric," "When Lilacs Last in the Dooryard Bloom'd," "O Captain! My Captain!"–all reprinted from an authoritative edition. Lists of titles and first lines. 128pp. 5³⁄₁₆ x 8¼. 0-486-26878-0

SONGS OF EXPERIENCE: Facsimile Reproduction with 26 Plates in Full Color, William Blake. 26 full-color plates from a rare 1826 edition. Includes "The Tyger," "London," "Holy Thursday," and other poems. Printed text of poems. 48pp. 5¼ x 7. 0-486-24636-1

THE BEST TALES OF HOFFMANN, E. T. A. Hoffmann. 10 of Hoffmann's most important stories: "Nutcracker and the King of Mice," "The Golden Flowerpot," etc. 458pp. 5⅜ x 8½. 0-486-21793-0

THE BOOK OF TEA, Kakuzo Okakura. Minor classic of the Orient: entertaining, charming explanation, interpretation of traditional Japanese culture in terms of tea ceremony. 94pp. 5⅜ x 8½. 0-486-20070-1

FRENCH STORIES/CONTES FRANÇAIS: A Dual-Language Book, Wallace Fowlie. Ten stories by French masters, Voltaire to Camus: "Micromegas" by Voltaire; "The Atheist's Mass" by Balzac; "Minuet" by de Maupassant; "The Guest" by Camus, six more. Excellent English translations on facing pages. Also French-English vocabulary list, exercises, more. 352pp. 5⅜ x 8½. 0-486-26443-2

CHICAGO AT THE TURN OF THE CENTURY IN PHOTOGRAPHS: 122 Historic Views from the Collections of the Chicago Historical Society, Larry A. Viskochil. Rare large-format prints offer detailed views of City Hall, State Street, the Loop, Hull House, Union Station, many other landmarks, circa 1904-1913. Introduction. Captions. Maps. 144pp. 9⅜ x 12¼. 0-486-24656-6

OLD BROOKLYN IN EARLY PHOTOGRAPHS, 1865-1929, William Lee Younger. Luna Park, Gravesend race track, construction of Grand Army Plaza, moving of Hotel Brighton, etc. 157 previously unpublished photographs. 165pp. 8⅞ x 11¾. 0-486-23587-4

THE MYTHS OF THE NORTH AMERICAN INDIANS, Lewis Spence. Rich anthology of the myths and legends of the Algonquins, Iroquois, Pawnees and Sioux, prefaced by an extensive historical and ethnological commentary. 36 illustrations. 480pp. 5⅜ x 8½. 0-486-25967-6

AN ENCYCLOPEDIA OF BATTLES: Accounts of Over 1,560 Battles from 1479 B.C. to the Present, David Eggenberger. Essential details of every major battle in recorded history from the first battle of Megiddo in 1479 B.C. to Grenada in 1984. List of Battle Maps. New Appendix covering the years 1967-1984. Index. 99 illustrations. 544pp. 6½ x 9¼. 0-486-24913-1

SAILING ALONE AROUND THE WORLD, Captain Joshua Slocum. First man to sail around the world, alone, in small boat. One of great feats of seamanship told in delightful manner. 67 illustrations. 294pp. 5⅜ x 8½. 0-486-20326-3

ANARCHISM AND OTHER ESSAYS, Emma Goldman. Powerful, penetrating, prophetic essays on direct action, role of minorities, prison reform, puritan hypocrisy, violence, etc. 271pp. 5⅜ x 8½. 0-486-22484-8

MYTHS OF THE HINDUS AND BUDDHISTS, Ananda K. Coomaraswamy and Sister Nivedita. Great stories of the epics; deeds of Krishna, Shiva, taken from puranas, Vedas, folk tales; etc. 32 illustrations. 400pp. 5⅜ x 8½. 0-486-21759-0

MY BONDAGE AND MY FREEDOM, Frederick Douglass. Born a slave, Douglass became outspoken force in antislavery movement. The best of Douglass' autobiographies. Graphic description of slave life. 464pp. 5⅜ x 8½. 0-486-22457-0

FOLLOWING THE EQUATOR: A Journey Around the World, Mark Twain. Fascinating humorous account of 1897 voyage to Hawaii, Australia, India, New Zealand, etc. Ironic, bemused reports on peoples, customs, climate, flora and fauna, politics, much more. 197 illustrations. 720pp. 5⅜ x 8½. 0-486-26113-1

THE PEOPLE CALLED SHAKERS, Edward D. Andrews. Definitive study of Shakers: origins, beliefs, practices, dances, social organization, furniture and crafts, etc. 33 illustrations. 351pp. 5⅜ x 8½. 0-486-21081-2

THE MYTHS OF GREECE AND ROME, H. A. Guerber. A classic of mythology, generously illustrated, long prized for its simple, graphic, accurate retelling of the principal myths of Greece and Rome, and for its commentary on their origins and significance. With 64 illustrations by Michelangelo, Raphael, Titian, Rubens, Canova, Bernini and others. 480pp. 5⅜ x 8½. 0-486-27584-1

PSYCHOLOGY OF MUSIC, Carl E. Seashore. Classic work discusses music as a medium from psychological viewpoint. Clear treatment of physical acoustics, auditory apparatus, sound perception, development of musical skills, nature of musical feeling, host of other topics. 88 figures. 408pp. 5⅜ x 8½. 0-486-21851-1

LIFE IN ANCIENT EGYPT, Adolf Erman. Fullest, most thorough, detailed older account with much not in more recent books, domestic life, religion, magic, medicine, commerce, much more. Many illustrations reproduce tomb paintings, carvings, hieroglyphs, etc. 597pp. 5⅜ x 8½. 0-486-22632-8

SUNDIALS, Their Theory and Construction, Albert Waugh. Far and away the best, most thorough coverage of ideas, mathematics concerned, types, construction, adjusting anywhere. Simple, nontechnical treatment allows even children to build several of these dials. Over 100 illustrations. 230pp. 5⅜ x 8½. 0-486-22947-5

THEORETICAL HYDRODYNAMICS, L. M. Milne-Thomson. Classic exposition of the mathematical theory of fluid motion, applicable to both hydrodynamics and aerodynamics. Over 600 exercises. 768pp. 6⅛ x 9¼. 0-486-68970-0

OLD-TIME VIGNETTES IN FULL COLOR, Carol Belanger Grafton (ed.). Over 390 charming, often sentimental illustrations, selected from archives of Victorian graphics–pretty women posing, children playing, food, flowers, kittens and puppies, smiling cherubs, birds and butterflies, much more. All copyright-free. 48pp. 9¼ x 12¼. 0-486-27269-9

PERSPECTIVE FOR ARTISTS, Rex Vicat Cole. Depth, perspective of sky and sea, shadows, much more, not usually covered. 391 diagrams, 81 reproductions of drawings and paintings. 279pp. 5⅜ x 8½. 0-486-22487-2

DRAWING THE LIVING FIGURE, Joseph Sheppard. Innovative approach to artistic anatomy focuses on specifics of surface anatomy, rather than muscles and bones. Over 170 drawings of live models in front, back and side views, and in widely varying poses. Accompanying diagrams. 177 illustrations. Introduction. Index. 144pp. 8⅜ x11¼. 0-486-26723-7

GOTHIC AND OLD ENGLISH ALPHABETS: 100 Complete Fonts, Dan X. Solo. Add power, elegance to posters, signs, other graphics with 100 stunning copyright-free alphabets: Blackstone, Dolbey, Germania, 97 more–including many lower-case, numerals, punctuation marks. 104pp. 8⅛ x 11. 0-486-24695-7

THE BOOK OF WOOD CARVING, Charles Marshall Sayers. Finest book for beginners discusses fundamentals and offers 34 designs. "Absolutely first rate . . . well thought out and well executed."–E. J. Tangerman. 118pp. 7¾ x 10⅝. 0-486-23654-4

ILLUSTRATED CATALOG OF CIVIL WAR MILITARY GOODS: Union Army Weapons, Insignia, Uniform Accessories, and Other Equipment, Schuyler, Hartley, and Graham. Rare, profusely illustrated 1846 catalog includes Union Army uniform and dress regulations, arms and ammunition, coats, insignia, flags, swords, rifles, etc. 226 illustrations. 160pp. 9 x 12. 0-486-24939-5

WOMEN'S FASHIONS OF THE EARLY 1900s: An Unabridged Republication of "New York Fashions, 1909," National Cloak & Suit Co. Rare catalog of mail-order fashions documents women's and children's clothing styles shortly after the turn of the century. Captions offer full descriptions, prices. Invaluable resource for fashion, costume historians. Approximately 725 illustrations. 128pp. 8⅜ x 11¼. 0-486-27276-1

HOW TO DO BEADWORK, Mary White. Fundamental book on craft from simple projects to five-bead chains and woven works. 106 illustrations. 142pp. 5⅜ x 8. 0-486-20697-1

THE 1912 AND 1915 GUSTAV STICKLEY FURNITURE CATALOGS, Gustav Stickley. With over 200 detailed illustrations and descriptions, these two catalogs are essential reading and reference materials and identification guides for Stickley furniture. Captions cite materials, dimensions and prices. 112pp. 6½ x 9¼. 0-486-26676-1

EARLY AMERICAN LOCOMOTIVES, John H. White, Jr. Finest locomotive engravings from early 19th century: historical (1804–74), main-line (after 1870), special, foreign, etc. 147 plates. 142pp. 11⅜ x 8¼. 0-486-22772-3

LITTLE BOOK OF EARLY AMERICAN CRAFTS AND TRADES, Peter Stockham (ed.). 1807 children's book explains crafts and trades: baker, hatter, cooper, potter, and many others. 23 copperplate illustrations. 140pp. 4⅝ x 6. 0-486-23336-7

VICTORIAN FASHIONS AND COSTUMES FROM HARPER'S BAZAR, 1867–1898, Stella Blum (ed.). Day costumes, evening wear, sports clothes, shoes, hats, other accessories in over 1,000 detailed engravings. 320pp. 9⅜ x 12¼. 0-486-22990-4

THE LONG ISLAND RAIL ROAD IN EARLY PHOTOGRAPHS, Ron Ziel. Over 220 rare photos, informative text document origin (1844) and development of rail service on Long Island. Vintage views of early trains, locomotives, stations, passengers, crews, much more. Captions. 8⅞ x 11¾. 0-486-26301-0

VOYAGE OF THE LIBERDADE, Joshua Slocum. Great 19th-century mariner's thrilling, first-hand account of the wreck of his ship off South America, the 35-foot boat he built from the wreckage, and its remarkable voyage home. 128pp. 5⅜ x 8½. 0-486-40022-0

TEN BOOKS ON ARCHITECTURE, Vitruvius. The most important book ever written on architecture. Early Roman aesthetics, technology, classical orders, site selection, all other aspects. Morgan translation. 331pp. 5⅜ x 8½. 0-486-20645-9

THE HUMAN FIGURE IN MOTION, Eadweard Muybridge. More than 4,500 stopped-action photos, in action series, showing undraped men, women, children jumping, lying down, throwing, sitting, wrestling, carrying, etc. 390pp. 7⅞ x 10⅝. 0-486-20204-6 Clothbd.

TREES OF THE EASTERN AND CENTRAL UNITED STATES AND CANADA, William M. Harlow. Best one-volume guide to 140 trees. Full descriptions, woodlore, range, etc. Over 600 illustrations. Handy size. 288pp. 4½ x 6⅜. 0-486-20395-6

GROWING AND USING HERBS AND SPICES, Milo Miloradovich. Versatile handbook provides all the information needed for cultivation and use of all the herbs and spices available in North America. 4 illustrations. Index. Glossary. 236pp. 5⅜ x 8½. 0-486-25058-X

BIG BOOK OF MAZES AND LABYRINTHS, Walter Shepherd. 50 mazes and labyrinths in all–classical, solid, ripple, and more–in one great volume. Perfect inexpensive puzzler for clever youngsters. Full solutions. 112pp. 8⅛ x 11. 0-486-22951-3

PIANO TUNING, J. Cree Fischer. Clearest, best book for beginner, amateur. Simple repairs, raising dropped notes, tuning by easy method of flattened fifths. No previous skills needed. 4 illustrations. 201pp. 5⅜ x 8½. 0-486-23267-0

HINTS TO SINGERS, Lillian Nordica. Selecting the right teacher, developing confidence, overcoming stage fright, and many other important skills receive thoughtful discussion in this indispensible guide, written by a world-famous diva of four decades' experience. 96pp. 5⅜ x 8½. 0-486-40094-8

THE COMPLETE NONSENSE OF EDWARD LEAR, Edward Lear. All nonsense limericks, zany alphabets, Owl and Pussycat, songs, nonsense botany, etc., illustrated by Lear. Total of 320pp. 5⅜ x 8½. (Available in U.S. only.) 0-486-20167-8

VICTORIAN PARLOUR POETRY: An Annotated Anthology, Michael R. Turner. 117 gems by Longfellow, Tennyson, Browning, many lesser-known poets. "The Village Blacksmith," "Curfew Must Not Ring Tonight," "Only a Baby Small," dozens more, often difficult to find elsewhere. Index of poets, titles, first lines. xxiii + 325pp. 5⅝ x 8¼. 0-486-27044-0

DUBLINERS, James Joyce. Fifteen stories offer vivid, tightly focused observations of the lives of Dublin's poorer classes. At least one, "The Dead," is considered a masterpiece. Reprinted complete and unabridged from standard edition. 160pp. 5$\frac{3}{16}$ x 8¼. 0-486-26870-5

GREAT WEIRD TALES: 14 Stories by Lovecraft, Blackwood, Machen and Others, S. T. Joshi (ed.). 14 spellbinding tales, including "The Sin Eater," by Fiona McLeod, "The Eye Above the Mantel," by Frank Belknap Long, as well as renowned works by R. H. Barlow, Lord Dunsany, Arthur Machen, W. C. Morrow and eight other masters of the genre. 256pp. 5⅜ x 8½. (Available in U.S. only.) 0-486-40436-6

THE BOOK OF THE SACRED MAGIC OF ABRAMELIN THE MAGE, translated by S. MacGregor Mathers. Medieval manuscript of ceremonial magic. Basic document in Aleister Crowley, Golden Dawn groups. 268pp. 5⅜ x 8½. 0-486-23211-5

THE BATTLES THAT CHANGED HISTORY, Fletcher Pratt. Eminent historian profiles 16 crucial conflicts, ancient to modern, that changed the course of civilization. 352pp. 5⅜ x 8½. 0-486-41129-X

NEW RUSSIAN-ENGLISH AND ENGLISH-RUSSIAN DICTIONARY, M. A. O'Brien. This is a remarkably handy Russian dictionary, containing a surprising amount of information, including over 70,000 entries. 366pp. 4½ x 6⅛. 0-486-20208-9

NEW YORK IN THE FORTIES, Andreas Feininger. 162 brilliant photographs by the well-known photographer, formerly with *Life* magazine. Commuters, shoppers, Times Square at night, much else from city at its peak. Captions by John von Hartz. 181pp. 9¼ x 10¾. 0-486-23585-8

INDIAN SIGN LANGUAGE, William Tomkins. Over 525 signs developed by Sioux and other tribes. Written instructions and diagrams. Also 290 pictographs. 111pp. 6⅛ x 9¼. 0-486-22029-X

ANATOMY: A Complete Guide for Artists, Joseph Sheppard. A master of figure drawing shows artists how to render human anatomy convincingly. Over 460 illustrations. 224pp. 8⅜ x 11¼. 0-486-27279-6

MEDIEVAL CALLIGRAPHY: Its History and Technique, Marc Drogin. Spirited history, comprehensive instruction manual covers 13 styles (ca. 4th century through 15th). Excellent photographs; directions for duplicating medieval techniques with modern tools. 224pp. 8⅜ x 11¼. 0-486-26142-5

DRIED FLOWERS: How to Prepare Them, Sarah Whitlock and Martha Rankin. Complete instructions on how to use silica gel, meal and borax, perlite aggregate, sand and borax, glycerine and water to create attractive permanent flower arrangements. 12 illustrations. 32pp. 5⅜ x 8½. 0-486-21802-3

EASY-TO-MAKE BIRD FEEDERS FOR WOODWORKERS, Scott D. Campbell. Detailed, simple-to-use guide for designing, constructing, caring for and using feeders. Text, illustrations for 12 classic and contemporary designs. 96pp. 5⅜ x 8½. 0-486-25847-5

THE COMPLETE BOOK OF BIRDHOUSE CONSTRUCTION FOR WOODWORKERS, Scott D. Campbell. Detailed instructions, illustrations, tables. Also data on bird habitat and instinct patterns. Bibliography. 3 tables. 63 illustrations in 15 figures. 48pp. 5¼ x 8½. 0-486-24407-5

SCOTTISH WONDER TALES FROM MYTH AND LEGEND, Donald A. Mackenzie. 16 lively tales tell of giants rumbling down mountainsides, of a magic wand that turns stone pillars into warriors, of gods and goddesses, evil hags, powerful forces and more. 240pp. 5⅜ x 8½. 0-486-29677-6

THE HISTORY OF UNDERCLOTHES, C. Willett Cunnington and Phyllis Cunnington. Fascinating, well-documented survey covering six centuries of English undergarments, enhanced with over 100 illustrations: 12th-century laced-up bodice, footed long drawers (1795), 19th-century bustles, 19th-century corsets for men, Victorian "bust improvers," much more. 272pp. 5⅜ x 8¼. 0-486-27124-2

ARTS AND CRAFTS FURNITURE: The Complete Brooks Catalog of 1912, Brooks Manufacturing Co. Photos and detailed descriptions of more than 150 now very collectible furniture designs from the Arts and Crafts movement depict davenports, settees, buffets, desks, tables, chairs, bedsteads, dressers and more, all built of solid, quarter-sawed oak. Invaluable for students and enthusiasts of antiques, Americana and the decorative arts. 80pp. 6½ x 9¼. 0-486-27471-3

WILBUR AND ORVILLE: A Biography of the Wright Brothers, Fred Howard. Definitive, crisply written study tells the full story of the brothers' lives and work. A vividly written biography, unparalleled in scope and color, that also captures the spirit of an extraordinary era. 560pp. 6⅛ x 9¼. 0-486-40297-5

THE ARTS OF THE SAILOR: Knotting, Splicing and Ropework, Hervey Garrett Smith. Indispensable shipboard reference covers tools, basic knots and useful hitches; handsewing and canvas work, more. Over 100 illustrations. Delightful reading for sea lovers. 256pp. 5⅜ x 8½. 0-486-26440-8

FRANK LLOYD WRIGHT'S FALLINGWATER: The House and Its History, Second, Revised Edition, Donald Hoffmann. A total revision–both in text and illustrations–of the standard document on Fallingwater, the boldest, most personal architectural statement of Wright's mature years, updated with valuable new material from the recently opened Frank Lloyd Wright Archives. "Fascinating"–*The New York Times*. 116 illustrations. 128pp. 9¼ x 10¾. 0-486-27430-6

PHOTOGRAPHIC SKETCHBOOK OF THE CIVIL WAR, Alexander Gardner. 100 photos taken on field during the Civil War. Famous shots of Manassas Harper's Ferry, Lincoln, Richmond, slave pens, etc. 244pp. 10⅝ x 8¼. 0-486-22731-6

FIVE ACRES AND INDEPENDENCE, Maurice G. Kains. Great back-to-the-land classic explains basics of self-sufficient farming. The one book to get. 95 illustrations. 397pp. 5⅜ x 8½. 0-486-20974-1

A MODERN HERBAL, Margaret Grieve. Much the fullest, most exact, most useful compilation of herbal material. Gigantic alphabetical encyclopedia, from aconite to zedoary, gives botanical information, medical properties, folklore, economic uses, much else. Indispensable to serious reader. 161 illustrations. 888pp. 6½ x 9¼. 2-vol. set. (Available in U.S. only.) Vol. I: 0-486-22798-7 Vol. II: 0-486-22799-5

HIDDEN TREASURE MAZE BOOK, Dave Phillips. Solve 34 challenging mazes accompanied by heroic tales of adventure. Evil dragons, people-eating plants, blood-thirsty giants, many more dangerous adversaries lurk at every twist and turn. 34 mazes, stories, solutions. 48pp. 8¼ x 11. 0-486-24566-7

LETTERS OF W. A. MOZART, Wolfgang A. Mozart. Remarkable letters show bawdy wit, humor, imagination, musical insights, contemporary musical world; includes some letters from Leopold Mozart. 276pp. 5⅜ x 8½. 0-486-22859-2

BASIC PRINCIPLES OF CLASSICAL BALLET, Agrippina Vaganova. Great Russian theoretician, teacher explains methods for teaching classical ballet. 118 illustrations. 175pp. 5⅜ x 8½. 0-486-22036-2

THE JUMPING FROG, Mark Twain. Revenge edition. The original story of The Celebrated Jumping Frog of Calaveras County, a hapless French translation, and Twain's hilarious "retranslation" from the French. 12 illustrations. 66pp. 5⅜ x 8½. 0-486-22686-7

BEST REMEMBERED POEMS, Martin Gardner (ed.). The 126 poems in this superb collection of 19th- and 20th-century British and American verse range from Shelley's "To a Skylark" to the impassioned "Renascence" of Edna St. Vincent Millay and to Edward Lear's whimsical "The Owl and the Pussycat." 224pp. 5⅜ x 8½. 0-486-27165-X

COMPLETE SONNETS, William Shakespeare. Over 150 exquisite poems deal with love, friendship, the tyranny of time, beauty's evanescence, death and other themes in language of remarkable power, precision and beauty. Glossary of archaic terms. 80pp. 5³⁄₁₆ x 8¼. 0-486-26686-9

HISTORIC HOMES OF THE AMERICAN PRESIDENTS, Second, Revised Edition, Irvin Haas. A traveler's guide to American Presidential homes, most open to the public, depicting and describing homes occupied by every American President from George Washington to George Bush. With visiting hours, admission charges, travel routes. 175 photographs. Index. 160pp. 8¼ x 11. 0-486-26751-2

THE WIT AND HUMOR OF OSCAR WILDE, Alvin Redman (ed.). More than 1,000 ripostes, paradoxes, wisecracks: Work is the curse of the drinking classes; I can resist everything except temptation; etc. 258pp. 5⅜ x 8½. 0-486-20602-5

SHAKESPEARE LEXICON AND QUOTATION DICTIONARY, Alexander Schmidt. Full definitions, locations, shades of meaning in every word in plays and poems. More than 50,000 exact quotations. 1,485pp. 6½ x 9¼. 2-vol. set. Vol. 1: 0-486-22726-X Vol. 2: 0-486-22727-8

SELECTED POEMS, Emily Dickinson. Over 100 best-known, best-loved poems by one of America's foremost poets, reprinted from authoritative early editions. No comparable edition at this price. Index of first lines. 64pp. 5³⁄₁₆ x 8¼. 0-486-26466-1

THE INSIDIOUS DR. FU-MANCHU, Sax Rohmer. The first of the popular mystery series introduces a pair of English detectives to their archnemesis, the diabolical Dr. Fu-Manchu. Flavorful atmosphere, fast-paced action, and colorful characters enliven this classic of the genre. 208pp. 5³⁄₁₆ x 8¼. 0-486-29898-1

THE MALLEUS MALEFICARUM OF KRAMER AND SPRENGER, translated by Montague Summers. Full text of most important witchhunter's "bible," used by both Catholics and Protestants. 278pp. 6⅝ x 10. 0-486-22802-9

SPANISH STORIES/CUENTOS ESPAÑOLES: A Dual-Language Book, Angel Flores (ed.). Unique format offers 13 great stories in Spanish by Cervantes, Borges, others. Faithful English translations on facing pages. 352pp. 5⅜ x 8½. 0-486-25399-6

GARDEN CITY, LONG ISLAND, IN EARLY PHOTOGRAPHS, 1869–1919, Mildred H. Smith. Handsome treasury of 118 vintage pictures, accompanied by carefully researched captions, document the Garden City Hotel fire (1899), the Vanderbilt Cup Race (1908), the first airmail flight departing from the Nassau Boulevard Aerodrome (1911), and much more. 96pp. 8⅞ x 11¾. 0-486-40669-5

OLD QUEENS, N.Y., IN EARLY PHOTOGRAPHS, Vincent F. Seyfried and William Asadorian. Over 160 rare photographs of Maspeth, Jamaica, Jackson Heights, and other areas. Vintage views of DeWitt Clinton mansion, 1939 World's Fair and more. Captions. 192pp. 8⅞ x 11. 0-486-26358-4

CAPTURED BY THE INDIANS: 15 Firsthand Accounts, 1750-1870, Frederick Drimmer. Astounding true historical accounts of grisly torture, bloody conflicts, relentless pursuits, miraculous escapes and more, by people who lived to tell the tale. 384pp. 5⅜ x 8½. 0-486-24901-8

THE WORLD'S GREAT SPEECHES (Fourth Enlarged Edition), Lewis Copeland, Lawrence W. Lamm, and Stephen J. McKenna. Nearly 300 speeches provide public speakers with a wealth of updated quotes and inspiration–from Pericles' funeral oration and William Jennings Bryan's "Cross of Gold Speech" to Malcolm X's powerful words on the Black Revolution and Earl of Spenser's tribute to his sister, Diana, Princess of Wales. 944pp. 5⅜ x 8⅜. 0-486-40903-1

THE BOOK OF THE SWORD, Sir Richard F. Burton. Great Victorian scholar/adventurer's eloquent, erudite history of the "queen of weapons"–from prehistory to early Roman Empire. Evolution and development of early swords, variations (sabre, broadsword, cutlass, scimitar, etc.), much more. 336pp. 6⅛ x 9¼. 0-486-25434-8

AUTOBIOGRAPHY: The Story of My Experiments with Truth, Mohandas K. Gandhi. Boyhood, legal studies, purification, the growth of the Satyagraha (nonviolent protest) movement. Critical, inspiring work of the man responsible for the freedom of India. 480pp. 5⅜ x 8½. (Available in U.S. only.) 0-486-24593-4

CELTIC MYTHS AND LEGENDS, T. W. Rolleston. Masterful retelling of Irish and Welsh stories and tales. Cuchulain, King Arthur, Deirdre, the Grail, many more. First paperback edition. 58 full-page illustrations. 512pp. 5⅜ x 8½. 0-486-26507-2

THE PRINCIPLES OF PSYCHOLOGY, William James. Famous long course complete, unabridged. Stream of thought, time perception, memory, experimental methods; great work decades ahead of its time. 94 figures. 1,391pp. 5⅜ x 8½. 2-vol. set. Vol. I: 0-486-20381-6 Vol. II: 0-486-20382-4

THE WORLD AS WILL AND REPRESENTATION, Arthur Schopenhauer. Definitive English translation of Schopenhauer's life work, correcting more than 1,000 errors, omissions in earlier translations. Translated by E. F. J. Payne. Total of 1,269pp. 5⅜ x 8½. 2-vol. set. Vol. 1: 0-486-21761-2 Vol. 2: 0-486-21762-0

MAGIC AND MYSTERY IN TIBET, Madame Alexandra David-Neel. Experiences among lamas, magicians, sages, sorcerers, Bonpa wizards. A true psychic discovery. 32 illustrations. 321pp. 5⅜ x 8½. (Available in U.S. only.) 0-486-22682-4

THE EGYPTIAN BOOK OF THE DEAD, E. A. Wallis Budge. Complete reproduction of Ani's papyrus, finest ever found. Full hieroglyphic text, interlinear transliteration, word-for-word translation, smooth translation. 533pp. 6½ x 9¼. 0-486-21866-X

HISTORIC COSTUME IN PICTURES, Braun & Schneider. Over 1,450 costumed figures in clearly detailed engravings–from dawn of civilization to end of 19th century. Captions. Many folk costumes. 256pp. 8⅜ x 11¾. 0-486-23150-X

MATHEMATICS FOR THE NONMATHEMATICIAN, Morris Kline. Detailed, college-level treatment of mathematics in cultural and historical context, with numerous exercises. Recommended Reading Lists. Tables. Numerous figures. 641pp. 5⅜ x 8½. 0-486-24823-2

PROBABILISTIC METHODS IN THE THEORY OF STRUCTURES, Isaac Elishakoff. Well-written introduction covers the elements of the theory of probability from two or more random variables, the reliability of such multivariable structures, the theory of random function, Monte Carlo methods of treating problems incapable of exact solution, and more. Examples. 502pp. 5⅜ x 8½. 0-486-40691-1

THE RIME OF THE ANCIENT MARINER, Gustave Doré, S. T. Coleridge. Doré's finest work; 34 plates capture moods, subtleties of poem. Flawless full-size reproductions printed on facing pages with authoritative text of poem. "Beautiful. Simply beautiful."–*Publisher's Weekly.* 77pp. 9¼ x 12. 0-486-22305-1

SCULPTURE: Principles and Practice, Louis Slobodkin. Step-by-step approach to clay, plaster, metals, stone; classical and modern. 253 drawings, photos. 255pp. 8⅛ x 11. 0-486-22960-2

THE INFLUENCE OF SEA POWER UPON HISTORY, 1660–1783, A. T. Mahan. Influential classic of naval history and tactics still used as text in war colleges. First paperback edition. 4 maps. 24 battle plans. 640pp. 5⅜ x 8½. 0-486-25509-3

THE STORY OF THE TITANIC AS TOLD BY ITS SURVIVORS, Jack Winocour (ed.). What it was really like. Panic, despair, shocking inefficiency, and a little heroism. More thrilling than any fictional account. 26 illustrations. 320pp. 5⅜ x 8½. 0-486-20610-6

ONE TWO THREE . . . INFINITY: Facts and Speculations of Science, George Gamow. Great physicist's fascinating, readable overview of contemporary science: number theory, relativity, fourth dimension, entropy, genes, atomic structure, much more. 128 illustrations. Index. 352pp. 5⅜ x 8½. 0-486-25664-2

DALÍ ON MODERN ART: The Cuckolds of Antiquated Modern Art, Salvador Dalí. Influential painter skewers modern art and its practitioners. Outrageous evaluations of Picasso, Cézanne, Turner, more. 15 renderings of paintings discussed. 44 calligraphic decorations by Dalí. 96pp. 5⅜ x 8½. (Available in U.S. only.) 0-486-29220-7

ANTIQUE PLAYING CARDS: A Pictorial History, Henry René D'Allemagne. Over 900 elaborate, decorative images from rare playing cards (14th–20th centuries): Bacchus, death, dancing dogs, hunting scenes, royal coats of arms, players cheating, much more. 96pp. 9¼ x 12¼. 0-486-29265-7

MAKING FURNITURE MASTERPIECES: 30 Projects with Measured Drawings, Franklin H. Gottshall. Step-by-step instructions, illustrations for constructing handsome, useful pieces, among them a Sheraton desk, Chippendale chair, Spanish desk, Queen Anne table and a William and Mary dressing mirror. 224pp. 8⅛ x 11¼. 0-486-29338-6

NORTH AMERICAN INDIAN DESIGNS FOR ARTISTS AND CRAFTSPEOPLE, Eva Wilson. Over 360 authentic copyright-free designs adapted from Navajo blankets, Hopi pottery, Sioux buffalo hides, more. Geometrics, symbolic figures, plant and animal motifs, etc. 128pp. 8⅜ x 11. (Not for sale in the United Kingdom.) 0-486-25341-4

THE FOSSIL BOOK: A Record of Prehistoric Life, Patricia V. Rich et al. Profusely illustrated definitive guide covers everything from single-celled organisms and dinosaurs to birds and mammals and the interplay between climate and man. Over 1,500 illustrations. 760pp. 7½ x 10⅛. 0-486-29371-8

VICTORIAN ARCHITECTURAL DETAILS: Designs for Over 700 Stairs, Mantels, Doors, Windows, Cornices, Porches, and Other Decorative Elements, A. J. Bicknell & Company. Everything from dormer windows and piazzas to balconies and gable ornaments. Also includes elevations and floor plans for handsome, private residences and commercial structures. 80pp. 9⅜ x 12¼. 0-486-44015-X

WESTERN ISLAMIC ARCHITECTURE: A Concise Introduction, John D. Hoag. Profusely illustrated critical appraisal compares and contrasts Islamic mosques and palaces–from Spain and Egypt to other areas in the Middle East. 139 illustrations. 128pp. 6 x 9. 0-486-43760-4

CHINESE ARCHITECTURE: A Pictorial History, Liang Ssu-ch'eng. More than 240 rare photographs and drawings depict temples, pagodas, tombs, bridges, and imperial palaces comprising much of China's architectural heritage. 152 halftones, 94 diagrams. 232pp. 10¾ x 9⅞. 0-486-43999-2

THE RENAISSANCE: Studies in Art and Poetry, Walter Pater. One of the most talked-about books of the 19th century, *The Renaissance* combines scholarship and philosophy in an innovative work of cultural criticism that examines the achievements of Botticelli, Leonardo, Michelangelo, and other artists. "The holy writ of beauty."–Oscar Wilde. 160pp. 5⅜ x 8½. 0-486-44025-7

A TREATISE ON PAINTING, Leonardo da Vinci. The great Renaissance artist's practical advice on drawing and painting techniques covers anatomy, perspective, composition, light and shadow, and color. A classic of art instruction, it features 48 drawings by Nicholas Poussin and Leon Battista Alberti. 192pp. 5⅜ x 8½. 0-486-44155-5

THE MIND OF LEONARDO DA VINCI, Edward McCurdy. More than just a biography, this classic study by a distinguished historian draws upon Leonardo's extensive writings to offer numerous demonstrations of the Renaissance master's achievements, not only in sculpture and painting, but also in music, engineering, and even experimental aviation. 384pp. 5⅜ x 8½. 0-486-44142-3

WASHINGTON IRVING'S RIP VAN WINKLE, Illustrated by Arthur Rackham. Lovely prints that established artist as a leading illustrator of the time and forever etched into the popular imagination a classic of Catskill lore. 51 full-color plates. 80pp. 8⅜ x 11. 0-486-44242-X

HENSCHE ON PAINTING, John W. Robichaux. Basic painting philosophy and methodology of a great teacher, as expounded in his famous classes and workshops on Cape Cod. 7 illustrations in color on covers. 80pp. 5⅜ x 8½. 0-486-43728-0

CATALOG OF DOVER BOOKS

LIGHT AND SHADE: A Classic Approach to Three-Dimensional Drawing, Mrs. Mary P. Merrifield. Handy reference clearly demonstrates principles of light and shade by revealing effects of common daylight, sunshine, and candle or artificial light on geometrical solids. 13 plates. 64pp. 5⅜ x 8½. 0-486-44143-1

ASTROLOGY AND ASTRONOMY: A Pictorial Archive of Signs and Symbols, Ernst and Johanna Lehner. Treasure trove of stories, lore, and myth, accompanied by more than 300 rare illustrations of planets, the Milky Way, signs of the zodiac, comets, meteors, and other astronomical phenomena. 192pp. 8⅜ x 11. 0-486-43981-X

JEWELRY MAKING: Techniques for Metal, Tim McCreight. Easy-to-follow instructions and carefully executed illustrations describe tools and techniques, use of gems and enamels, wire inlay, casting, and other topics. 72 line illustrations and diagrams. 176pp. 8¼ x 10⅞. 0-486-44043-5

MAKING BIRDHOUSES: Easy and Advanced Projects, Gladstone Califf. Easy-to-follow instructions include diagrams for everything from a one-room house for bluebirds to a forty-two-room structure for purple martins. 56 plates; 4 figures. 80pp. 8¾ x 6⅜. 0-486-44183-0

LITTLE BOOK OF LOG CABINS: How to Build and Furnish Them, William S. Wicks. Handy how-to manual, with instructions and illustrations for building cabins in the Adirondack style, fireplaces, stairways, furniture, beamed ceilings, and more. 102 line drawings. 96pp. 8¾ x 6⅜. 0-486-44259-4

THE SEASONS OF AMERICA PAST, Eric Sloane. From "sugaring time" and strawberry picking to Indian summer and fall harvest, a whole year's activities described in charming prose and enhanced with 79 of the author's own illustrations. 160pp. 8¼ x 11. 0-486-44220-9

THE METROPOLIS OF TOMORROW, Hugh Ferriss. Generous, prophetic vision of the metropolis of the future, as perceived in 1929. Powerful illustrations of towering structures, wide avenues, and rooftop parks–all features in many of today's modern cities. 59 illustrations. 144pp. 8¼ x 11. 0-486-43727-2

THE PATH TO ROME, Hilaire Belloc. This 1902 memoir abounds in lively vignettes from a vanished time, recounting a pilgrimage on foot across the Alps and Apennines in order to "see all Europe which the Christian Faith has saved." 77 of the author's original line drawings complement his sparkling prose. 272pp. 5⅜ x 8½. 0-486-44001-X

THE HISTORY OF RASSELAS: Prince of Abissinia, Samuel Johnson. Distinguished English writer attacks eighteenth-century optimism and man's unrealistic estimates of what life has to offer. 112pp. 5⅜ x 8½. 0-486-44094-X

A VOYAGE TO ARCTURUS, David Lindsay. A brilliant flight of pure fancy, where wild creatures crowd the fantastic landscape and demented torturers dominate victims with their bizarre mental powers. 272pp. 5⅜ x 8½. 0-486-44198-9

Ted Seth Jacobs
'Mes Illusions'
Les Cerqueux sous Passavant
49310
France

near Vihiers

airports: Nantes (1½ hours)
Tours (")
Poitiers
or train to Angers (45 mins)

0033 2 41 59 57 55